The Subject of Prostitution

The Subject of Prostitution offers a distinctive analysis of the links between prostitution and social theory in order to advance a critical analysis of the relationship of law to sex work.

Using the lens of social theory to disrupt fixed meanings, the book provides an advanced analytical framework through which to understand the complexity and contingencies of sex work in late modernity. The book analyses contemporary citizenship discourse and the law's ability to meet the competing demands of empowerment by sex workers and protection by radical feminists who view prostitution as the epitome of patriarchal sexual and economic relations. Its central focus is the role of law in both structuring and responding to the 'problem of prostitution'. By developing a distinctive constitutive approach to law, the author offers a more advanced analytical framework from which to understand how law matters in contemporary debates and also suggests how law could matter in more imaginative justice reforms. This is particularly pertinent in a period of unprecedented legal reform, both internationally and nationally, as legal norms simultaneously attempt to protect, empower and criminalise parties involved in the purchase of sexual services. *The Subject of Prostitution* aims to overcome the current aporia in these debates and suggest new ways to engage with the subject and law.

As such, *The Subject of Prostitution* provides an advanced theoretical resource for policymakers, researchers and activists involved in contemporary struggles over the meanings and place of sex work in late modernity.

Jane Scoular is a Professor in Law, based at the University of Strathclyde, Scotland, UK.

'Most debates about regulating prostitution assume that feminists all want to use criminal law to punish male customers and 'send a message' that prostitution exploits women. In this important and timely book, Jane Scoular develops an analysis of sex work laws, including anti-trafficking efforts, that is feminist but rejects the use of coercive law. Scoular's nuanced approach is a breath of fresh air, and should be read both by feminists and by anyone interested in criminal law and criminal justice policy.'

– *Mariana Valverde, University of Toronto*

The Subject of Prostitution

Sex work, Law and Social Theory

Jane Scoular

Routledge
Taylor & Francis Group
a GlassHouse book

First published 2015
by Routledge
2 Park Square, Milton Park, Abingdon, Oxfordshire OX14 4RN

and by Routledge
711 Third Avenue, New York, NY 10017, USA

First issued in paperback 2016

Routledge is an imprint of the Taylor & Francis Group, an informa business

British Library Cataloguing in Publication Data
A catalogue record for this book is available from the British Library

Library of Congress Cataloging-in-Publication Data
Scoular, Jane, author.
The subject of prostitution : sex work, law and social theory / Jane Scoular.
pages cm
"A GlassHouse Book."
Includes bibliographical references and index.
ISBN 978-1-904385-51-6 (hbk)—ISBN 978-1-315-77843-3 (ebk)
1. Prostitution—Law and legislation. 2. Prostitutes—Social conditions. I. Title.
K5295.S36 2016
306.74—dc23 2015027179

ISBN13: 978-0-415-79227-1 (pbk)
ISBN13: 978-1-904385-51-6 (hbk)

Typeset in Baskerville
by Keystroke, Station Road, Codsall, Wolverhampton

For Mum, with love, and to Benny, Luke and Liam, grá mo chroí

Contents

Acknowledgements

This book, like many, has endured a particularly long gestation. This has been, in part, due to positive interruptions in life and in work, including opportunities to be involved in other projects with great colleagues whose insights have almost certainly advanced my thinking.

It has also taken me some time to work through the central argument in the book. This has less to do perhaps with the earth-shattering nature of my insights and more to do with my interminable procrastination, but the less said about that the better, or maybe yes, or perhaps in the conclusion – oh, hold on, I need to read more . . .

For all of these reasons I must thank the patience and forbearance of my dear family, friends and colleagues who have supported and endured the protracted development of this book, not least the publishers who have been incredibly patient with me. Beverly Brown's initial vision and encouragement helped me form the project and Colin Perrin and his team have kept faith and helped me to nurse it to its final publication.

This book would simply not have been anything like as coherent were it not for insights of Mariana Valverde, Neil Hutton and Thérèse O'Donnell, who were all so very generous with their time. Thank you. I am also grateful for the guidance provided by Judith Walkowitz in Chapter 2 and for the research assistance of the incredibly talented Emma Boffey and Stewart Cunningham. Stewart, in particular, has provided invaluable support and input and I am sure will be glad that I've finally 'Let it go!'.

On a personal level, I have been greatly supported by my family and dedicate the book to them, although they probably want never to hear about it again. My mum, Helen, in particular, has provided incredible support to help me sustain a young family while working and even helped to proofread the final text. My partner, Benny, has injected humour and a blunt realism into a project that I managed to turn into a production to match that of the Great Wall of China! And, finally, to my precious Luke and Liam, for bringing so much fun that it's been hard to pull myself from them and refocus. I know it is somewhat of a disappointment that mum/Princess Leia was busy all this time producing something other than a further *Star Wars* trilogy, but I hope as you grow older you come to understand the importance of political and intellectual projects that seek increased understanding and are orientated towards social justice (not that the fight against the Empire isn't without its colonial subplot) – knowing you both, I think you will.

I will stop now before I start thanking each cast member of my favourite box sets, although Stringer Bell *did* play his part!

Chapter 1

The subject of prostitution: an introduction

> Gender equality will remain unattainable so long as men buy, sell and exploit women and children by prostituting them . . . Prostituted persons are the weaker party, exploited by both the procurers and the buyers . . . By adopting the legislation Sweden has given notice to the world that it regards prostitution as a serious form of oppression of women and children and that efforts must be made to combat it. (Swedish Government 2003)

> The Supreme Court of Canada has struck down the country's major prostitution laws, saying that bans on street soliciting, brothels and people living off the avails of prostitution create severe dangers for vulnerable women and therefore violate Canadians' basic values. (Fine 2013)

> A New Zealand prostitute has won substantial damages for sexual harassment by a brothel owner . . . 'Sex workers are as much entitled to protection from sexual harassment as those working in other occupations', the ruling said. New Zealand Prostitutes Collective national coordinator Catherine Healy told Fairfax News the decision showed New Zealand had become a world leader in sex workers' human rights after legalising prostitution in 2003. 'It's one up for decriminalisation, it's a significant ruling because it could never have happened when sex work was illegal.' (ABC News 2014)

Overview

As these accounts, taken from recent press accounts and government reports, demonstrate, prostitution is, at the beginning of the twentieth-first century, characterised and governed in strikingly different ways. Fiercely polarised battles have emerged between those who, on the one hand, view the practice as a form of sexual violence, and as a form of exploitation and, on the other, those who regard the activity as work like any other, as a form of sexual labour that individuals have a basic human right to engage in (safely).

What is striking about this current debate is not only the seemingly mutual incompatibility of each perspective (according to the current orthodoxy, prostitution can only ever be *either* the epitome of modern day slavery *or* the expression of a fundamental human right, of sexual freedom and economic liberty – but never both) but also the central role that law is assigned in adjudicating between these competing constructions. Although each side disagrees vehemently on the very meaning, and, indeed, morality of commercial sexual exchange, they are united in their belief that law is the panacea to this Solomonic dilemma. Whether by criminalising the purchasing of sex or by providing increased rights and labour recognition for those in the sex industry – law, it would seem, is the answer. Yet is it?

In this work, I take a step back from the issue as it is currently presented and question the central role of law in framing and responding to the subject of prostitution. This book asks the critical, yet often overlooked, question of *how law matters in contemporary sex work.* Is law simply a neutral arbiter that comes down from above to ordain the right normative answer to this moral dilemma, or, is this presentation of 'the law', as a singular sovereign power, part of the very problem that many seem to want to 'resolve'?

The latter is very much my contention as I seek to challenge formalist accounts and develop a constitutive approach to the subject of prostitution *and* to the subject of law. This reveals a more complex relationship between law, society and the subject that requires a reorientation of the search for justice as it shows that the insistence on 'a' legal solution to this issue can do more harm than good.

This work is motivated by fact that there is surprisingly little written *on* law in this area. I should clarify, of course, there is indeed a great deal written *about* law – calling for increased legal sanction, or conversely reduced legal intervention. There have also been myriad reports and studies *describing* the content of various laws, empirical studies of policing and a great deal of political rhetoric, yet these rarely *engage* with the discipline of law itself. Despite massive regulatory complexity, analysis has become ever more narrowed in a binary of legalisation/criminalisation with decriminalisation appearing to fall somewhere in between. Laws are described and debated at great length, but rarely are they analysed in more than these narrow analytical terms.

My methodology resists the legal centrism of formalist accounts, which, in assuming that the 'law' regulates prostitution, in a particular way according to its sovereign expression, overstates law's coherence (as if 'law' is a singular power), wrongly attributes 'intention' (as if 'law' has a controlling mind and is unified in its actions) and over-determines its influence (as if 'law' acts alone and not in the context of other discourses and actors).

By contrast, a constitutive approach sees law as an inseparable dimension of social relations. It looks beyond what law 'says' and instead examines what law 'does', as it operates alongside other discourses and practices to shape the subjects, spaces and forms of power in sex work.

Examining these social processes gives a greater insight into what law 'does' and the significance of legal processes, actors and norms in the context of a wider system of meaning as prostitution emerges as a problem of governance at particular times and spaces (Rose and Valverde 1998).

This analytical method helps to more clearly elucidate how law matters in contemporary societies, without either over-privileging it or rendering it obsolete (Agustín 2009)[1] or ephemeral to other structures such as the economy (Bernstein 2010) or gender in radical feminist accounts (Jeffreys 1997a).

In this book, I offer a genealogy of the modern subject of prostitution. Each chapter looks at the relationship between dominant constructions of the 'problem of prostitution' and the associated norms of regulation and governance, across various historical epochs. My attention to 'history' is necessarily selective as I focus on changing representations of prostitution as it moves from being depicted predominantly as an issue of sin, to being understood largely as a question of public health, to more recent portrayals as the epitome of gendered violence and as an issue of sex workers' rights.

Such an analysis is particularly pertinent, in a period of unprecedented legal reform, both internationally and nationally, as legal norms simultaneously attempt to protect, empower and criminalise parties involved in the purchase of sexual services. These feature, at their most reductive, on one side, a flat victimised subject that dictates an abolitionist approach pitted against a hyper mobile rights-bearing subject that appears to prescribe legal recognition and rights.

This book intervenes in the debate and questions whether, in the context of modern governance, these approaches are as distinctive as they appear. By asking how law matters, this book offers a way out of the current political and analytical impasse. It analyses law's ability to meet seemingly competing demands for protection, made by radical feminists (who view prostitution as the epitome of patriarchal sexual and economic relations), and for empowerment, by those who advocate sex worker rights. It warns of the dangers of fixed positions and unproductive identity politics, and suggests a constitutive methodology as a means to radically rethink the relationship between the subject of prostitution and law and to break out of the current aporia of many contemporary politics and legal debates on sex work.

Introduction

This book considers the subject of prostitution. In the last 40 years, both the supply and demand for commercially available sexual services *appear* to have risen exponentially. The contemporary period has witnessed far reaching sociocultural changes, brought about by increased globalisation, technological advancement changing patterns of migration, the breakdown of previous political structures

1 See Scoular 2010, in which I argue that Agustín's 2009 claim that law did not matter while appearing as an example of post-structural evisceration is not an accurate post-structural account of the role of law in modern societies, which would recognise that law does matter but just not as formalist accounts describe.

(such as nation states, borders and the 'family') and a loosening of traditional sexual mores – which have, it is claimed, not only served to increase the desire for commercial sex, but also optimised the conditions for its realisation (Bernstein 2007a: 188). The result is a highly visible and highly varied market in sexual services that is 'ever more specialised, diversifying along technological, spatial and social lines' (Bernstein 2007a: 115). Writers describe, and some denounce, an increasing 'raunch culture' (Levy 2005) and a seemingly 'unbridled ethic of demand', as 'pornography, strip clubs, lap-dancing, escorts, telephone sex and "sex tours" in developing countries' appear to be in inexhaustible and immediate supply, at the click of a button (Bernstein 2001: 389).

I use parentheses when presenting this account. While changes in late modern society have undoubtedly altered the meanings and increased the visibility of sex, which now includes a myriad of commodified and mediated forms, I dispute the frequently assumed correlation between these changes and a rise in real terms in the amount of sex sold. There are simply no reliable data to measure historical change in quantitative terms.

Such concerns are, of course, those of a social scientist, rather than those of a politician or activist. Many ideologically driven governments and campaigners habitually talk in exaggerated terms, citing vastly inflated figures, invoking metaphors of floods and epidemics (in both demand and supply), in order to rationalise and justify increased regulation. To give a typical example:

> Germany has been flooded with foreign sex workers, mostly from Eastern Europe. Their sheer number, and willingness to accept lower rates, has driven prices so low one American punter, who takes three sex trips to Germany each year, calls the country 'Aldi for prostitutes'.
>
> (Diu 2014)

This story features familiar tropes commonly utilised in reports across many jurisdictions: EU accession is blamed for an 'explosive increase in human trafficking' (Der Spiegel 2013) and for having 'triggered an apparently unstoppable growth in the country's sex industry' (Diu 2014), with public services 'like schools, housing and the NHS being stretched to breaking point' as 'vice girls flood in' (Sheldrick 2014)[2]. The conclusion drawn from this apparent rise in sex work, is, of course, not that the presence of migrants (who for many reasons make up a large section of the industry) (Agustín 2007) may make prostitution more *visible* but rather that legalising the activity has failed and that tougher measures are required (Der Spiegel 2013).

2 Another example comes from the *Scotsman* newspaper: 'Organised crime groups flooding Scotland with Brazilian prostitutes', which notes that: 'Senior police sources say that in just two years they have seen a "several hundreds per cent" increase in the number of sex workers who are either from Brazil or claim to be'. http://www.scotsman.com/news/organised-crime-groups-flooding-scotland-with-brazilian-prostitutes-1-1363254

Alongside this popular hyperbole, vastly inflated and unsubstantiated numbers are recirculated between media, politicians and campaigners so that they are transformed into 'fact'. Figures on sex trafficking are notoriously exaggerated, often overestimating numbers by conflating sex trafficking with *all* forms of prostitution (forced and otherwise) and with other forms of forced labour. The US State Department claimed for many years that between 600,000 and 800,000 people were trafficked for forced labour and sex worldwide each year, 80 per cent of whom were women and girls and the majority of whom were trafficked for sexual exploitation (US State Department 2005: 6). Statistics such as these have been challenged by many commentators for their lack of empirical grounding (Agustín 2007; Weitzer 2007; Doezema 2010). The International Labour Organization (2012) estimates that there are 20.9 million forced labourers in the world, 4.5 million (22 per cent) of whom are victims of sexual exploitation. Even these estimates, which are, in the first place, high, when repeated, are frequently misrepresented and exaggerated. By way of example, a fact sheet produced by the international NGO Equality Now, refers to the ILO report highlighting *only* the 20.9 million total figure and states that '80% of all trafficking victims are used and abused as sexual slaves', which grossly exaggerate the ILO estimates (Equality Now 2012).

In the UK the figure of '25,000 sex slaves' was used across a number of media outlets (the *Daily Mirror* warned of '25,000 Sex Slaves on the Streets of Britain' (see Edwards 2005)) and by many prominent governmental ministers, including Denis MacShane (the UK's former Minister of State for Europe) and others. These figures have been strongly criticised as lacking any scientific veracity (Davies 2009). O'Connell Davidson for example wryly ponders why this number, which amounts to more than the entire workforce of one of Britain's largest department stores, was not detected by the police (O'Connell Davidson 2007). Further reports, widely circulated in media outlets state that 80 per cent of all prostitutes were trafficked and controlled. These figures emanated from a study where 'researchers' called up brothels and asked how many foreign women were working there and from this deduced that the majority of the workforce were trafficked. This flawed research was later debunked by many including Agustín 2009).

Nevertheless, these figures and reports have fuelled a renewed and intense focus on trafficking at both national and international levels. Contemporary nation states are responding to seismic societal changes by shoring up their increasingly fluid sexual and geopolitical borders, to protect the security, not just of 'victims', but of all 'regular' citizens (Aradau 2008). To support this pursuit, alongside increased border controls, international protocols have been passed, such as the Palermo Protocol, which has been ratified by 166 countries (as at December 2014), which requires signatories to put in place measures to 'prevent and combat' trafficking as well as to 'protect and assist' victims. In order to meet these international obligations, national laws have been instituted against traffickers and associated penalties increased in order to deter and punish those who intentionally or unintentionally[3] facilitate this 'trade in human misery' (Aronowitz 2009).

What could be described as a current hysteria over sexual slavery (Weitzer 2007) is reminiscent of an earlier century's moral panic over an imagined 'white slave trade' (Burton 1994; Doezema 2010). Once again, an inordinate attention is being paid to the issue of trafficking in Western industrialized economies, which is vastly disproportionate to the problem. As Kotiswaran notes:

> Only 7% of the world's 20.9 million forced labourers are in developed economies and the EU, while 56% are in Asia Pacific where the subject has much less policy resonance.
>
> (Kotiswaran 2014a: 353)[4]

Regulatory responses

Reponses display similar colonial dynamics to Victorian campaigns, with modes of governance utilised by Western governments to combat the problem, stressing dependence and rescue (Agustín 2007; see also Chapter 2 of this book). Foreign aid is increasingly made dependent on beneficiaries adopting anti-trafficking laws that often do more harm than good (GAATW 2007; Doezema 2010; Kotiswaran, 2014a). These initiatives tend to ignore the material context in which labour exploitation takes place and simply replicate relations of ruling, rather than supporting resistance already practiced by those governed. Such unbalanced representations create the conditions for sexual humanitarianism whereby developed countries shape international trafficking law and policy, transporting legal norms while ignoring legal conditions.

This leads to an overreliance on criminal justice interventions, dictated by international protocols rather than local solutions that tend to prioritise labour controls and forms of self-regulation and representation (Kotiswaran 2014a;[5] see Chapter 5, more generally).

3 Intention is becoming increasingly unnecessary in certain purchasing offences. For example, in England and Wales section 14 of the Policing and Crime Act 2009, which renders purchasing sex from those who have been 'forced' a strict liability offence, representing a significant departure from criminal legal standards (see Chapter 3).

4 Kotiswaran elaborates 'According to the ILO, forced labor, one of the forms of exploitation listed in Article 3, is to be found largely in Asia and the Pacific. Thus, in 2005, of the 8.1 million victims of forced labor (excluding sex work) the world over, nearly 6.2 million were in the Asia-Pacific region while the industrialized economies had only 113,000 victims of forced labor. Similarly, one million of these victims of forced labor were trafficked into it, of which 408,968 were trafficked in the Asia-Pacific region and 74,113 in the industrialized economies' (Kotiswaran 2014a: 361).

5 Sex workers account for 60 per cent of members (40 per cent are lawyers, doctors, and social workers). As of 2006, these boards operated in 27 different red light districts in Kolkata. The idea is that people working in the industry are best placed to identify victims of trafficking, if someone new is identified as working in the area the board convenes, interviews her to find out if she is trafficked

The same is true in Western contexts: at a national level, sustained and sensationalist media accounts of a growing trade in prostitution have induced a flurry of inquiries and government commissions, leading to significant changes in many countries' legislative frameworks for domestic prostitution in recent years. On the one hand, these reforms seek either to stymie the supply of, or demand for, commercial sex (described as prohibitionism/abolitionism) or, on the other, to recognise it as a social fact to be managed through processes of bureaucratic regulation. Finally, decriminalisation often features as a desirable 'third way solution' between these two extremes. Much political activism follows this binary pattern, with one group (abolitionists) such as the Coalition Against Trafficking in Women (CATW)[6] seeking to harness governmental power to protect those exploited by commercial sex. This 'protection' comes in the form of enticements to exit sex work, in addition to criminalising purchasers, with the overall goal being the elimination of the sale of sex. Other campaigners, such as the Global Network of Sex Work Projects (NSWP), seek governmental recognition of 'sex work' as a form of legitimate labour in order to gain the protection and rights that workers should enjoy.

Prohibitionism, abolitionism and neo-abolitionism

The terms prohibitionism and abolitionism are frequently conflated in popular discourse, as both view the activity in a negative light. Moral opprobrium, often religiously based, informs a prohibitionist approach which seeks to deter parties from engaging in prostitution by punishing one (usually female sellers) or, increasingly, both parties. This reasoning informs the position in all but one of the states in the USA, where prostitution is illegal.[7]

Abolitionism takes a similarly dim view of the activity but rather than relying solely on Christian moralism, it is informed by certain strains of feminist ideology which situates prostitution on a spectrum of male violence against women. As Weitzer notes, abolitionism:

> [d]iffers from the religious right's objections to commercial sex, which centers on the threat it poses to marriage, the family, and society's moral fiber . . . [but rather] holds that sex work is the quintessential expression of patriarchal gender relations and male domination.
>
> (Weitzer 2012: 10)

or working voluntarily. If trafficked, she is offered assistance, if working voluntarily, an induction to the industry and the area is carried out. See Kotiswaran (2014a: 399–403) and Chapter 5 for other constructive uses of workplace sex workers' rights.

6 CATW is a coalition of academics, activists and NGOs committed to ending human trafficking. Its website states that it 'engages in advocacy, education and prevention programmes for victims of trafficking and prostitution in Asia, Africa, Latin America, Europe and North America, including the United States' and that it is 'a leading architect of the end demand strategy to end human trafficking'. See www.catwinternational.org

7 Nevada is the one exception (see Brents, Jackson and Hausbeck 2010).

As Chapter 2 will describe in more detail, the early abolitionist movement was inspired by the activities of mainly middle-class feminists and philanthropists, such as the Victorian pioneer Josephine Butler and her Ladies National Association (LNA) in the UK and the Progressive era's great social reformer Jane Addams in the USA. Such women campaigned to save, rather than punish, fallen women, and to focus attention instead on discriminatory laws and male depravity and licentiousness. In the UK, together with moral puritans and members of the 'respectable working class' the National Vigilance Association successfully overturned the discriminatory regime of compulsory testing under the Contagious Diseases Acts of 1864, 1866 and 1869. Yet through the anti-vice activities of some of its members, campaigners helped to reinstitute an equally, if not, harsher regime of protectionism, further strengthened in subsequent legal reforms (an issue I return to in subsequent chapters when I discuss the politics of legal reform).

Such efforts have been revived in recent years by another alliance, this time between moral conservatives, radical feminists and social democrats, who seek to combat prostitution, which they consider to be a form of 'modern day sexual slavery' and an activity incompatible with gender equality. This new wave of abolitionist activity is often termed as 'neo-abolitionist' – a term used to describe the more exclusive focus on clients. In this approach, any distinction between voluntary commercial sex and forced sexual exploitation or trafficking is collapsed, being replaced with the broad term 'commercial sexual exploitation' – which covers a myriad of activities – which is then used in official discourses to justify increasingly punitive approaches against clients and the promotion of exiting and the 'rehabilitation' of sex workers.

The most notable example of 'neo-abolitionism' is in the Swedish law, the Prohibition of the Purchase of Sexual Services Act 1998, which, for the first time in history, criminalises *only* the purchase, not the sale, of 'casual sexual services'. At the time of writing, and this is a rapidly changing scene, this approach has been adopted, in the large part, by parliaments in Norway and Iceland,[8] and Northern Ireland[9] and implemented in part, or in tone, by Finland,[10]

8 The Swedish position's influence in neighbouring Scandinavian countries has led to its description as the 'Nordic model', although careful empirical examination of the variations between different Scandinavian regimes questions the assumed homogeneity and suggests this term may be misleadingly overbroad (Skilbrei and Holmström 2011). Following a review completed in 2012 the Danish Ministry of Justice decided not to criminalise the purchase of sex. http://politiken.dk/indland/politik/ECE1819574/justitsministeren-forbud-mod-koebesex-ville-kraeve-alt-for-mange-ressourcer/

9 S.15 of the Human Trafficking and Exploitation (Criminal Justice and Support for Victims) Act (Northern Ireland) 2015.

10 Finland explicitly rejected the full Swedish model in 2006 and instead criminalises only the purchase of sex from minors or victims of trafficking. There is debate as to whether it is aligned with the 'Nordic model' or not (see Skilbrei and Holmström 2013). http://nppr.se/2009/10/12/finlands-prostitution-law-and-the-hope-of-nordic-unity/

South Korea, South Africa,[11] Lithuania[12] and the United Kingdom,[13] and is being actively considered by other legislatures such as in the Republic of Ireland,[14] France and Israel (Livneh 2013).

Regulationism

Prohibitionist and abolitionist approaches are frequently contrasted with efforts to recognise and positively influence the activity of sex work. Governments at different levels have approached the issue pragmatically, and tried to 'manage' the social reality of prostitution, by implementing systems of regulation, such as licensing, inspections, working permits and the promotion of forms of self-organisation and unionisation. Such 'regulatory' approaches are said to operate in the Netherlands, in parts of Germany, Nevada, Switzerland, Austria, Greece, Latvia, Turkey and in regions in Australia, such as Queensland, Victoria and New South Wales, although implementation at a local level is quite varied.

Decriminalisation

Finally, decriminalisation is often featured in policy discussions as a desirable 'third way solution' between the two aforementioned extremes: as an idyll of non-interference that circumvents both the harms of legal sanction and bureaucratic regulation. In 2003, the New Zealand parliament pioneered decriminalisation when the Prostitution Reform Act swept away centuries of criminal law proscription. The New Zealand model is often cited in policy discussions as emblematic of a possible and indeed desirable middle ground in what are, increasingly, polarised debates.

Political and analytical stalemate

As the opening quotations demonstrate, the debate on how best to regulate prostitution has, in recent years, been fiercely polarising, divided around these ostensibly adversarial positions. Abolitionist campaigners have attempted to universalise their understanding of commercial sex as an affront to human dignity and to ensure that the criminalisation of the demand and purchase of sexual services (i.e. the Swedish position) is adopted at national and international levels.

11 South Africa criminalises clients (s.11 of the Criminal Law Sexual Offences and Related Matters 2007) and sex workers.

12 Like South Africa and South Korea, Lithuania extended the laws to criminalise clients while retaining the criminalisation of sex workers (see Global Network of Sex Work Projects, Briefing Paper #2, 'Criminalisation of clients': http://www.nswp.org/sites/nswp.org/files/Criminalisation%20of% 20Clients-c.pdf

13 See Chapter 3.

14 Criminal Law (Sexual Offences) Bill 2014: http://www.justice.ie/en/JELR/Pages/PB14000350

Some progress has been made in this respect.[15] Not only have a number of jurisdictions already implemented or are considering adopting the Swedish approach, but the campaign has also been further strengthened by a recent resolution of the European Parliament which states:

> [P]rostitution and forced prostitution are intrinsically linked to gender inequality in society and have an impact on the status of women and men in society and the perception of their mutual relations and sexuality.
>
> (European Parliament 2014: para E)[16]

While this body does not have law-making power (any legislative change would need to come from the European Commission), it does carry significant symbolic and political weight. Press accounts, for example, claim that the passing of the resolution 'formally establishes the EU's stance on prostitution and puts pressure on member states to re-evaluate their policies on sex work', pushing them towards the Nordic model (Oppenheim 2014). Indeed the British MEP Mary Honeyball, who was instrumental in proposing the motion, has since been encouraging states 'to be radical and ambitious enough to go Swedish' (Osbourne 2014).

As neo-abolitionism takes hold in Europe, there seems to be less of an appetite for regulatory measures. The idea of legalising or tolerating aspects of commercial sex has become less tenable in Europe. Notably, local authorities and legislatures in both the Netherlands and Germany are revisiting their previous legalised stance[17] (Outshoorn 2012; Frommel 2014).

Yet, critics of abolitionism, a loose alliance of sex work activists, dissenting feminists, NGOs, libertarians and pragmatists point to the many harms of

15 The European Women's Lobby (which describes itself as the largest umbrella organisation of women's associations in Europe) has publicly endorsed this position, stating that the 'persistence of systems of prostitution in EU Member States is a strong indicator of the failure of Europe as a whole to engage in reaching gender equality and promoting women's rights' (European Women's Lobby 2010).

The group also states that: Women state that their wish to be respected by their partners and work colleagues is constantly undermined because of the normalisation of prostitution. This clearly shows how urgent it is to address the EU's tolerance for prostitution in light of its commitment to gender equality' (European Women's Lobby). http://www.womenlobby.org/publications/Position-Papers/article/towards-a-europe-free-from-all?lang=en

16 The motion, emanated from the women's committee of the parliament, and was sponsored by British MEP Mary Honeyball. It was endorsed by the parliament in a vote on 26 February 2014 in which 343 MEPs voted for the motion, 139 MEPs against and 105 abstained.

17 Outshoorn notes that 'the Netherlands is reneging on its original progressive legalisation by adopting a strict regulation of all prostitution' (Outshoorn 2012). A new bill, the Law Regulating Prostitution and Suppressing Abuse in the Sex Industry, was introduced to the Dutch parliament in 2009, with stricter measures to combat human trafficking and crime, but also featuring greater control of the sex industry and sex workers.

criminalisation. They cite the benefits of New Zealand's experience of decriminalisation (Abel et al. 2010b; Abel 2014) and point to international examples where sex workers' rights have been recognised (such as the recent Canadian Supreme Court decision of *Canada (Attorney General)* vs. *Bedford* 2013 SCC 72)[18] as they seek to harness human rights' instruments and labour laws in their campaigns for justice.

The current situation has reached something of a stalemate, with both 'positions' becoming entrenched and each side increasingly talking past the other. Any recognition of ambivalence or contradiction is frequently viewed as a concession to the 'other side'. Sadly, as I will demonstrate, such fixed positions do little to help mitigate the risks and harms involved in sex work, neither do they lead to better policy solutions. Accounts that describe prostitution in terms of binaries of 'forced *or* free' (see Bindman and Doezema 1997: 5; Doezema 1998: 34–50) and as *either* a form of work *or* sexual abuse miss the complexity of an activity that can act as *both* a form of 'work *and* exploitation' (Sullivan 2004).[19] This more complex and ambivalent lived experience is increasingly recognised in the sociology of sex work (Bell 1994; O'Connell Davidson 1998; Phoenix 1999; O'Neill 2001; Scoular 2004b; Bernstein 2007a). Building on a poststructuralist account of the liberal, Enlightenment subject more generally (Haraway 1985), post-structural feminists have done much to complicate the idea of the subject of prostitution beyond binaries of forced and free (Bell 1994; Doezema 1998; O'Connell Davidson 1998; Phoenix 1999; O'Neill 2001; Scoular 2004b; Bernstein 2007a). Yet the potential of such analysis is stymied when the desire is expressed for 'a' legal response. The entry of law into this frame seems to always push the debate back into legal/illegal constraints. This stunts not only a more contextual and ambivalent understanding of the subject (as an effect of power) but also of law – of its power and also its possibilities. This situation can, I argue, be overcome but only if we move away from an enduring legal formalism that dominates and stymies the analytical field and develop instead a more critical account of law.

An enduring legal formalism

Legal formalism casts a long dark shadow over the field of legal inquiry. In this schema, law is presented as a science, as a system of 'rational' rules, an independent and objective body of knowledge that can be examined deductively. The

18 This decision struck down three of Canada's prostitution laws on the basis that they breached sex workers' constitutional right to security of the person, and has been hailed, perhaps prematurely, as a victory for sex workers' rights, as it has been undermined by the Canadian government's recent Protection of Communities and Exploited Persons Act 2014, which seeks to prohibit the purchase of sex and communicating in any place for that purpose (see, further, Chapter 5).

19 Phoenix similarly notes that prostitution can be 'both a means of securing material and social survival and a set of relationships that threatens that survival' (Phoenix 1999: 2).

application of formal law is considered to operate in purely instrumental ways – according to an internal logic – and changes in behaviour in society are assumed to follow its prescribed codes. Fidelity to law is measured according to an internal consistency or by abstract conjecture, rather than by examining how it operates as a practice in a wider social context.

Formalism is a common approach in the presentation and interpretation of law in prostitution studies. Discussion of the regulation of sex work typically begins with a review of the distinctions between different regulatory approaches (Kilvington et al. 2001; Council of Europe, Resolution 1579 (2007); Phoenix 2009) as outlined earlier. Researchers, campaigners and policymakers frequently rehash the broad terms prohibitionist, abolitionist, regulationism and decriminalisation before recommending or adopting an approach which best supports their own particular socio-political and ethical contexts and projects.

Closer, empirical examination shows that such neat normative classifications are often misleading. They describe general political and social aspirations regarding how best to regulate commercial sex, rather than how law works on the ground. For all the considerable time and energy spent debating the relative merits and demerits of criminalisation versus legalisation, the problem with these forms of classification which currently dominate the terms of the debate, is that neither of these idealised accounts is empirically accurate, bearing little resemblance to how law works in practice.

Legal-centric approaches tend to assume that the sex industry on which it acts is homogeneous, when in fact it is highly differentiated, meaning that 'sex workers' interests are not uniformly served, or harmed, by the same legislation' (O'Connell Davidson 1998, 2006).[20] 'State-centred' approaches also fail to account for local conditions, which often appear at odds with the terms of the formal law. Formal classification and top-down approaches give a misleading impression of legal coherence. It relays a false impression of unity in policy settlements that are always provisional, often contradictory, and generally reflective of 'the varied and complex political influence of competing discourses and organised interests' (West 2000).[21]

Formalist approaches also give a misleading impression of legal coherence, which tends to disintegrate when legal practices are examined. The mediating influence of the exercise of discretion by officials, non-compliance by those whose conduct law is intended to regulate and the unintended social impact of laws,

20 Stakeholders in sex markets vary greatly according to location, capital and other social factors such as race, sex and sexuality. This means that forms of regulation will have a differential impact on what is a complex and varied market (see Kotiswaran 2011).

21 Considerable variation in policy practices exists between regions and cities. Some local areas operate quite autonomously from the national level, and discretion in designing and implementing policy, on matters such as public health, public order and spatial planning, all lead to significant differences.

policies and techniques, put in place in good faith by governments and other social actors, are often overlooked in many formal accounts which describe policy aspirations for law and are much less concerned with how law works in practice.[22] Of course, we cannot expect legal classificatory systems to do otherwise but we can expect more of analytical work. Yet, critical legal work is not sufficiently developed in the field of prostitution, with studies tending to focus on legal rules and their shortcomings, yet failing to properly elucidate the ways in which law operates in modern societies. While there is increasing recognition that 'law shapes but does not determine the extent of sexual exchange' (Neave 1985), there is little by way of analytical explanation, or connection to wider theories on the operation of law in late modernity. Existing treatises on the subject of prostitution, no matter how sharp the philosophical analysis (Nussbaum 1998; Anderson 2002; De Marneffe 2009), how critical the eye (Bernstein 2007a; Agustín 2009) and or how careful the empirical methodology (Weitzer 2012), fail to adequately comprehend the complex relationship between law and society.

Even feminist legal studies, usually critical of legal formalism have become ensnared in its binary framework.[23] A lot of time and energy has been spent on adopting the correct ideological and normative position, then using this to campaign for either the criminalisation of commercial sex or for its legal recognition as work. Unfortunately, these debates, like similar polarised debates in the women's movements regarding pornography, have 'generated a lot of heat and not necessarily very much light' (Valverde 1987: 21). As Kotiswaran, whose work is a rare exception,[24] notes:

> [F]or all the sophistication of feminist theorizing of sex work, when it comes to the law, feminists demonstrate signs of legal formalism.
>
> (Kotiswaran 2011: 186)[25]

22 A law may look good on paper but as Kennedy notes, '[P]aper rules may or may not be enforced' (Kennedy 2002) – and they will most definitely be enforced in selective ways, in particular spaces and times and for particular people. They may even be disregarded, a good example being the case of Germany, where despite being described as an example of legalisation par excellence, the reality, due to political convention, has been a system of regional control working counter to the intention of the state legalisation (Pates 2012).

23 Notable exceptions are Sullivan 1997, 2004; O'Connell Davidson 1998; Phoenix 1999, 2009; O'Neill 2001; Scoular 2004a, 2004b, 2010; Kotiswaran 2011.

24 Prabha Kotiswaran's *Dangerous Sex, Invisible Labor* provides a rich ethnography of sex work and its organisation, contrasting brothels in Sonagachi (Calcutta) with the more disparate sex work in temple town of Tirupati. Utilising insights from legal realism, legal pluralism and materialist feminism, she reveals the complex interactions of rules and their multiple and varied effect on the differently placed protagonists in different sectors of the sex market. I return to her work, as an example of the benefits of critically engaging with law, in Chapter 5.

25 She continues: [F]eminists, irrespective of whether they are of an abolitionist persuasion or not, all display an unwavering faith in the power of the criminal law' (Kotiswaran 2011: 14).

Feminist and other critical legal analyses have been stymied by an enduring legal formalism, ensnared in ideological battles between victims vs. sex workers and criminalising vs. legalising commercial sex. This has meant that less attention has been spent on the more convoluted task of understanding the complexities of how law works in practice.[26] Without this critical work, law may appear as removed from social life and as increasingly irrelevant, as some recent analyses suggest – an approach that takes us further and further away from the task of developing more pragmatic, inclusive and less dogmatic legal strategies.

Does law matter?

The gap between what law says and what law does leads to anxiety about the role of law in contemporary societies. Not only do the same laws work differently in practice, but different laws may have similar results on the ground, as recent empirical studies, including my own work with colleagues, attest (Bernstein 2007a; Hubbard et al. 2007). Our work, which examined the impact of regulation on the spaces of sex work, in the apparently distinctive systems in the Netherlands, Sweden and the UK systems, found a number of correlations:

> [S]treet prostitution is being increasingly repressed (and displaced) by the state on the grounds that it is benignly seeking to protect both prostitutes and communities. Through a contrary set of moves, prostitutes hence 'disappear' beyond the bounds of respectable visibility (and often the protection of the state and law): even in instances where prostitution has been brought within the ambit of state licensing systems (e.g. the Netherlands), critics allege a failure to address many of the issues of gendered inequality occurring in such off-street spaces.
>
> (Hubbard et al. 2008: 149)

These and analogous findings (Bernstein 2007a),[27] have provoked a long overdue consideration of the current role of law in society but the conclusions drawn in

26 This work is motivated by fact that there is surprisingly little written *on* law in this area. I should clarify, of course, there is indeed a great deal written *about* law – calling for increased legal sanction, or conversely reduced legal intervention. There have also been myriad reports and studies *describing* the content of various laws, empirical studies of policing and a great deal of political rhetoric, yet these rarely *engage* with the discipline of law itself. Despite massive regulatory complexity, analysis has become ever more narrowed in a binary of legalisation vs. criminalisation with decriminalisation appearing to fall somewhere in between. Laws are described and debated at great length, but rarely are they analysed in more than these narrow analytical terms. There are, of course, exceptions: Carol Smart 1989, 1995; Drucilla Cornell 1995; Nicola Lacey 1998, but no scholar has yet developed a sustained or detailed analysis of law and prostitution thus far.

27 These findings were echoed in a contemporaneous study by Elizabeth Bernstein, which contrasted the Dutch and Swedish systems with her native San Francisco. She found, as we did, that apparently distinctive policy approaches effected similar changes on the ground:

initial work I have found to be insufficient. Many commentators are left oscillating between two extremes – neither of which is particularly satisfactory; law is either irrelevant to the social scene (according to Agustín's expulsion thesis) or appears as a mere instrument of the economy (as suggested by Bernstein's more structural thesis).

For Agustín (2009) the fact that all systems are characterised by non-compliance, and much of sexual commerce takes place despite its supposed legal status, means that law does not matter:

> [I] dispute the usual assumption that these laws make reality on-the-ground very very very different. On the contrary, if someone were to come to Earth from Mars, they would look at commercial sex in the USA, which mostly has meant criminalising laws, and look at it in New Zealand or the UK or Germany, and not see much difference at all. The endless debating about legal systems to control prostitution is bizarrely irrelevant, except for its symbolic value.
>
> (Agustín 2009)

Bernstein appears to suggest that the commonality between different legal models is the product of larger structural forces:

> While the broad constellation of attitudes towards gender and sexuality as well as other components of national and local cultures, histories and regulatory strategies are by no means irrelevant to the configuration of sexual commerce in these cities, the shared realities ushered in by larger patterns of political economy have been more definitive in shaping its predominant forms.
>
> (Bernstein 2007a: 146)

These analyses highlighted to me the pressing need to find new analytical tools to better understand the contemporary significance of legal structures, processes and practices.

Such conclusions have, understandably, caused some sociological unease. Ron Weitzer, for example, questions the empirical basis of these findings, preferring a more grounded sociological explanation of the different systems (Weitzer 2012). The danger with any broad structuralist approach (which I do not think Bernstein

> [T]hree quite disparate versions of policy reforms in the late 1990s resulted in a common series of alterations to the social geography of sexual commerce: the removal of economically disenfranchised and racially marginalised street walkers and their customers from gentrifying city centres; the de facto tolerance of a smaller tier of predominantly white and relatively privileged indoor clients and workers; and the driving of illegal migrant sex workers further underground.
>
> (2007a: 146)

intends to offer but is what Weitzer attributes to her) is that, in the absence of an explanation of how the law interacts, reproduces, or diverges with the economy or other structures, the law simply appears as a tool of the market – an instrument of the political economy.[28]

While the economy is clearly a key factor in shaping the current configuration of commercial sex, this cannot be explained by economic factors alone. Empirical analysis of practices demonstrates that explanations of change are complex and cannot be reduced to single general factors such as 'the economy'. More attention needs to be given to how this works on the ground, how structures manifest themselves, and, indeed, how they may be resisted. This criticism also applies to the role of law in her analysis, which similarly lacks elaboration. Without further analysis of what is meant by 'regulatory strategies are by no means irrelevant' and an explanation of how 'larger patterns of political economy' come into play (Bernstein 2007a: 146), Bernstein's analysis risks giving the impression of structural determinism, with the market always operating behind the scenes.

And, while I agree with much of Agustín's description of the practical effects of many law reforms, I find her prescriptive conclusion that law 'just doesn't matter', that it is as she states 'bizarrely irrelevant' (Agustín 2009: 21) less convincing and somewhat concerning. While it is certainly the case that legal doctrine is over-privileged in most analyses of prostitution and while I would agree that blind faith in the law is unsustainable as a political and intellectual position, it does not necessarily follow from this that law does not matter in any significant way in shaping the contours of contemporary sex work.[29]

These concerns are not due to any unwavering belief in legal formalism but rather by the knowledge that law does matter, albeit not in the all encompassing way envisaged by formalists but yet in a more significant way than Agustín allows. By a conviction that by dismissing law's relevance, either by way of structural determinism or cultural evisceration, not only will the ways in which modern legal power operates be missed, but also the opportunities that law may sometimes be able to offer to mitigate the risks and harms of prostitution will be lost. Law can and should be used to make a difference in the contemporary politics of prostitution but this can only happen with a more sensitive understanding of what law is, how law works in practice and how law intersects with other structural forces in society.

28 Yet, by presenting sociological data without a governmental framework, Weitzer may miss the normative aspects of governance (see Scoular 2010).

29 Given the calibre of Agustín's work and the real insights she has brought to the field of sex work by pioneering a cultural, post-structural approach more generally, and given that empirical findings would appear to support the conclusion that the law is no longer relevant, it is necessary to take this account seriously. I did this in Scoular 2010, arguing that her analysis took a narrow sovereign understanding of law and showing how a constitutive approach could better explain these similarities.

To appreciate its contemporary significance and potential, it is necessary to view law through a governmental lens which highlights the part played by law in constituting the practices of prostitution.

Methodology – a new analytic of legal power

In this work, I seek to develop the first post-structural account of *both* the socio-political subject of prostitution *and* of law. I add a much needed critical analysis of 'law' to the already established post-structural account of the subject of prostitution, which recognises the political and constitutive nature of the 'prostitute subject', best captured by Bell's observation:

> [T]hat the referent, the flesh-and-blood female body engaged in some form of sexual interaction in exchange for some kind of payment, has no inherent meaning and is signified differently in different discourses.
>
> (1994: 1)

I show that law is part of this constitutive process. A constitutive sociology assumes that law – which is often assumed to sit outside society – is one of the many forces involved in producing 'the social'. My thesis rests on the liberating or perhaps unsettling insight, depending on your perspective, that the law *too* has no *inherent meaning*. As Rose and Valverde brilliantly observe, there is no such thing as 'The Law', except as a jurisprudential fantasy:

> There is no such thing as 'The Law'. Law, as a unified phenomenon governed by certain general principles is a fiction. This fiction is the creation of the legal discipline, of legal textbooks, of jurisprudence itself, which is forever seeking for the *differentia specifica* that will unify and rationalize the empirical diversity of legal sites, legal concepts, legal criteria of judgement, legal personnel, legal discourses, legal objects and objectives.
>
> (1998: 545)

My use of the term 'post-structural' signals a rejection of 'structural' explanations for social phenomena, which includes those who want to reduce explanation to concepts such as neo-liberalism, capitalism, the economy, individual agency, gender, sexuality and legal ideology. This does not mean, as some argue when critiquing post-structural work, that these factors are irrelevant or that nothing takes place, it simply means that the way in which social phenomena are constituted has to be explained. This is not to suggest that power is absent; neither is it to ignore the contexts in which its intersections create hegemonic effects (see Lloyd 2005 for an account of post-structuralism that recognises forms of global dominance). But it is to recognise that, as Deleuze notes, referencing Valvery: 'Le plus profond, c'est la peau' (Deleuze 1995: 119) – there is nothing deeper than the skin,[30] an insight that reminds us that social phenomena, whether termed the economy, the market, the family, or indeed the 'law', and the relationships between them, have to be observed, described and accounted for – not simply alluded to.

A constitutive approach is a helpful way to understand changes in legal power. Legal formalism is a methodology best suited to a particular operation of legal power, with absolute monarchies exercising sovereign power but is increasingly unable to cope with modern forms of power.

Foucault's work is particularly instructive as it attributes no particular form to law, but rather highlights its changing rationalities. His work focused in particular on the move from sovereign to normalising, disciplinary and bio-political power – the modern forms of power that are so pertinent to prostitution regulation. He noted:

> We must eschew the model of Leviathan in the study of power. We must escape from the limited field of juridical sovereignty and state institutions, and instead base our analysis of power on the study of the techniques and tactics of domination.
>
> (Foucault 1980: 102)

This does not mean that law has become irrelevant, but rather that the legal complex has become embedded within governmental strategies that increasingly centre on the routine administration of lives (Veitch et al. 2007). The legal complex has been governmentalised and, as Veitch, Christodoulidis and Farmer note:

> [W]hile it may no longer provide the model for power relations in society as sovereign and formal accounts maintain . . . remains a vital process through which modern power relations operate; 'a medium rather than a principle of power'.
>
> (Veitch et al. 2007: 242)

As law adapts to the wider social and political culture of neoliberalism, typified by a decentred economy and forms of governance that operate at a distance, it too increasingly reflects its 'economised model' (Rose and Valverde 1998) of power, operating through, not simply over, lives. Legal processes and actors and norms are increasingly drawn into forms of normalising, disciplinary and bio-political power 'which seek to produce subjects as effects of power and to 'structure the[ir] possible field of action' (Foucault 1982b: 221).

30 See Valverde 2003: 12–13: 'When asked to explain Foucault's method, Gilles Deleuze observed that a metaphor Foucault might well have used to describe his method is one drawn from Paul Valery's remark "le plus profond, c'est la peau"' (Deleuze 1995: 119).

A constitutive approach

This constitutive approach has been further developed by law and society scholars in the United States (Yngvesson 1988; Sarat and Kearns 1995, 1997: 7; Ewick and Silbey 1998; Silbey 2005; Merry 2006). Their work views law as an inseparable dimension of social relations. Law is not a separate system: rather, it is embedded in the social relations that it helps to constitute. Law does not simply reflect society – it works on and in it – as legal processes and norms participate in the constitution of culture, shaping consciousness, practices and social relations.

This requires that we ask different questions of law beyond its formal pronouncements and its binary categories of legal/illegal. To understand the contemporary power of law, we need to look not *simply at its sovereign expression* but rather at the way legal processes and norms operate, alongside other discourses, to construct the fabric of the modern subject. In order to understand law's more complex, constitutive role, it is necessary to decentre law from the outset.

Questioning formalist ideology (which, as Valverde notes 'dreams' of, rather than exhibits, a common knowledge) means that law loses its elite position and has no privilege in a more complex system of meaning. This does not, however, mean that law is irrelevant as some have previously argued (Hunt and Wickham 1994; Agustín 2009). Legal mechanisms, legal arenas, legal functionaries, legal forms of reasoning *are* involved in strategies of regulation, but they lack unity and privilege, whether as a unique source of legitimate authority or as a unique form of reasoning. As Rose and Valverde explain:

> The codes, techniques, discourses and judgements of law are only one element in the assemblages that constitute our modern experience of subjectivity, responsibility, citizenship both public and private, even of rights, or of guilt and innocence. The workings of law are always intermixed with extra-legal processes and practices.
>
> (Rose and Valverde 1998)

Rather than assume that law regulates 'prostitution' – it is necessary to move beyond sovereign power and beyond law's rhetoric, to look at what law does, rather than what law says it does. By doing so, we see it as part of wider processes that constitute certain subjects as objects of knowledge and as targets for governments and then authorises and informs system of governance that then act on these subjects. Law has no privilege in this process, but is one of a number of discursive and non-discursive practices that constitutes prostitution as a social fact. This does not mean we ignore law or legal actors but rather see their significance in context and in relation to all the elements of a wider system of meaning. The analytical device of problematisation is very helpful here (Rose and Valverde 1998: 545, citing Castel 1994).

> [A problematisation] is the ensemble of discursive and non-discursive practices that makes something enter into the play of true and false and constitute it as an object of knowledge.
>
> (Rabinow and Rose 2003:18)

Such an approach recognises that problems do not emerge from law itself but from the intersection of legal and extra-legal discourses, practices and institutions. Rather than ask how 'the law' regulates 'prostitution', it moves us to question how prostitution comes to emerge at various times as a target for government and 'what role is played by legal institutions, functionaries and calculations in this?' (Rose and Valverde 1998: 544–546).

Approaching the subject in this way not only allows us to understand better how law matters in contemporary settings and debates but also to begin to think how it could matter in different ways.

Structure of the book: a selective genealogy of prostitution

Grounded in a constitutive methodology, *The Subject of Prostitution* offers a selective genealogy of the subject of prostitution, focusing on the changing constructions of the 'problem of prostitution'.

While the exchange of sex for a price might be eternal, it only comes to the attention of government from time to time. The ways in which prostitution is constituted as an object of governance – in the context of changing forms of power – has implications for prostitution as a social practice that I outline in the sections that follow.

I use the lens of problematisation to identify three key epochs: the period in which prostitution moves from being conceived predominantly as an issue of sin to being understood as a significant governmental issue; recent representations of the subject either as a problem of male exploitation and campaigns that feature the prostitute as a 'rights-bearing subject'; as key to understanding the constitutive nature of the subject and changing rationalities of governance.

I begin in Chapter 2 by tracing the 'creation' of the modern prostitute subject in the Victorian era. This is not to suggest that commercial sex was invented at this time, or is to imply that attempts to control it were anything new. Rather, I argue that during this particular period of late nineteenth-century history, characterised by rapid social change (industrialisation, changing social norms and the birth of the social sciences), the problematisation and governance of certain forms of commercial sex took a particularly modern turn,[31] as prostitution emerged as 'governmental' issue.

31 In reference to 'modernity', although I locate this at a particular historical juncture – a period often defined as modernist by some – I am not making a temporal claim. Modernity is not a temporal

Prior to this, prostitution was often classified under the more general categories of vagrancy, drunkenness and other public disturbances and the tendency was to offer salvation through pastoral forms of governance, backed up by sovereign modes of repression. The economic and social changes of this period generated new modes of governance which developed more normative systems of social control, which collectively aimed to empower, protect, cure and reform the prostitute, to socially integrate rather than exclude. Only when such measures failed, were punitive measures utilised, legitimated as being necessary to protect the health of the population.

An important part of my analysis is to show that law is integral to these changing forms of governance. Despite overwhelming attention on the sovereign 'juridico-discursive apparatus of power', which is expressed vividly in the brutality of the forced testing sanctioned by the Contagious Diseases Acts, the legal complex, at this time, mirrored changes in wider governance, and was also very much part of the wider normative apparatus of power. 'Law' at this juncture does more than simply punish. Legal processes, norms and officials also operated to construct risky bodies, to demarcate public and private spaces, and to inform and authorise the normative controls and interventions of 'petty officials' (Rose and Valverde 1998), such as those involved in newly established public health initiatives, and the many in charitable organisations that sought to rescue their fallen sisters and put them back on the right path.

These transformations in legal power (in which law can be seen to have been governmentalised) are vital to understanding the significance of law in this area and indeed in contemporary forms of regulation. They help to explain why the Acts' later repeal (brought about from pressure from early feminists and the public concerned at their brutal regime of forced testing), does not signify the end of the 'loving power of the norm' (Tadros 1998). Legal processes continue to be involved in constituting and then regulating 'lives'. This normative function persists and is redeployed around new problematisations, often supported by further sovereign enactments, around the issues of; the protection of youthful or vulnerable sexualities, public nuisance, commercial sexual exploitation or sex workers' rights, as subsequent chapters will illustrate.

In Chapter 3, I examine the re-emergence of the prostitute as a victimised subject in the late twentieth and early twenty-first century. I trace particular processes whereby, in the context of what some have termed a moral panic over

but rather a qualitative state, a coming together of epistemologies and practices. Note it is not universal; neither is it complete. When stating 'the "prostitute" becomes a modern subject', I am aware that this process is not complete, fragile and resisted. John Gray in *Straw Dogs* (2002), documents the fallacy of enlightenment progress via science, as Latour and Porter note: 'We have never been modern' (1993). But this has not stopped modernist discourses from trying to attempt to control nature through science. The regulation of prostitution in the late nineteenth and early twentieth centuries is a prime example of this process and my discussion of the Contagious Diseases Acts and their wider context show the centrality of legal reasoning to this project.

'modern' sexual slavery (Weitzer 2007), prostitution has, in some states, been problematised as a form of gendered violence and as a barrier to gender equality. In this schema, increasingly pathologised male consumers act in concert with a rapacious market to exploit the apparent 'inherent' imbalance of power between the sexes. This leads to an increased emphasis on abolitionism and criminal censure in reform measures, as the state and law are called upon to save victims from the exploitation that is considered to be synonymous with the demand for commercial sex.

I use Sweden as a model of this process of problematisation. That this relatively small Scandinavian country has pioneered such a radical move that has enjoyed considerable international attention and influence is quite remarkable. To understand how this situation came about, it is important to understand the distinctive context of the Swedish law, which was formed against a backdrop of a panic about the influx of 'trafficked' women from Eastern Europe, fears around EU enlargement and anxiety over an assumed permissiveness in society and prostitution policies in other parts of Europe. Moreover, a history of paternalism in social policy, a hegemonic feminist movement and decades of social science work on the much neglected client, all help to make sense of the country's unique approach. My governmental approach not only sheds light on this process of problem construction, it also is useful in understanding policy transfers and in analysing efforts to pathologise clients and rescue victims of 'modern day slavery'.

While this has clear parallels to the earlier period's efforts to rescue 'fallen women', it is important to appreciate the contemporary drivers and the distinctive features of late modern governance, which operates primarily at a distance, through a system of self-governance, responsibilisation and in the wider context of a retrenched welfare system and conditional citizenship. Moreover, for the first time, men have been brought into the frame as, under the auspices of gender equality, the purchaser is increasingly the subject of concern, control rehabilitation and, failing that, censure. While this approach is packaged as the only way to achieve gender equality, this chapter looks at implications and politics of these emerging forms of regulation and questions their link to social justice.

Chapter 4 charts the emergence of the prostitute as a 'rights-bearing' subject, a characterisation that is gaining increasing salience via the discourse of sex workers' rights and is frequently invoked as an alternate to victim models. This chapter highlights both the promises and paradoxes of rights. In contrast to my final chapter, which takes a more nuanced approach to rights claiming, here I present 'sex workers' rights' at their most reductive, fixed, rudimentary and most singular: as either claims for recognition as 'work' or 'sexual identity'. I do this deliberately to make the connection between a modernist legal construction and some of the more mixed regulatory consequences that have been highlighted in work that assesses the impact of legalising and decriminalising prostitution (Hubbard et al. 2008; Sullivan 2010; Harrington 2012).

These emerging critical studies reveal the regulatory capacity of rights. When sex workers' rights are asserted as 'fully constituted and bounded' identities, around either the idioms of sex or work, these flattened subjects (i.e. economic entrepreneur or sexual liberator) risk being co-opted by systems of liberal and neoliberal governmentality (Scoular 2010), and may only be meaningful for a small section of self-governing individuals at the upper end of the marketplace. These forms of governance, which operate via responsibilisation, function in similar ways to the forms of exiting that apply to their victim counterparts.

Sex workers' rights, therefore, must be viewed in a critical light. This does not mean abandoning them altogether but it does mean embracing ambivalence, and recognising that sex workers' rights, like rights in general, are as replete with paradoxes as they are fecund with promise. This does not mean that rights are not meaningful or useful but it is to argue that the radical potential of rights is not guaranteed by their mere invocation but rather requires careful attention to their empirical effects and a more critical engagement with the supposedly stable subject of rights and the apparently modern discourse of law than has been the case up until now.

My point, as in the previous chapter, is that care needs to be taken to examine and critically reflect on the forms of governance that these apparently liberatory discourses of rights or exiting may support. By viewing the relationship between law and society as constitutive not merely instrumental, we open up a wider field of power which helps explain why similar reforms have different effects and apparently distinctive approaches (such as legalisation and criminalisation) may make little difference to many on the ground, as regards the practice of prostitution.

While such conclusions may appear discouraging, I argue that a post-structural methodology not only elucidates how law matters in a complex system of governance (operating in ways that so often simply consolidate power), but also suggests ways that law *could* be reconfigured to have more progressive effects in wider justice campaigns.

This leads me to Chapter 5, where, having offered a critique of modernist approaches that attempt to fix subjects in law and their negative regulatory consequences, I move to consider the implications of a post-structural approach to the subject. In this final chapter, I engage with critiques that argue that without a foundational subject, post-structuralism fails to offer a clear programme for action and risks moral relativism. These claims are even more pertinent in the context of current legal reform given the omnipotence of the liberal subject and liberal concepts in this discourse. Yet I dispute claims of nihilism and argue instead that acknowledging the political nature of the subject serves to invigorate legal engagement.

Given the centrality of legal reform in governmental projects, I show that it is necessary to pragmatically engage with legal norms but that one can do so without recourse to universals. I am interested in how we can manipulate tensions in the current normative order, to suggest new futures, the outcomes of which we cannot know in advance (Rorty 1989) and suggest ways to do this. By engaging creatively with the constitutive work that norms such as consent and rights do, I highlight some possibilities for increased justice, thus demonstrating that 'law(s)' can play a more constructive and effective role in mitigating certain risks and harms that are experienced by workers and clients in the sex industry.

Yet, however well intentioned reforms may be, or how carefully they are post-structurally conceived, there are always unforeseen consequences as governmental projects are produced by and implemented in varying social contexts. Thus an eye must always be kept on the empirical effects of any policies, including those I suggest at the end of this work. To understand how law matters, we must engage with the legal complex, in all its sociological complexity, and approach it pragmatically and critically rather than ideologically.

My conclusion reminds readers that a post-structural exposition does not intend to aspire to be in any way a 'programme' for legal reform, but that does not mean that my work is not underpinned by the search for a more progressive or constructive approach to addressing some of the negative outcomes of prostitution and its governance. I seek to break from current modernist thinking and offer a more modest, yet intellectually apposite, example of how a deconstructive engagement with law can offer a better understanding of the limits of using law as a means of regulation but also some hope as to where it may provide some leverage for justice.

Rather than being a comprehensive account or a final word on the subject or even a manifesto, it is hoped that this book inspires a new generation of scholarship that looks beyond the binary of illegal/legal to the complexities and to the possibilities of commercial sex and its regulation, and marks the beginning of a period of more critical engagement with the subject of prostitution and law.

Chapter 2

The prostitute subject as a metaphor of modernity: from sin to social problem

> [Life] passed into knowledge's field of control and power's sphere of intervention. Power would no longer be dealing simply with legal subjects over whom the ultimate dominion was death, but with living beings, and the mastery it would be able to exercise over them would have to be applied at the level of life itself; it was the taking charge of life, more than the threat of death, that gave power its access even to the body.
>
> (Foucault 1976: 142–143)

> What is a prostitute? . . . She is a woman with half the woman gone, and that half containing all that elevates her nature, leaving her a mere instrument of impurity; degraded and fallen she extracts from the sins of others the means of living, corrupt . . . a social pest, carrying contamination and foulness to every quarter . . . who like a disease, creeps, no precaution used, amongst the crowd . . . and poisons half the young.
>
> (Acton 1870: 166)

Introduction: frameworks of understanding: from theories of social control to a governmental approach

Contrary to the cliché that prostitution is the 'oldest profession' (Kipling 1899), much of what we understand today as the problem of prostitution is a relatively modern invention. Far from being a perennial problem, the common image of prostitutes as a special group of outcasts, requiring specialist forms of intervention and management, is a relatively new phenomenon.

Prostitution emerged as a mainstream social problem during the Victorian era. Many analyses of this period attribute the growing significance of prostitution as a social problem to the 'moral panic' induced by changes in the economy and social structures, brought about by the advent of industrial capitalism (see Table 2.1).[1]

In the sections that follow, I outline the limitations of this model, highlighting the problems with a structuralist approach more generally but also arguing that by

1 Elizabeth Bernstein in *Temporarily Yours* develops a typology that seeks to explain the changing meanings of sexual commerce in relation to broad shifts in the wider economic and social structures.

Table 2.1 Typology of changes of meaning of sexual commerce

	Early modern capitalism	*Modern-industrial capitalism*	*Late capitalism*
Work	Domestic production	Wage labour	Service work; 'creative' and 'flexible' jobs
Kinship	Extended kin networks	Nuclear	Recombinant families/ isolable families
Sexual ethic	Procreative	Companionate/promiscuous (gendered double standard)	Bounded authenticity

Source: Bernstein (2007a)

focusing on the negative effects of power, such approaches miss the constitutive nature of modern power, including modern legal power.

Moral panic

Stan Cohen argued that the process of creating identifiable groups requiring control and regulation is central to maintaining social order and preserving dominant power relations (Cohen 1972). According to this theory, periods of intense regulatory change are often preceded by moral panics. The threat and experience of social rupture provokes considerable anxieties on the part of certain groups, who seek to maintain control of social order to preserve existing power relations. This anxiety is assuaged by the creation and censure of 'folk devils' (Cohen 1972). These figures become particularly important during periods of significant change when power may be in flux and outsider groups are perceived as a threat to the social fabric and its associated norms. Thus the creation of the outsider figure and their sanctioning, often via repressive laws, gives the impression that social order has been re-established in the public imagination and permits the reassertion of hegemonic values.

She contrasts an early modern capitalist period (characterised by a focus on domestic production, wage labour and procreative sex) with modern industrial capitalism (characterised by wage labour, nuclear families, companionate and promiscuous forms of sex that are subject to a gendered double standard) and late capitalism (typified by service work, creative and flexible jobs, recombinant families and isolable individuals and a sexual ethics of bounded authenticity).

In the best Weberian style, it offers important insights into the relationship between sexual ethics and social structure. Yet, while this framework appears familiar to many, care should be taken not to generalise from this. As Kotiswaran notes, the typology is predicated on a particularly Western history (Kotiswaran 2011). Moreover, the typology gives the impression of temporality of progress, when in fact many cultures display many features simultaneously. I think Bernstein does recognise these factors, nevertheless, it is important to stress that this typology should be used as a loose explanatory framework to be used alongside careful empirical study, which the author provides, rather than as a formula.

This schema would appear to explain why, during periods of social flux, dangerous identities and issues of problematic consumption, such as alcohol, gambling and prostitution are familiar and convenient 'targets' for new laws, and programmes of social control and repression (Hunt 1999b). Indeed, the device of moral panic is commonly used to explain how prostitution in the Victorian era became an important focus for state, legal and societal attention, with this newly 'created' prostitute subject being expelled in order to assuage widespread cultural anxieties over the overlapping processes of urbanisation, immigration and women's shifting roles, during the intense social and economic transformation that characterised this era (Walkowitz 1980; McLeod 1982; Smart 1989, 1995; Edwards 1993; Spongberg 1997; Self 2003).

While this explanation certainly resonates with historical accounts of this period and offers a useful insight into some aspects of prostitution control, there are a number of analytical limitations to the social control framework that hinder its general applicability.

Limitations of the model

The first limitation that social control theories exhibit, in the context of modern prostitution regulation, is that they give the impression of a newly created figure of censure, when, in fact, prostitution has been a perennial problem. While moral panic may be a useful lens through which to understand some aspects of prostitution control (for example, it seems well suited to contemporary concerns over trafficking and its earlier antecedent, the 'white slave trade'), it is less suited to the changing representations of the subject in general.

The prostitute subject was always stigmatised, her identity already spoiled.[2] Indeed, she appears throughout history, as 'a dense signifier through which a variety of social anxieties' can be expressed (Phoenix 2007). What *does* change at this juncture, and what *is* novel, is not the problematisation of prostitution per se but the *nature* of her problematisation;[3] she is no longer simply a vehicle of sin but is also increasingly represented as a vector of disease, a form of deviant sexuality, a social malady.[4] The more expansive framework of governmentality, developed in this book, is better able to explain how new forms of governance both constitute and act on this ever popular site.

2 Thanks to Jo Phoenix for this point made in relation to my contribution to her 2009 collection, *Regulating Sex for Sale*. Her insight has stayed with me and motivated me to work through its implications here.

3 The female gender is important here and is intended to specifically refer to the construction of a particularly 'female' prostitute. It is important to note that both are social constructions but that male prostitution has its own etiology. As Scott notes, male prostitution only becomes a 'social problem' in the mid-twentieth century and follows distinctive processes of signification and problematisation. For a wonderful account of the making of the male prostitute subject, see Scott 2005: Chapter 6.

4 The framework of moral panic and folk devils may be more apt when used in the context of trafficking; see for example, Weitzer 2007.

A further problem with the lens of social control and its image of panic and censure is that it limits a proper investigation of power. Power operates 'behind the scenes' in this structuralist account and in a vertical, repressive manner.

The implication arising from the use of the term 'moral panic' is that the underlying 'anxiety' is irrational and responses to it represent an overreaction (Hunt 1999a). This gives the impression that there is something else going on behind the scenes; that moral panics are, in fact, a media conspiracy or a result of the economy. Hunt sees this as misleading or even as a variant of structuralism. That is not to say these factors are not involved in the apparatus of power, but it is to question the assumption that they are the whole story. It is important to note that moral panics *do* address real issues but in complex and, of course, power-laden, but not necessarily structurally determined ways. They are empirical events not structural smokescreens.

The more complex way in which power operates tends to be obscured in models of sovereign power that operate from the 'top down', in which 'law' acts on 'society' or a defined group of outcasts. Hunt (1999b) critiques social control theories for their tendency to ignore the critical issue of agency: the role of regulators and those subjected to regulation, the important issue of translation, discretion and resistance. He notes that power emanates from the middle (from helping professions, philanthropic interventions and forms of professional knowledge) and even from the self, via the promotion of self-governance, as much as from the command and control of others. To accommodate this more expansive field of power, it is necessary to abandon a singular focus on sovereign forms of power, as Hunt argues:

> It is necessary to expunge the Durkheimian focus on 'social control' by insisting that it is never 'society' that acts, but always and only people who act . . . on others or in so doing on themselves.
>
> (Hunt 1999b: 19)

For Hunt, it means abandoning the vertical image of power operating on or by a homogeneous group such as 'society'. For Hunt, there is no such thing as society. This is meant, not in a neo-conservative sense (which implied there were no bonds between individuals),[5] but rather in the post-structural or indeed sociological sense, which sees such terms as 'society' and 'nation state' as myths, which fulfil ideological purposes. As Hunt notes, rather than a 'society' that acts, there is an 'aggregate of people, their relations, conflicts and interactions' (Hunt 1999b: 19).

I would also argue that legal power is incompletely characterised in these accounts. Social control theory links the censure of prostitution to social structure, with the law operating as a lever for society's anxieties over changing social structures

5 The statement 'There is no such thing as society' was the famous mantra of the conservative leader Margaret Thatcher (UK Prime Minister, 1979–1990); interview 23 September 1987, as quoted by Douglas Keay, *Woman's Own*, 31 October 1987: 8–10.

and roles. The Contagious Diseases Acts of 1864, 1866 and 1869, a series of statutes that instituted a regime of compulsory medical testing of 'public' women, figure centrally in these accounts. Law in this context appears as a lever for social anxiety, brought down to punish the outcast group and in so doing it appears to secure the protection of the public's individual moral and social health (Smart 1989: 94). This imagery while appealing and familiar gives an incomplete account of legal power which operates well beyond the realm of negative sovereign power.

Indeed, Hunt's quote is reminiscent of Foucault's call to 'eschew the model of Leviathan when studying power' (Foucault 1980: 102). For Foucault this meant 'moving away from the limited field of juridical sovereignty and state institutions' and looking instead to 'the techniques and tactics of domination' (Foucault 1980: 102). This does not mean that law is irrelevant, but that its tactics and techniques change as it too becomes a medium for changing forms of governance that operates as much by inclusion and normalisation as it does by censure.

Governmentality provides a methodology that can trace the processes through which prostitution and the modern prostitute subject becomes constituted and regulated as a social problem, amid the social upheaval of the early nineteenth century.[6] The advent of prostitution as a major social issue coincides with the centralised and normative political power that accompanies the formation of the state and the changing dynamics of power, in what Foucault called the city–citizenry game (Valverde 2007: 164–165). Contrary to moral panic approaches that focus on the creation of a *new* folk devil, this approach, which focuses on changes in the problematisation of prostitution (from sin to social problem) offers a more nuanced and empirically rich account of the links between social constitution and political governance. It also offers a more subtle understanding of the operation of legal power, as the Victorian era displays a more complex and diverse approach to policing prostitution that cannot be reduced to 'a caricature of repressive moralism' (Howell 2009: x).

Prostitution as a 'sinful problem'

The construction of the female prostitute as an abject subject has a long history that predates the Victorian period. Throughout history she had been a figure of censure and an object of punishment. While there was no systematised approach to its regulation, with many temporal and regional variations,[7] what can be said is that in most parts of Europe in the pre-modern and early modern period prostitution was primarily regarded as a problem of sin.

6 For these reasons, Hunt's study of the regulation of prostitution forms a small part of a much larger examination of moral politics, which looks at prostitution, pornography, temperance, drugs and sex. My field of enquiry is different. I am attempting to present a critical account of legal power in the context of the regulation of prostitution across different epochs.

7 See, for example, studies such as Rossiaud 1988.

Scott notes that the prostitute was 'an anomalous figure' in this period, being neither fully in nor out of the symbolic realm (Scott 2005: 100). Within this schema, the prostitute subject, although frequently cited as an abject figure, was not straightforwardly banished. Like the leper in medieval society, she embodied pollution and defilement and thus performed important symbolic functions; she was a sinner as she had sex outwith marriage and outwith its prescribed procreative place but she could also repent and be saved. She was a useful reminder for all of humanity and performed a useful lesson for all of society – which balanced on the precipice of mortal sin and was in constant need of pastoral and spiritual care and the exercise of self-control.

The prostitute was an abject, sinful, morally polluting subject, whom society was encouraged to avoid. Rossiaud's work on medieval prostitution describes various forms of segregation and quarantining practices, such as the periodic closing of brothels and bathhouses during times of epidemic as well as temporal restrictions such as curfews imposed by local magistrates (Rossiaud 1988: 8–9, 58–59, 81). There were also rules in some cities on what clothes prostitutes could wear. In parts of France in the fifteenth century, for example, prostitutes were required to wear an *aiguillette*, a knotted cord of contrasting colour worn from their shoulder to waist, others were not permitted to wear silk, amber necklaces, gold or other signs of status. Such vestementary restrictions (which also applied to lepers and Jews in many parts of medieval Europe) indicated their 'spoiled identities' and were used to distinguish them from other members of the community (Rossiaud 1988). These interventions, whether they took the form of quarantine, punishment or vestementary restriction, all helped to emphasise the association between prostitution and sin, which continued throughout the eighteenth century (Scott 2005).

Law's sovereign power was used to repress or punish visible signs of sin but functioned in the main as a backup for pastoral forms of control. If a prostitute's sin was not remedied by penitence and pastoral guidance and absolution, performed by the church and its ministers, she could be punished under sovereign regimes that sanctioned punishment on the bodies of juridical subject. Thus floggings, branding and banishment (transportation) were intermittently inflicted on the bodies of prostitutes to reinforce the idea of the prostitute as a sinful 'other' but they were neither systematic nor organised but, rather, were individualised and sporadic (Mahood 1990: 21–22).

Laws were, at this time, silent on prostitution. It was managed as one of the many symptoms of a burgeoning population growth and policed by local officials under more general laws of nuisance and disorder (Henderson 1999: 76).[8] In most

8 Griffiths' study of the court records of London's Bridewell show a disproportionate number of sexual offences in the sixteenth century, with charges of vagrancy increasing in the seventeenth century, and women formed an increasing proportion of those arrested after 1600. This reveals how the capital's local government dealt with symptoms of burgeoning population growth, with an increasing number of women brought before the court as its focus moved away from sexual matters to those pertaining to the 'dangerous side effects of growth' (2008: 202), such as vagrancy and street crimes.

parts of the United Kingdom, centuries' old vagrancy laws governed policing and cast prostitutes alongside beggars, gamblers, thieves and vagrants, as common sources of nuisance and disorder.[9] The evidential basis for this nuisance was unclear and highly discretionary. Policing consisted of a mixture of informal and vaguely defined tactics. As Henderson notes: '[F]lexibility, compromise and the absence of a system were almost the defining characteristics of the policing of street prostitution in this period' (Henderson 1999: 140).

While the term 'common prostitute'[10] was used for the first time in the Vagrancy Act 1824, its use denoted a category that existed alongside the rest of the urban poor. It was decades before 'prostitutes' were singled out for particular attention and the term was used as a means of specific and dedicated governance (Henderson 1999).

Change can be attributed to a number of factors: increasing urbanisation, developments in local policing in the eighteenth century (including the advent of a new professional police force,[11] which was established in London in 1829 and was, by 1846, operating throughout the country) and the introduction of salaried magistrates. These developments led to an increased tightening of local control and ever increasing crackdowns on commercial sex and petty crime over the next two centuries (Walkowitz 1980; Henderson 1999).

The rationality for policing also changes at this time. The formation of the modern state and developments in medical and social science meant that prostitution was increasingly cast as a 'distinctive' bio-political problem bringing with it an increasing emphasis on the medical policing of prostitution.

9 These acts date back to before the Elizabethan era. The earliest vagrancy laws date from around 1380s – the Statute of Cambridge passed in 1388 established controls on the movements of labourers, servants and beggars. In the fifteenth century the Vagabonds and Beggars Act 1494, in the sixteenth century Henry VIII's Vagabonds Act of 1530, followed by Edward VI's Vagabonds Act of 1547 all made similar provisions. In the nineteenth century the Vagrancy Act 1824 was passed, elements of which are still in force in England and Wales today. This act was widely used to control and arrest all sorts of people including prostitutes. The Vagrancy Act 1824 was extended to Scotland and Ireland in 1871 via the Prevention of Crimes Act 1871. The entire act was repealed from Scots law by the Civic Government (Scotland) Act 1982 but certain elements are still in force in England and Wales.

10 The legislation did not define the term, and despite the fact that it was expressed in gender neutral language, it was only ever applied to women. This gendered application of the term was confirmed in the case of *DPP* vs. *Bull* [1994] 4 All ER 411 in which the court held that '"common prostitute" [was] a term honoured by common law usage as referring specifically to women' (Diduck and Wilson 1997: 505). The language of 'common prostitute' was removed from statute by s.16 of the Policing and Crime Act 2009 with Alan Campbell MP, then Parliamentary Under Secretary of State for the Home Office noting that it was 'outdated and offensive' (Hansard, HC Public Bill Committee, 9th Sitting, col.318 (10 February 2009)).

11 Reynolds 1998 notes that professional policing had beginnings in the watch practices in certain West End parishes. These watches, she argues, evolved into the modern police force of the late eighteenth century. Walkowitz notes that one of the aims of the reform was to create some distance between working class communities and police on the beat, which was not fully achieved.

In noting this change, I am by no means arguing that the association between sex work and sin is some historical anachronism that no longer applies. The conviction that prostitution is deeply immoral, against the laws of nature or god's will, remains and is shared by many, who, due to religious faith, moral conviction or political identity, or a combination of all three, hold particular values about the 'proper' place of sex and money. Such moralism continues to inform governmental and legal strategies, but it is no longer a singular signifier as during this particular period of history it was displaced and joined by newly formed modern epistemes: emerging scientific, 'psy' knowledges and legal discourses, which piled on, and augmented, an underpinning Christian moralism, to problematise prostitution as a governmental issue.[12]

Prostitution as a social problem: the modern subject of prostitution

> [T]he history of modern prostitution control offers a dynamic perspective on the private lives of women as well as the public functioning of medicine, patriarchy and the nation state.
>
> (Guy 1995: 182)[13]

The increased importance of prostitution as a social issue and its emergence as a distinct identity has to be understood in the context of the increasing importance of sexuality and sexual identity to the emerging social order. By the eighteenth century sexuality had become a focus of public and private attention, as it had never been before. In contrast to popular portrayals of earlier periods in history as sexually repressive, the Victorian era was actually a notably productive period in terms of the proliferation of sexual discourse (Foucault 1976). The Victorians may have covered up the legs on their pianos but to assume that this period is signified by repression and prudery misses the constructive role that sexuality played during this period of history.[14] As Foucault explains:

12 Modernity should not be read as radical discontinuity – elements present before remain – but they are joined by new features of modern governance (Howell 2009: 6). While recognizing that there is rarely a 'diachronically-neat transition from one rationality of governance to another' (Szymanski 2000: 558) with 'rationalities' of governance 'piling up' rather than replacing one another, my point is that it is the meanings and stigma surrounding prostitution that are now informed by a much wider range of discourses, with religion being just one of the many.

13 'The quote continues . . . and emphasizes the need to understand how gender and sexuality are interrelated inextricably to race, cultural diversity and economic circumstances' (Guy 1995: 182).

14 Foucault's (1976) work questions assumptions that sexuality is a domain of increased 'enlightenment' of freedom or liberation, rather, he shows it to be a site of struggle and politics. Thus, contrary to common understandings that cast previous periods as marked by repression moving through time towards increased 'rationalism', it is rather often in great flux.

> Toward the beginning of the eighteenth century, there emerged a political, economic, and technical incitement to talk about sex . . . This need to take sex 'into account', to pronounce a discourse on sex that would not derive from morality alone but from rationality as well, was sufficiently new that at first it wondered at itself and sought apologies for its own existence. How could a discourse based on reason speak like that?
>
> (Foucault 1976: 25)

The emergence of the middle class as a social and political force is key to understanding the increasing significance of sex and the, related, creation of the modern prostitute subject. In the context of fundamental changes in the modes of economic and social production and in kinship models, sexual identity comes to the fore as means of delineating social standing, supplementing and overlaying class distinctions (Ridgway 1997).

Dabhoiwala (2012) describes this as the 'first sexual revolution', in which previous understandings of sex were unsettled. It is important to recognise that this is a distinctly political process, one of social constitution rather than the result of economic determination (Mahood 1990: 12). Three centres of knowledge, medical, legal and psychiatric discourses, were deployed to constitute a new public sexual discourse (Foucault 1976). Whereas previously sex was to be confined to its procreative function or be repressed, sexual desire could now fulfil positive social functions. The polarisation of public and private spheres became the foundation upon which the ascendant bourgeois constructed the family and its sexuality. Sexual desire was increasingly viewed as a natural drive that had to have an outlet, meaning that sex outside marriage was increasingly tolerated *for some*. Promiscuity and adultery were more acceptable for heterosexual men.

Alongside this, women were seen to be naturally more virtuous than men. Overt displays of female sexuality were frowned upon and stigmatised. They were to be seduced by men; an assumption that created a double standard of sexual morality with enduring effects on women's sexual autonomy. The notion of the companionate marriage (Dabhoiwala 2012) and the figures of the publicly and competitive orientated husband and his passionless reproductive wife, confined to a private life of domesticity, are central reference points for the development of a new normative sexual order[15] which no longer simply revolved around licit/illicit.

In processes of cultural formation, as Foucault and Mary Douglas have so clearly articulated, the construction of insiders cannot avoid the construction of outsiders (Douglas 1970). In generating new normative standards for appropriate

15 This was further augmented by the development of psychiatry and sexology in the period from 1890 to 1910, which effected a major transformation in theories of sexuality (Ellis 1897; Freud 1912).

sexual identities, those who failed to meet these qualifications were also constituted. As Foucault noted:

> The pervert, child masturbator, homosexual, hysteric, prostitute, primitive and nymphomaniac, all emerged as distinctly classified sexual species possessing their own internal 'secret' which had been revealed by the penetrating gaze of science.
>
> (Ridgway 1997)

In this normative context, the modern prostitute body was produced as a negative image of the bourgeois subject, as Bell notes, she was 'an empty symbol filled from the outside with the debris of the modern body/body politic, a sign to women to sublimate their libidinal body in their reproductive body' (Bell 1994: 72).

Prostitutes were seen as spreading contagion and weakening the modern social body as they disrupted the boundaries of the emergent bourgeois family. They threatened the symbolic order and were increasingly pathologised as contrary to the norm. While prostitution was already contrary to some accepted ideal of sex (its procreative role) and had been for centuries, it only began to be seen as deviant with the advent of social sciences and increasing normative expectations regarding sexuality. While some studies and laws in Europe had connected prostitution with syphilis, without the whole discipline and apparatus of public health: a whole systematised body of thought connecting contagion with sex, the association with disease was much more socially muted. The advent of public health, developed through the new epistemologies of social and medical science, meant that they could now be classified as a bio-political problem.

The science of prostitution

> The prostitute body was mapped – marked out and defined – as a distinct body, and 'the prostitute' was actively produced as a marginalized social-sexual identity, part during the latter half of the nineteenth century and the beginning of the twentieth century.
>
> (Bell 1994: 40)

During the nineteenth century prostitution began to be researched by social scientists. Emerging social science methodologies of social anthropology, statistical inquiry, empirical survey, phrenology, and physiognomy were central in defining the contours of the prostitute social body (Bell 1994: 41). In this 'age of reason', science was elevated to the previous position of religion, and scientific studies allowed prostitution to be understood and problematised in new ways: on a scientific rather than moral basis. Walkowitz notes that the regulation of prostitution was partly informed by some of the earliest applications of population statistics and qualitative research interviews to social problems (Walkowitz 1980: 32–47). The emerging fields of public health, sanitation and hygiene were of central importance to this process, in particular the epidemiologies provided by Alexandre-Jean-Baptiste Parent-Duchâtelet and William Acton, whose work was instrumental to the process of 'making up' this new identity.

Parent-Duchâtelet was one of the most eminent social hygienists of the nineteenth century, with studies on a range of subjects from food waste, the effects of tobacco, the sewers of Paris to prostitution. *De la prostitution dans la ville de Paris* (On Prostitution in the City of Paris), published in 1836, provided a model for subsequent research around the world and led him to be dubbed 'the Newton of Harlotry' (White 1990: 3). The study based on 12,000 registered prostitutes, it was one of the first epidemiological studies of prostitution. In it, Parent-Duchâtelet applies the same rationality to prostitution as he did his previous subjects:

> I have been able . . . to penetrate into the sewers, to handle putrid matter, to spend part of my time in refuge dumps, in a sense to live in the midst of the most abject and disgusting products of large groups of people, why would I blush to enter into a sewer of another type (a sewer more impure, I swear, than all of the others) in the hope of doing some good.
>
> (Parent-Duchâtelet 1836: 6, in Harsin 1985: 108)

While there is an obvious moral dimension to the association between prostitution and disease and pollution, with references to prostitutes as 'putrid matter' and being 'happy in mire and filth' (Parent-Duchâtelet 1836: 135, in Bell 1987: 48), these studies are about more than the simple imputation of moral censure. By making a link to his previous work on sewers, Parent-Duchâtelet extends a public hygiene discourse, setting the scene for a new public health framework and management of prostitution (Gilman 1985; Corbin 1990).

His work, which includes interviews with women and observations of their lifestyle alongside statistical analysis (Walkowitz 1980: 36), helped to create an anthropological category, described, delineated by social science methods and went on to inform future studies and regulatory strategies.

The pathological and social 'taxonomy of prostitution' that emerges from his work is interesting. The subject that emerges from the descriptions is both ambivalent and contradictory. The prostitute body, while diseased, is not inherently different from the bodies of any other women. Parent-Duchâtelet notes that the virtuous and prostitute are 'somatically the same'; their genitals and reproductive organs, for example, are 'surprisingly similar' (!). Yet, he notes, their genitals are '*situationally* more prone to disease' (Bell 1994: 47, emphasis added). This is significant, as Bell notes, as in contrast to work that casts the prostitute as an inherently or somatically diseased body (for instance, Ellis 1910), Parent-Duchâtelet renders the prostitute body *socially* prone to disease, which must then be kept clean of disease via social regulation (Bell 1994: 48). This construction is crucial in terms of the modes of governance that follow. The fact that the prostitute body is territorialised as a socially, pathologically and environmentally risky body, justifies a range of normative (and punitive) controls, spatial as well as medical interventions, which are instituted in order to protect the newly formed 'public health'.

Social regulation and surveillance can then be justified on the basis of the permeability of the boundary between the prostitute and the non-prostitute, as the identity of the prostitute is the same but different. Reintegration into society is still possible, provided she conforms to newly establishing norms regarding health and social acceptability (especially sexual virtue).

Acton

The framework set out by Parent-Duchâtelet was followed closely in Acton's 1870 publication *Prostitution Considered in its Moral, Social and Sanitary Aspects*. This work has been described as 'a combination of scientific observation and analysis, social criticism and open propaganda' (Humphreys 1972: v). This is evident in the quotation featured at the opening of this chapter, where in response to the rhetorical question, 'What is a prostitute?', Acton answers with a combination of moral censure and scientific data gleamed from his own classificatory study, which attempts to provide social science data about the prostitute from a larger typology of women.

In this work, prostitutes are described according to physical characteristics (such as eye and hair colour, eyebrows (?!) and voice), social and economic determinants, conduct and cleanliness (Scott 2005: 98). Subjects are then classified according to levels of visibility and deportment as Acton differentiates between different 'classes' of prostitutes, including 'common prostitutes', a term taken from the Vagrancy Acts but used here as a form of social categorisation:

> The order may be divided into three classes – the 'kept woman' [a repulsive term, for which I have in vain sought an English substitute]. Who has in truth, or pretends to have, but one paramour, with whom she, in some cases, resides, the common prostitute, who is at the service, with slight reservation, of the first comer, and attempts no other means of life; and the woman whose prostitution is a subsidiary calling.
>
> (p.28)

Much of the analysis in the study appears contradictory; at times the prostitute subject is healthier than others then at other points she is 'ridden with disease'. Such apparent inconsistencies, however, make sense when viewed in the context of modern normative power, where, as Foucault notes, power operates according to relation not separation:

> [T]he principle of power is not some absolute system of difference that acts to demarcate between good and bad instead power operates more broadly and more subtly, visible as a constant anxiety or pressure to conform to shifting and forever unattainable norms.
>
> (Scott 2011: 54)

The scientific examination of the prostitute population meant that prostitution could be understood, problematised, regulated and punished in new ways. The behaviour of prostitutes is not classed according to a binary schema that differentiated good from bad as in the previous model. Rather than producing the prostitute as 'other', new scientific technologies multiplied and differentiated the body of the prostitute with 'classes of prostitutes distributed along normalising scales, according to measures of sociability' (Scott 2011: 60) on a continuum of normalcy ← → deviance. As Scott notes, 'power differentiates the bad from the bad and pluralises in order to bind populations' (Scott 2011: 54). These classificatory systems fed into models of regulation that governance operated by inclusion not simply exclusion.

Regulation

By the mid-nineteenth century most European states had moved the regulation of family life and 'its alternatives' (Mahood 1990) out of the purview of church courts and under aegis of secular state control (Luker 1998: 602). Populations, health and productivity became increasingly a key governmental concern of a newly delineated social body (Foucault 2003: 239–263). Problematic sexual practices and identities, such as prostitution, adultery, and homosexuality, became a 'police' matter in the sense that there was a need to make them align with the public welfare (Mahood 1990: 10).

The system of regulationism and medical policing of prostitution that was developed was an elaboration of this 'bio-politics'. Regulation was to become more 'enlightened', but that did not necessarily mean progressive, but rather having recourse to reason, to 'medical and social science', which became authoritative forms of knowledge in dealing with the challenges of modern urban industrial life due to developments in social science and modern state craft. Prostitution did not cease to be an object of punishment but the mode of its problematisation and forms of governance changed. As Mahood (1990) notes, efforts to cure or reform did not signal a shift to a more tolerant or humane system – rather they represented a shift to medical responsibility where new technologies of power emerged, designed to penetrate the soul. The idea was not punish less but to punish better and more deeply within the social body (Foucault 1975: 82).

This process was furthered by the development of specific institutions such as the Magdalene asylums and lock hospitals which were set up in this period to manage prostitution via public health control. Moral reformers were increasingly concerned that the treatment of the urban poor, paupers, orphans and wayward women, via incarceration or corporal punishment, tended to harden rather than reform. Instead philanthropists advocated for the care and moral reform of these unfortunates, for them to be trained in middle-class values and behaviour and standards of femininity in order to successfully reintegrate into society.

The London Asylum was established in 1750 as a place where poor girls at risk of seduction could be sent, to be trained as servants. In 1758 the London Magdalene Hospital in Whitechapel was established as a reformatory for penitent prostitutes.

These institutions quickly spread throughout Western Europe and Australia. Their aim was not simply repression but the moral reform of working-class women, through religious instruction, moral education and training in domestic service.

Subjects could also be detained in lock hospitals, established for the medical treatment of syphilis and VD and curative measures forced on them in the interests of public health. This practice was strengthened by later acts of parliament that introduced a codified system of medical regulationism in some parts of the UK.

Regulationism

With origins in the pre-Napoleonic code and informed by the work of Parent-Duchâtelet and fellow epidemiologists, a regulationist model of state-supported medical policing of prostitution was developed in France. This model combined pre-modern and modern practices. Enclosure and surveillance techniques installed prostitutes in strictly monitored locales or in other disciplinary institutions such as reformatories, hospitals or prison. This was combined with the registration of prostitutes and the licensing and inspection of brothels (*maisons de tolerance*), which were under state control. Policing operated to enforce administrative regulations and repress prostitution where necessary. The system operated through much of the nineteenth and early twentieth century and became a model for many European states. Howell (2009) describes the key components of medical policing as being:

1 Identification: this was carried out via policing which itself was a diffuse practice and was increasingly informed by medical models and modes of classification.
2 Inscription: this involved the entry of known, and hence tolerated, prostitutes into police registers.
3 Inspection: regular medical inspections were carried out, and, if necessary, curative steps taken.
4 Incarceration: commitment of those considered a risk to special lock hospitals or equivalent, until they were no longer a threat to newly established public health services.

Influenced by the continental system (many leading regulationists in the UK were venereologists[16] who had studied medicine in Paris (Walkowitz 1980)), the UK parliament[17] enacted a series of statutes, collectively known as the

16 Venereology is the study and treatment of sexually transmitted diseases.

17 This was at the time the parliament of the United Kingdom included Great Britain and Ireland. I refer mostly to England and Wales and Ireland – where the acts operated. Similar processes of governance operated in the USA, and the colonies of Canada, Australia and India, all of which were under British rule. In each case, the laws interacted with distinctive cultures and thus had varied effects. Some generalisations can be made but we should not ignore the contingencies of these distinct cultures.

Contagious Diseases Acts, 1864, 1866 and 1869, which introduced a muted form of regulationism.[18]

The Contagious Diseases Acts

These measures were part of a wider movement for sanitary protection[19] that aimed to provide an infrastructure to protect the newly created 'public health'. They were just one of a number of pieces of 'scientific' legislation aimed at eradicating hazards to health, via the incorporation of expert knowledge and increased centralised regulatory control (Hunt 1999b: 144). The acts were heavily influenced by developments in social scientific knowledge, for example the second edition of Acton was published in support of the acts and his work was cited in support of them.

The main aim of the acts was to prevent the spread of venereal disease in the military (and thus protect the integrity of the nation) but there was a secondary aim: to protect women, especially young girls, from prostitution. The first of the statutes was passed in 1864 and authorised a compulsory medical regime of 'sanitary [or surgical] inspection' of women suspected of being prostitutes in a number of military areas of southern England and Ireland. Those who were found to be diseased or who resisted inspection could be detained in a lock hospital for three months. Later acts, passed in 1866 and 1869, extended both the scope and techniques of the statutory regime. On recommendations of the medical committee, who advised periodic inspection 'under a well-organised system of medical police' (Mort 1987: 81), the 1866 Act permitted the compulsory examination of every 'common prostitute', and extended the area of spatial control to 11 more garrison towns and increased the period of detention to six months.

Fortnightly examinations of all known prostitutes were introduced in 1869 and detention further extended to a period of nine months, in which moral and religious instruction of those confined was to be provided.

The extension of sovereign powers under the later acts meant that the police were given unlimited powers to pick up any and every female they considered suspicious. Suspected prostitutes could be excluded from parts of cities and forced to wear distinguishing apparel. Women were also forced to undergo invasive medical examinations to determine whether or not they were carrying the disease and to establish their general sexual standing. The government issued cards to women who were medically checked as 'clean' and who could return to the streets.[20]

18 A 'proctorial system' set up under medieval charter in university towns, was an early antecedent to the Contagious Diseases Acts. This regulatory system, which aimed to protect the sexual health of the undergraduate population operated in Cambridge and involved a small zone of tolerance, repression of street prostitution and the compulsory inspection of women and detention if diseased.

19 Examples include the Food Adulteration Act 1860; Vaccination Act 1861; Diseased Meat Act 1863; Sanitary Act 1866; Public Health Act 1876.

20 There was resistance to the Acts. Walkowitz 1980 describes the influence of Mrs E. M. King, feminist and free thinker, whose agitation encouraged 75 cases of non-compliance in Plymouth in 1870.

For those women who refused to be surgically examined or who were found to be diseased, the consequences were severe. They could be imprisoned, forced to undertake hard labour and detained in lock hospitals. During such stays 'fallen women' were subject to moral and religious instruction, in order to relearn their feminine virtue, and make them fit for re-entry into domestic life in service or in marriage.[21]

Attempts were made to further extend the acts into other parts of the UK, but this was not successful and public opposition to them began to surface in the early 1870s. Opposition became increasingly formalised as repeal associations were formed, which drew thousands of women into the political arena for the first time. Among which was the newly formed Ladies National Association (LNA),[22] which under the leadership of Josephine Butler, sought to challenge male centres of power – such as the police, parliament, and the medical and military establishments, involved in the administration of the contagious diseases regime. In coalition with middle-class evangelicals and radical workingmen, opponents decried the acts as immoral and unconstitutional, and called for their repeal. A main focus of these campaigns was to highlight the cruelty of the medical examination (described as an act of 'instrumental rape' (Walkowitz 1980), which was successful in igniting widespread public opprobrium and support for repeal which was eventually secured in 1886.[23]

The legacy of repeal

Accounts of the operation of the acts and the repeal movements they inspired have been well documented. While this period has been described by some as 'a golden era of feminist politics' in which 'feminist attitudes were much more homogeneous', united in viewing prostitution as the 'profanation of the dignity and individuality of women' (Elmy, quoted Jeffreys 1997a: 1),[24] a more complex history is provided by feminist and critical historians such as Lucy Bland and Philippa Levine, Alan

21 It would be interesting to compare the moral instruction of women at that time with the content of contemporary exiting programmes which may also (unwittingly) advance some fairly unchallenging norms, for example by encouraging women to enter into low-tier, unstable service sector work and urging conformity with acceptable forms of domestic sexuality (see Scoular and O'Neill 2007).

22 The two most significant repeal movements, the largely male National Association for the Repeal of the Contagious Diseases Act and the Ladies National Association (LNA), were organised along sexist lines. The former were to concentrate on developing a 'rational', 'scientific' critique of the acts ('leave the science to the men, dear'), while the LNA, formed in 1869 under the leadership of Josephine Butler, was to focus on the public aspects of the act. Interestingly, the structure of the repeal movements, while intended to perpetrate a strict gendered division, unintentionally effected a radical change, as, for the first time, women entered into the public sphere.

23 A parliamentary motion noting disapproval of forced examinations of women under the Contagious Diseases Act was a precursor to their later suspension in 1883 and repeal in 1886.

24 Jeffreys portrays what she regards as the heroic efforts of the National Vigilance Association in her book, *The Spinster and Her Enemies* (1997b).

Hunt and Judith Walkowitz. Their work casts doubt on the notion of a singular feminism and shows that 'feminist objectives' in this area were deeply contested[25] (as indeed they still are). The class and colonial dynamics of the movement and their campaign is also shown to inform both the tenor and legacy of reform (Smith 1971; McHugh 1980; Walkowitz 1980).

Maternal feminism

Writers highlight the 'maternal' feminism deployed by the Ladies National Association (LNA) which sought to rescue women from the brutal regime (but also from prostitution more generally),[26] while a useful trope to use at this time as a means to lever entry to the political realm, concealed both class and colonial divisions with harmful effects on those it sought to save.

As Walkowitz notes: '[W]hile female victimisation was a sincere concern of feminists, it also served diverse political interests' (Walkowitz 1980). It was used to appeal to men to protect, rather than emancipate, women.[27] The needs of poor women were often interpreted through the lens of campaigners' own class interests and overlooked the state and the economy's role in structuring and maintaining a distinction between women. These campaigns did not advocate liberating women from traditional roles, from their primary sexual, reproduction, maternal and domestic functions but instead relied on these tropes in order to gain a political voice for the middle class.

Moreover, claims for protection by middle-class feminists on behalf of their 'poor sisters' at home cast prostitute and young working-class women as objects of care and concern while, at the same time, positioning themselves as moral custodians. This construction, which both distanced the campaigners from the mass of working-class women and drew them closer to the politically enfranchised male (while retaining their virtue and femininity) was to prove important to an emerging suffrage movement (Walkowitz 1980). Opposition to the acts provided a vehicle for political solidarity, helping to gain political recognition for some women and is often cited as a precursor to the later enfranchisement of some, notably propertied, women over 30, which was to follow in 1918.

25 Hunt identifies four strands in the oppositional discourse of the repeal movement. This includes the suppression of vice; a critique of double standards; anti-regulationism, (i.e., liberal opposition to state intrusion) and radical populism (Hunt 1999b: 146–147). From this, we can see where the tensions in feminism comes from as many repealers, understandably, utilised a number of competing discourses in mounting their dissent.

26 Feminist censure, while potentially counter-hegemonic, often became normative when extending to a more general crusade against prostitution as degrading to women, often forming uneasy alliances with moral puritans in the process.

27 Walkowitz notes that respectable working-class parents shared many of these paternalistic and sexist sentiments: 'Despite the fact they often sent their own daughters out to work at thirteen, they nonetheless took pains to restrict their social independence and sexual knowledge and experience' (Walkowitz 1982: 84).

Colonial dynamics

Burton extends this critique, revealing colonial dynamics as the LNA sought to extend its campaign to reach women in the colonies as it rallied against the expansion of the acts but also against commercial sex as a form of oppression for all women. Butler and her circle turned their attention to similar measures that had been 'exported' to the colonies[28] and to saving their 'poor' sisters abroad who suffered under the tyranny, not only of the discriminatory regime but also from the existence of prostitution more generally. Burton highlights that Victorian feminists' relationship to the 'injured identities' of 'colonial others' (and their poor sisters at 'home') was central to feminist desire to (re)focus the attention of the state on 'their own desire for inclusion in the body politic' (1994: 339) as these campaigns helped in a larger struggle for enfranchisement.[29] The campaign against the Contagious Diseases Acts was transported to rescue, civilise the poor unfortunates and in the process reaffirmed Britain as the centre of democracy and by claiming rights on behalf of others, feminists were able to claim their right to participate in the empire (Burton 1994: 499).[30]

These perspectives are interesting as they assign a discursive power to feminism – it is not assumed to be above power, but is actively involved in relations of power. These insights also highlight the limitations of a feminism that views gender as a universal signifier and is inattentive to class and racial dynamics.

My contribution to this scholarship is to show that an analysis of modern legal power can augment this critical history. A governmental approach that moves beyond law's symbolism, beyond a singular focus on statutory law and frameworks of repressive power, to seeing law as a series of practices, allows us to appreciate the constitutive and productive role that law plays, as part of a wider normative system of governance. This is not to deny the impact and the symbolism of the

28 Prevention of Contagious Diseases Act 1868 (Queensland), Conservation of Public Health Act 1878 (Victoria); Contagious Diseases Act 1879 (Tasmania). In India, East India Contagious Diseases Act 1887. In Canada, Contagious Diseases Act 1865 (Province of Canada).

29 The LNA and some of its individual members were involved in the wider campaign for women's votes.

30 Not content to only represent their 'poor sisters' at home, by 'invoking ideas of women's supposed ability', based on 'essential feminine characteristics, to identify with the suffering bodies and therefore, to represent them politically' (Doezema 2001: 22), these Victorian feminists reproduced hierarchies of age, race and class in their efforts to save fallen sisters abroad.

The spectre of slavery employed in campaigns at this time (present in many contemporary trafficking campaigns), conceals a colonialist discourse that casts subaltern women's identity as 'homogenised, backward, helpless and inferior' (Burton 1994). For example, in May 1887 Butler told the *Sentinel*:

> [O]ur poor Indian sisters claim our sympathy even more than our own country women who were subjected to the Contagious Diseases Acts, for not only are they women oppressed by men, but they are the women of a conquered race oppressed by their conquerors. Their hope of deliverance must seem to them so very far off.
>
> (Burton 1994: 146)

acts but recognises that they are not 'the be all and end all of Victorian regulationism or policing which is more than mere repression moralism' (Howell 2009: 22).

The legal legacy: how law matters

> [The Contagious Diseases Acts are] the single most important legal intervention addressing sexuality through the 19th century.
>
> (Mort 1987: 53)

While the Contagious Diseases Acts are certainly 'the most prominent and by far the most studied legislation for the policing of prostitution in Victorian Britain', they were, in effect, a very 'localized intervention in the economy of sex' (Howell 2009: 1) in place for a relatively short period of time, just over 20 years, and in a small number of districts,[31] although the geopolitics of the empire meant that this 'local intervention' could operate on an imperial scale.

Despite efforts to expand their reach, the acts never extended into the more highly populated urban centres in the UK, including the capital, London, where prostitution was most prevalent. In the districts in which they operated, the acts were superimposed on local modes of policing, were inconsistently applied, highly contested and often resisted by those who were subject to their power[32] (Walkowitz 1980).

More grounded historical research shows a much more varied map of policing in the nineteenth century. The acts were part of a much more complex plural rule network, which consisted of formal legal rules and informal social norms (Kennedy 2002). Vagrancy law continued to structure the culture of negotiation between police and prostitutes (Howell 2009; Lee 2012). Some of the most populated cities developed their own approaches to prostitution. For example, a

31 By 1869 the Acts operated in 18 districts, mostly naval ports and army towns in Britain and Ireland.

32 Some women publicly refused to comply with the acts, encouraged in some places by feminist campaigners. Others subverted them by recasting the practice of inspection as a form of 'licensing' or 'registration'. Calling themselves 'Queen's Women', women used the cards to attract custom. Walkowitz notes that this was a great irony, as the laws were, in part, designed to eradicate prostitution, yet through their operation, as he notes, it became virtually a state-run industry, as the acts created card-carrying prostitutes (Walkowitz 1980). In terms of the operation of the law, there was inevitably a real difficulty in identifying targets due to the fact that intimacy and commerce were, and indeed are, routinely combined. This was a period of significant urban poverty and many women, even those in paid employment and service, commonly sold sex to supplement their bare incomes. This meant that there was a real difficulty in deciding precisely who was a prostitute and who was not. With such wide discretion and unlimited powers of arrest, the potential for corruption was great. Plainclothes police officers picked up women at random, often on the basis of gossip and bribes and sex was commonly exchanged for clemency. The most sociologically sound studies recognise that prostitution was a transitional occupation for a predominantly working-class group of young women, at that time daughters of artisans, those who had previously been domestic factory workers.

system of regulationism continued at a local level in Liverpool from 1872 until 1890. This combined proactive municipal policing with the containment of tolerated brothels in one part of the city (Howell et al. 2008; Howell 2009).[33]

Other apparently 'voluntary' systems operated, such as the Glasgow system of police repression, which was pioneered in the city under the Police Act 1866 and later adopted in Manchester, Leeds, Edinburgh and other Scottish towns. The system combined repression and reform with the police and the Magdalene Institution acting in partnership with the shared aim of eradicating prostitution from the city. According to the city's Chief Constable McCall, the police endeavored to make the trade 'so hard and unprofitable' that women were 'glad to take refuge' in the Magdalene Institution (Mahood 1990: 145). It was presented by city officials as 'morally superior to the compulsory systems of state regulation like the Contagious Diseases Acts' as it was a 'voluntary system of care and cure', which, they claimed, did not violate women's civil rights as women 'chose' to enter the lock hospital for medical treatment or the Magdalene Institution for 'rehabilitation' (Mahood 1990: 129). This 'choice' was, however, exercised in the context of relentless police repression, which subjected women involved in prostitution, or identified as such, to repeated fines, imprisonment and police harassment.[34] While the proponents of the Glasgow system were keen to argue that it was 'effective' in reducing prostitution in the city, Mahood argues that it 'is doubtful that the system had any permanent effect on prostitution in Glasgow' and instead that working women were displaced and adopted more discreet working practices (Mahood 1990: 149). Thus the system operated to spatially restructure prostitution, moving it from public to private spaces in line with bourgeois morality.

A myopic approach to law, which is confined to the Contagious Diseases Acts, overshadows what is, in fact, 'a patchwork of local informal regimes directed towards disease and disorder' (Howell 2009: 1). Moreover, simply looking to

33 Liverpool's managed system came under fire when it drew the attention of moral reformers who considered tolerance as similar to the pernicious contagious diseases regime and as out of step with an increasingly national repression of vice (practised in the Glasgow system and Liverpool's neighbouring Manchester). Brothels also became a target after repeal with vigilance groups encouraging concerned 'respect' to individuals to initiate proceedings against brothels in this area sought to help and encourage the police to enforce the terms of the Criminal Law Amendment Act (Howell et al. 2008).

34 The Police Act 1866 gave the police extensive powers to crack down on both indoor and outdoor prostitution. Police constables were given the power to obtain a warrant from the magistrate to enter any establishment at any time of the day or night and arrest the proprietor if prostitution were taking place on the premises. Those arrested for brothel keeping were subject, on first offence, to a fine of £10 or 60 days in prison. If a second charge were made the brothel was officially closed and a six-day prison sentence was handed down. Women convicted of soliciting in public places for the 'purposes of prostitution' were subject to a fine of 40 shillings or 14 days' imprisonment. Convictions could be secured purely on the basis of the testimony of a police constable with the '"test of a prostitute" [being] that she was "known to be going about the streets by the police, following no other occupation, and earning her livelihood in that way"' (Mahood 1990: 124–125).

overthrow the repressive power of the acts and replace it with more enlightened reform, obscures the productive nature of legal power that endures and operates in ways that both complicates and stymies reform efforts.

Enduring legal power

Earlier insights into the productive aspect of modern power can complement the critical account of history by scholars such as Walkowitz (1980). A governance approach inspired by Foucault (Hunt 1993; Hunt and Wickham 1994; see also Valverde 1991, 2003) advances an understanding of power beyond the focus on its location in a specific site to an awareness of its changing techniques and rationalities of control (Foucault 1976). Modern forms of power, he notes, break from earlier sovereign regimes of control, which are subsequently characterised as inhumane and unworkable, and increasingly use the rationality of science to justify powers which operate not with the aim of exclusion but normalisation (Scott 2005). Central to my analysis is the fact that law is part of this changing apparatus of modern power:

> We must eschew the model of Leviathan in the study of power. We must escape from the limited field of juridical sovereignty and state institutions, and instead base our analysis of power on the study of the techniques and tactics of domination.
>
> (Foucault 1980: 102)

Escaping from the limited field of juridical sovereignty does not mean law is redundant or that sovereign power is irrelevant, it simply means that law's significance changes as it becomes 'a medium rather than a principle of power' (Veitch et al. 2007: 242).

Following changes more generally, law (which consists of legal mechanisms, legal arenas, legal functionaries, legal forms of reasoning) increasingly operates constitutively, shaping the subjects, spaces and norms and modes of power in modern life (Rose and Valverde 1998).

Legal power does not stand in one position – as either enabling or repressive, rather, it regulates by constituting bodies in particular ways. Law has recourse to both methods – control through the allocation of rights and penalties and regulation through the increased significance of medicine, psychiatry, social work and other professional discourses of the modern episteme. This creates new terrains as law extends governmental authority, not just in terms of discovering new objects for scrutiny, but also in terms of new techniques of control.

The Contagious Diseases Acts can be read in this light. Their purpose was not simply to confer sovereign power but to facilitate a wider system of normative power. They operated alongside other discourses, such as medical science, to identify sex as a public issue, to differentiate male from female sexuality, to mark certain types of sexual activity as dangerous, and produce the prostitute body as a site of disease and pollution (Bell 1994: 55).[35]

Rather than simply repress prostitution, the acts for the first time created prostitution as a 'distinctive legal category' and 'inscribed a disciplinary regime on the body of the prostitute' (Bell 1994: 55). They performed an important constitutive function in helping, alongside other discourses, to create the prostitute as a separate class of women, dislocating them from their working-class communities. Its justification lay in the fact that prostitutes were a special group, outside the normal boundaries of society, as a consequence of their own undesirable attributes, rather than as a consequence of the effects of law (Smart 1989). Having created this pariah group, governments were able to pass legislation which devised more and more specialised modes of regulation to control their behaviours. Law operates not only through censure but through the bodies of prostitutes and working-class women caught up in this regulatory frame.

The acts are not superseded by normative power but merged with medical and welfare-orientated knowledges and practices, becoming part of a complex normative model of regulation and surveillance. Thus despite the fall of the acts, routine normative power persists. Repeal signalled the end of their *sovereign* power but not the end of normative power.[36] As Tadros notes:

> [L]iberation from the blunt technology of the juridical does not prevent the individual being subjected to the loving force of bio-power.
>
> (1998: 103)

This 'loving power' or bio-power continues to be exercised through subjects, spaces and techniques, with certain shifts as it refocuses on new targets, for example the vulnerable (in vigilance campaigns and in the Criminal Law Amendment Act, discussed later), the disorderly (in the post-war focus on public nuisance)[37] and in

35 Modern discourses are, in this context, mutually reinforcing – medical and social scientific norms influenced and informed the creation of new legal measures, which, in turn, authorised the medical policing of prostitution and fed into a prevailing scientific typology – perfectly illustrating the cyclical, mutually constitutive process of modern governance. This circular process is repeated in later periods, for example, during the AIDS pandemic in the early twentieth century, research on prostitution, funded by the Rockefeller Foundation, operated in a similar way in the USA and Europe (Bullough and Bullough 1987).

36 The acts operated in the context of a complex of rules network. When they are repealed, many other norms and sovereign acts continue and structure the field of prostitution, e.g., the Vagrancy Acts (which remain in some form even today) and the Police Acts 1866 that sanctioned the Glasgow system, to give but a few examples.

37 The twentieth-century's major reform of prostitution took place during the moral restructuring of the post-war era (Self 2003). A 'liberal' approach was heralded by the Wolfenden Committee Report 1957, which sought to move away from the explicit moral censure of earlier decades and replace it with a system of private morality. This was implemented via the Street Offences Act of 1959. I have written on this period previously, critiquing the idea of non-interference (Scoular

recent abolitionist and sex workers' rights campaigns. Each of these problematisations is often buttressed by enactments of further sovereign powers.

As Howell (2009) notes, the acts signified the excess of a more general regime of public health which persisted long after they fell. Regulationism does not go away, it limps on for some time in Liverpool, it continues to structure compulsory strategies of VD management until at least the 1940s (Davidson and Hall 2001; Cox 2007) and resurfaces again as an official programme in the crisis of the two world wars, when both women and soldiers were subject to compulsory inspection and continues to be applied in the management techniques of the empire (Burton 1994; Howell 2009). This classificatory system of public health control remains to this day. As Scott notes, it 'has enabled the regulation of prostitution in both "private" and "public" spaces, where technologies of control have often operated inconspicuously' (Scott 2003: 279). It rests on the distinction routinely made (using the medical 'knowledges' and classifications derived from Parent-Duchâtelet and Acton) between 'hygienic', 'normal', brothel-based sex workers and 'unclean', 'dangerous', street-based prostitute (Scott 2003). This leads to forms of governance that ensure 'public' prostitutes are subject to official scrutiny and criminal sanctions, while 'private' (brothel) prostitutes are 'supported' if they embrace the public health model of self-care and harm reduction. This model of governance via responsibilisation was particularly evident during the HIV/AIDS panics in the mid-1980s and, is, as I will demonstrate in a later chapter, common in many contemporary 'legal' systems of sex work regulation.

Yet, this more extensive, normative and constitutive character of modern legal power continues to be overlooked in reform efforts, which tend to focus on the rhetoric and symbolism of law, rather than its practice, which, as I will show, remains unchallenged and is simply augmented in new constructions of the problematisations of prostitution and new 'legal' initiatives. Indeed, this is what happened when feminists, after successfully overturning the acts, turned their attention to the 'protection' of the vulnerable (see Figure 2.1).

The politics of protection

Despite this complex palette of tactics and techniques for bringing prostitution under the sway of government (Howell 2009: 4), feminist opposition was focused on repealing sovereign Acts. While this performed a useful rallying point for mobilising opposition, it also circumscribed the repeal movements' conception of power, which remained closely associated with the functioning of the criminal justice system and a juridico-discursive apparatus of power, with little attention

et al. 2007), although not specifically from a governmental point of view. In many ways, this 'liberal' approach may be more significant in terms of cultural perceptions of sex work than the epochs and problematisations I have selected. Yet it is cultural perceptions of law that I want to consider and feel that the symbolism of the repressive law (as exemplified by the Contagious Diseases Acts) still has a significant hold on the cultural imagination of law.

Figure 2.1 Protecting the vulnerable?

being paid to more routine normalising practices (Foucault 1980). As Howell notes, campaigners constructed a political map consistent with a liberal tradition based on sovereignty, power and empire. This meant that they failed to question sexual double standards or attack colonial rule, and simply replaced the previous system with a new focus on protectionism which, though cast as a new problem, utilises the same medical and moral policing to similar ends (Howell 2009: 26).

The repeal movements' efforts were increasingly associated with a growing social purity movement that mounted a general crusade against prostitution and the vulnerabilities of youthful sexuality. After the success of the repeal, feminist anti-regulationists formed a number of voluntary associations and continued in their crusade against vice and to protect the vulnerable. They went on to build a vast array of institutions to help with this task. In addition to rescue homes for prostitutes, reformatories for wayward girls, single mothers and young women considered to be mentally defective, were set up in many cities in the 1880s (Bartley 2000). They offered guided leisure and religious instruction, training for service and menial labour, rather than, as Walkowitz notes, jobs in a developing economy.

Many feminists joined their campaigns *against* an apparent emerging foreign 'traffic in women' and the supposed entrapment of children into prostitution in London and *for* an increase on the age of consent, in order to 'protect' innocents from abuse. Assisted by the moral panic generated by fabricated accounts of virgins being sold in the 'Maiden Tribute of Modern Babylon',[38] an 'unholy' alliance of feminists, Anglican bishops and socialists used it to force through the Criminal Law Amendment Act (CLAA) of 1885, legislation aimed to counter the aristocratic abuse of vulnerable sexualities.

The Criminal Law Amendment Act of 1885 (An Act to make Further Provision for the Protection of Women and Girls, the Suppression of Brothels and other Purposes)

In order to advance the cause of 'social-purity', this Act sought to protect 'innocence' by restricting the sexual autonomy of young women[39] and men

38 Reformers were helped greatly in these efforts by the publication in 1885 of the 'Maiden Tribute of Modern Babylon', W.T. Stead's exposé of child prostitution in London. Published in the *Pall Mall Gazette*, this was one of the most successful pieces of scandal journalism in the nineteenth century. It described in lurid detail the sale of 'five pound' virgins (the title of a subsequent book on the same subject) by aristocratic old rakes. Like the image of the instrumental violation of the Contagious Diseases Acts, the story of aristocratic corruption of virgins 'generated a sense of outrage with which a wide spectrum of public opinion sympathised' (Weeks 2012: 108). The working class were attracted to the radical message in Stead's exposé of aristocratic vice and feminist campaigners to the apparent assault on male power. Riots broke out at the publishers' offices as great numbers attempted to obtain copies of the third installment of *Gazette* and an estimated 250,000 members of the public demonstrated in Hyde Park against the aristocratic corruption of young innocents. The demonstration and public furore whipped up by the 'Maiden Tribute' was used to good effect by an unholy alliance of feminists, Anglican bishops and socialists who used it to force through the enactment of measures to deal with their concerns.

Subsequent academic work, however, casts real doubt that the slave trade existed in the sensationalist ways presented. Evidence of widespread entrapment of British girls in London and abroad is slim. There was a light traffic in women between Britain and Europe during the 1870s and 1880s. Yet, it was the *conditions* of commercial sex in state-licenced brothels in Antwerp and Brussels rather than its existence that troubled those women involved. There undoubtedly were some child prostitutes on the streets of major cities, but most of these young girls were not victims of false entrapment, but were on the streets due to the, less sensationalist, yet nevertheless still harrowing, impact of poverty and severely limited choices. Yet attention in the campaigns does not focus on the structural issues related to prostitution, but rather on class dimensions undercut by sentimental moralism, prurient details of passive, innocent female victims and individual evil men, fuelled by the salacious publications.

39 The increase in the age of consent for young women can be attributed to the efforts at this time to protect young women from exploitation by men. Constructions of young women as powerless victims and the failure to empower by addressing their economic vulnerability meant that any

engaged in homosexual relations (homosexuality was associated with the corruption of working-class youth by the same upper-class profligates who bought the services of young girls). The act made sexual acts between consenting male adults a crime (forming the legal basis of persecution of male homosexuals in Britain which persisted until 1967, but with much wider, and lasting, social ramifications), raised the age of consent for girls from 13 to 16 and gave police powers to close brothels 'for the protection' of women and children.

This legislation has been described as a 'particularly nasty and pernicious piece of legislation' (Walkowitz 1982: 85). Despite the fact that this reform was designed to tackle corrupt aristocrats and international traffickers, the clauses of the new bill were mainly enforced against working-class women. The new act extended police summary jurisdiction over poor working-class women and children. In many locales, legal repression dramatically affected the structure and organisation of prostitution. Campaigners enlisted the support of local police in cracking down on brothels and street prostitution. The National Vigilance Association (NVA) was formed to ensure the local enforcement of the CLAA.[40] While they opposed the expansion of national state policing powers under the Contagious Diseases Acts, they seemed content to expand local policing powers, when they thought that they would operate under their control. Police powers were used to clear streets, removing any suspected prostitutes. Between 1890 and 1914, the systematic repression of lodging-house brothels was carried out in almost every major city in Britain (Walkowitz 1980), often with the support of vigilance campaigners. Prostitutes were uprooted from their neighbourhoods and displaced to other areas of the city. As their activity became more covert and furtive, the number of third parties, with a strong interest in prolonging women's stay on the streets, increased. Cut off from any other sustaining relationship, they were forced to rely increasingly on pimps for emotional security as well as protection against legal authorities, meaning that prostitution shifted from a female- to a male-dominated trade in the early twentieth century. As Walkowitz argues:

> In these and other respects, the 1885 Act drove a wedge between prostitutes and the poor working-class community. It effectively destroyed the brothel as a family industry and a center of a specific female subculture, further undermined the social and economic autonomy of prostitutes; and increasingly rendered them social outcasts.
>
> (1982: 86)

'protection' was tendered at the expense of female sexual autonomy. This pushed attention away from material realities and onto subjectivities – vulnerable femininity and predatory men – and operated to increase state control and surveillance of 'wayward girls', which continues to this day (see Phoenix 2002b: 35). This mode of control continues in recent efforts to protect vulnerability of young people, where material needs are obscured as attention becomes narrowed into the 'control' of vulnerable women and predatory men. Phoenix cites the Department of Health guidance, *Safeguarding Children involved in Prostitution* (2000: 368) as an example.

40 The NVA also turned its attention to other targets such as obscene publications and pornography. Pornographic literature was considered by these crusaders as a vile expression of the same 'undifferentiated male lust' that ultimately led to homosexuality and prostitution.

The great irony of this period is that anti-regulationism movements had more significant effects on prostitute women than regulation itself (Laite 2012). Historical scholarship offers a critical perspective on the politics of repeal and highlights the role of a 'maternal' feminism that augments rather than challenges power differentials. To this work, I add important insights with regards the role of law in their campaigns. Campaigners' conceptualisations and use of law had no negative consequences for those they sought to 'protect'. The feminist critique of the Contagious Diseases Acts and failure to appreciate the complexities of modern legal power also played a significant role in the *reconstitution* of prostitution in ways that did not necessarily reduce but in fact increased control.

The reform movement's focus on overturning the acts meant that they often missed and sometimes worked, to strengthen these more heterogeneous and local forms of policing. Moreover by engaging with law as a sovereign entity they miss the productive nature of legal power, which both complicates and stymies their reform efforts.

These lessons need to be borne in mind to contemporary feminist campaigning in this area.

Conclusion – the modernist legacy

In this chapter, I present a genealogy of the *modern* subject of prostitution, tracing the processes by which the subject of prostitution was transformed from being predominantly a marker of sin, subject to pastoral forms of control and sovereign power into a social problem, amenable to a variety of techniques of normalising power.

This has led to the prostitute subject being described as a metaphor of modernity (Gilfoyle 1999), an association that evokes the association between the subject and the modern epistemes which played a key role in helping to define prostitution in ways that meant it could operate as a vehicle for distinctly new modes of governance in the late nineteenth and early twentieth century in many common law countries.

In this chapter, I also argue that the prostitute subject has an indexical relationship to modern legal power. I show that the governance of prostitution as a social problem proved to be a fertile site for the operation of distinctly modern forms of legal power which combines both sovereign and normative control.

This modernist idea that prostitution is a social problem to be tackled via disciplinary and bio-power has had a significant and enduring legacy. It remains as a method of classification, in modes of thinking, in legal and policy approaches that continue to utilise the tropes of diseased body, violence and even rights, as later chapters will demonstrate. These normalising powers persist, augmented by other discourses such as the post-war focus on public nuisance[41] and more

41 I have written on Wolfenden, and, although not specifically from a governmental point of view, I did critique the idea of non-interference (Scoular et al. 2007). See also note 37.

contemporary concerns over sex work's anti-social elements and its relationship to exploitation as later chapters will show.

This productive feature of modern legal power has been largely ignored by many involved in prostitution reform; from the campaigners of the Victorian age (such as the renowned Josephine Butler and her supporters) to contemporary feminists and politicians, activists and academics. The more extensive, normative and constitutive power of modern legal power is often overlooked by campaigners who tend to focus on the rhetoric of repressive law, rather than its wider social practice. In doing so, they miss its more insidious normative power that constitutes the bodies of certain women as objects of governance, often trying to use it in new problematisations. A prime example being the repeal movements' efforts to harness law for its protectionist concerns, which helped to institute similarly divisive legislation in the form of the CLAA.

Endnote

These dynamics of modern legal governance and resistance are important to bear in mind when considering calls by contemporary feminists 'to return to golden age of feminist consensus' (Jeffreys 1997a) and by politicians who in recent years, when reforming prostitution laws, have set out to 'do what Josephine Butler attempted over 100 years ago, in a very different era and in a very different way' (UK Home Office 2003).[42]

In drawing these parallels, I do *not* suggest that contemporary moves are simply 'the same old story' of prostitution reform. Contemporary reforms have their own specificity. History, however familiar, never exactly repeats itself. But what I *do* want to argue is that a *critical* understanding of 'modern' legal power can offer some insight into the contemporary politics of prostitution and law reform. In light of the critical account just presented, the next chapter considers the implications of just what might be at stake in these contemporary calls to a return to Victorian values and modes of governance in the twenty-first century.

42 The full quotation from the then Home Secretary David Blunkett reads: 'We must now focus our efforts on working with agencies and voluntary organisations with practical experience of what works so that we can reach out and protect those trapped in prostitution and offer them exit routes . . . We in this century must do what Josephine Butler attempted over 100 years ago, in a very different era and in a very different way' (UK Home Office 2003).

Chapter 3

The object of prostitution and the pathological 'punter': problematising the purchase of sex in the twenty-first century

> The cultural shift in Sweden was that we went from seeing prostitution as separate from other forms of male violence to naming it as a serious form of male sexual violence against women. And if prostitution is male violence against women, then it is a crime and consequently, there is a perpetrator. So, we need to focus on all the perpetrators in the debate on prostitution, not just the traffickers or the pimps, but the immediate perpetrator – the man who commits the prostitution act on the prostituted woman who is no different than a rapist.
>
> (Ekberg 2008)

> Like Foucault's nineteenth-century homosexual, the twenty-first-century Swedish client is a site at which particular configurations of knowledge, power, and discourse converge and kindle. The deployment of sexuality continues to produce new species. By identifying them and examining them, we advance Foucault's work of illuminating the processes through which modern life is constituted.
>
> (Kulick 2005: 225)

Introduction

In 1998 the Swedish Parliament took the unprecedented step of prohibiting the purchase, but not the sale, of sexual services (Act Prohibiting the Purchase of Sexual Services 1998). The law was informed by a certain interpretation of radical feminist ideology which considers commercial sex to be a form of violence against women and an activity inimical to equality between the sexes.

That this relatively small Scandinavian country pioneered such a radical move that has enjoyed considerable international attention and influence is quite remarkable.[1] To understand how this situation came about, it is important to appreciate the distinctive context of the Swedish law. National anxiety regarding

1 Something that is often missed in these debates is the fact that prostitution was never particularly significant in Sweden. It amounted to no more than 650–1,000 known instances when the law was introduced (Kulick 2005: 207). This seems at odds with the amount of energy spent in devising, implementing, defending and exporting the law to other countries.

an apparent 'influx' of 'trafficked' women from Eastern Europe and associated fears with regards Sweden's entry to the European Union (EU), a history of paternalism in social policy, a hegemonic and politically influential feminist movement, and decades of social science work on the much neglected client: all help to make sense of this country's unique approach.

Appreciating that the governmental processes that *constitute* the purchase of sex as a problem of male power are social, not simply ideological, help in both anticipating policy transfer (as policies do not simply jump across borders) and evaluating the impact of such models. The move to criminalise purchasing sex tends to be analysed in binary terms; as either a positive step towards gender equality by supporters of the law, or an example of unenlightened repression. In this chapter, however, I seek to move the debate beyond the binaries of personal liberty versus paternal state repression. These binaries, I argue, ignore the unique constitutive processes and modes of governance that have come to problematize selling sex in a number of twenty-first-century sites. This approach requires us to ask not simply whether criminalisation is either good or bad, but to consider a number of different questions such as: what technologies and modes of power are authorised and what subjects and spaces are permitted or denied under this schema?; how do abolitionist systems transform relations between men, women and the 'state' as it is envisaged in this framework; does increasing men's criminalisation produce increased equality for women and what gains and losses arise from embracing a politics of protection?

The Swedish context: national integrity, the spectre of trafficking and fear of the foreign

Prostitution became visible to Swedes during the 1990s when, as a result of the breakdown of the Eastern bloc, migrants from neighbouring Baltic countries flocked across its borders. Anxieties around immigration were fuelled by the media, which reported that hundreds of thousands of women were literally 'flooding' into Sweden to make money through prostitution.[2] For example, *Dagens Nyheter*, Sweden's largest daily newspaper warned that:

2 Lucas Moodysson's film, *Lilya-4-Ever*, offers an excellent visual narrative of the way in which prostitution and trafficking is being increasingly problematised in parts of the global North and provides an insight into the thinking behind contemporary Swedish and abolitionist approaches to prostitution. The film is based on the real-life story of Dangoule Rasalaite, a 16-year-old Lithuanian who, after being forced into prostitution in Sweden, killed herself in June of 2000. It documents the young woman's harrowing experience of rape and exploitation by a range of men, and ends with the fictional Lilya jumping to her death from a bridge. *Lilya-4-Ever* has become a popular portent of the horrors of trafficking and prostitution. It is frequently used as an educational and awareness-raising tool by the anti-trafficking movement and those campaigning for the abolition of prostitution, including the Swedish government. Yet, as Kulick notes, Lilya tells us more about Swedish anxiety about migration than it does the problem of human trafficking. The epilogue, which shows her

> [A] a new form of prostitution is spreading in Europe . . . a mobile prostitution where about 100,000 young women from the Eastern bloc travel out into Europe to make money by prostituting themselves.
>
> (*Dagens Nyheter*, 2 February 1993)[3]

In these reports, migration and trafficking were frequently conflated (as they commonly are in academic and policy discourse) and linked to organised crime, drugs, and a 'new wave of HIV'[4] (Kulick 2003: 202). In the two years prior to the 1994 referendum on entry into the EU, these stories were commonplace, meaning that prostitution emerged 'as a way for Swedes to talk about and negotiate their relationship to the EU' (Kulick 2003: 330). Those who opposed European integration utilised the spectre of trafficking and fear of the spread of unfettered markets in commercial sex to support their opposition to integration. For example, the leaflet *Bordell Europa* (Månsson and Backman 1992) (which appeared during the Swedish referendum on EU membership in 1992, co-written by Professor Sven-Axel Månsson, one of the Swedish government's most relied upon experts on prostitution) urged Sweden not to join the EU as, it stated, most European countries 'actively encouraged' organized trafficking in sex. Further political integration, it warned, would mean that Sweden would be flooded with foreign prostitutes and the country's progression toward gender equality would be undermined.

A Swedish government commission on trafficking in the same year expressed similar concerns about an 'altogether more liberal view' emerging from other EU countries (quoted in Gould 2001: 440) such as the Netherlands and Germany, which were actively considering legalising prostitution.[5] Alarm was expressed at

playing as an angel, 'back home' – in an unspecified post-Soviet country – is bleak, suggesting that the only happy ending for Lilya was to have never left her homeland in the first place. This resonates with an increasingly abolitionist approach taken in Swedish policy, where the answer to the vulnerability that Lilya faces, is to close borders and adopt an increasingly intolerant position towards migration and prostitution, which is routinely equated with trafficking. Inclusion or recognition of sex work is simply not consonant with Swedish, and increasingly European, citizenship.

3 *Dagens Nyheter* has a daily circulation of around 380,000.

4 By invoking the rhetoric of drugs, the press 'drew on language and symbolism which had a nation-wide resonance' (Gould 2001: 450), as Sweden has had a particularly paternalistic approach to drugs policy. Harm reduction and decriminalisation are considered to be dangerous liberal ideas and the route to a drug-free society is thought to be via compulsory care and treatment. This approach is transferred to prostitution, where eradication via criminalisation and exiting is prioritised and any harm-reduction approaches considered akin to tolerance.

5 Governments who pragmatically decide to regulate prostitution are simply disparaged as supporting the prostitution industry – which is portrayed as a homogeneous market that feeds off commercial sexual exploitation. For example, the Swedish women's minister Margareta Winberg argued that:

> [E]fforts to combat prostitution and trafficking in women can only succeed if we refuse to be the stooges of the international prostitution industry . . . Instead of adopting the superficial and individualised arguments put forward by advocates of legalisation, we must take a stand against a society in which women and children are regarded as commodities for trade.
>
> (Hubbard et al. 2007: 13)

the proximity to, and increasing influence of, what was now termed an increasingly 'pro-prostitution lobby' in the rest of Europe, which could potentially swallow a culturally (and apparently morally) homogeneous Swedish society if the EU were to further enlarge. As Kulick argues:

> [T]he combination of 'Eastern bloc' women eager for intercourse in Sweden and 'pro-prostitution' policies in other European countries raised the truly frightful spectre of Sweden being penetrated on all fronts.
>
> (Kulick 2003: 220)

These overlapping anxieties helped to generate support for a firm stance against an external threat. The law against purchasing sex can be read, at one level, as an attempt to assert a rational image; a coherent state identity in the face of moral, economic and national insecurity. Indeed, Gunilla Ekberg, a former Swedish government-appointed expert on prostitution and trafficking (and prominent advocate of the Swedish model), represents the Swedish state as standing alone against neoliberal commodification of women and girls by making a governmental commitment to a 'democratic society where full gender equality is the norm' (Ekberg 2004: 1188).[6]

Yet, the fact that the law, which, however one views it, represents an audacious move, achieved such a broad consensus amongst a diverse group of actors, across political parties and has received consistent support by the public, cannot be explained simply by the assumed 'threat' of migration and rhetoric of trafficking alone. The law's success also owes much to the coherence of the 'feminist' message that strongly resonates with certain 'paternalistic' strands of Swedish social policy tradition.

A weak liberal tradition

Using the ideological function of law to express a particular vision for society is not new in the Swedish context. Despite popular images of Sweden as a 'liberal' nation (particularly in sexual matters), in reality Swedish social policy in many areas demonstrates a weak liberal tradition with strong paternalist overtones. While such a background may have a number of advantages, not least in terms of generating support for social democracy and social welfare, it also explains a broad consensus for forms of state intervention and social engineering that are considered to be in the public good. Gould explains: 'Swedes . . . have a tendency to take a strict line

6 When Sweden voted narrowly to join the EU, Swedish 'Eurocrats' spent a great deal of time and energy in Brussels trying to persuade the rest of Europe to adopt the 'Swedish position' as a prophylactic against the spread of the market from centres of vice in mainland Europe (Kulick 2005: 222). The Swedes have been actively promoting their position internationally whenever the opportunity arises and their influence is clear from debates in other parliaments, such as those of Canada, Scotland and Northern Ireland and Eire where similar reforms have recently taken place.

on something other countries treat in a liberal or pragmatic manner' (2001: 437). Much of this is due to the fact that Sweden was, until relatively recently, a predominantly agrarian country with a largely homogeneous population. This is exemplified by the term the Swedes have for their country – *folkhem* – the people's home. Without a strong urban culture, the liberal ideas and moral pluralism that influenced European public thought have been less evident in Sweden, which has instead 'tended to favour a strong state' and a 'strong society' (Gould 2001: 452).[7] Politicians, therefore, see their role as 'a fostering one, one of legislating particular moral stances that the populace, guided by them in this way, will come to adopt' (Kulick 2003: 228). Many issues that would be recognised as morally ambiguous in other political cultures have been defined as clear-cut in the Swedish context, with the government confidently assuming the role of moral guardian when others would be more cautious. This moral paternalism has characterised a number of areas of Swedish social policy in the twentieth and twenty-first centuries, including the widespread sterilization programme (which took place between 1934 and 1976 and encompassed 65,000 people – 95 per cent of them women (Runcis 1998)), the outright ban on corporal punishment, and restrictive approaches, including compulsory testing, instituted for drug users and those with HIV/AIDS (Gould 1994: 450; Gould 1999: 12; Gould 2001: 450; Kulick 2003: 221). The ban on purchasing sex, regardless of consent, can also be read in this context.

The patriarchal subject of prostitution: radical feminist discourse and the women's movement in Sweden

The law criminalising the purchasing of sex was a culmination of nearly a decade of work by feminist groups in Sweden to convince lawmakers that they should 'send a message' that 'society' does not accept prostitution. Despite the image of Scandinavian countries as sexually liberated, there has been some unease over the legacy of the sexual revolution. Feminists, in particular, have highlighted the continued inequality and sexual violence that women experience and have been active in promoting more egalitarian forms of sex, which they consider have not been realised in earlier decades and which could act as a moral barrier to increasing commodification. What is interesting is that in the context of modern and late modern governance, notions of 'good sex' do not simply represent an oppositional challenge to established hierarchies and meanings, but that they also take on a normative force.[8]

7 Gould suggests that Swedish modernism has led to a sense of moral superiority and a fear of the outside world (2001: 82).

8 Thus contemporary feminism has played a role in establishing a new normative order. In the same way as the bourgeois Victorians used sexuality as a way to define their social standing, so too contemporary societies wrestle with sexuality as a means of defining the parameters of citizenship. Again, as in the Victorian era, this pressure comes as much from the middle as from those in powerful

An official Swedish sexuality

In Sweden, in order to qualify as 'good sex', sex has to accord with sexual equality (*jämställdhet*) which as Kulick notes means:

> [I]t has to be socially approved, mutually satisfying sexual relations between two (and only two) consenting adults or young adults who are more or less sociological equals. It must not involve money or overt domination, even as role-playing. It should occur only in the context of an established social relationship.
>
> (Kulick 2005: 208)

When measured against this version of 'official sex', many sexual 'identities' and activities appear as problematic. Thus, alongside the promotion of good sex, there has been a parallel problematisation of a number of activities,[9] including commercial sex, which are presented as the antithesis of loving, caring and equal sex that characterises the 'official' Swedish model. The governmental impulse then is to change or to exclude these pathological and foreign 'others', via normative control and criminal sanctions that are increasingly seen to be legitimate.

Prostitution, already a 'dense signifier' of the boundaries of the contemporary nation state and its sexual citizenship, takes centre stage in this process of normative reconstruction with feminist discourse, and actors playing a particularly influential role in its exclusion.

A radical feminist imaginary

As already noted, a great deal of the impetus for the reform of prostitution came from the women's movement in Sweden, which, in contrast to other countries, is a largely homogeneous body, well represented at a political level (Gould 2001; Svanström 2004). It was striking that the feminist movement in Sweden was so

elites in society, and feminists have been particularly active in helping to reiterate the ideals of 'good' sex that they consider have not been realised in earlier decades. And just as the Victorians needed the homosexual, the prostitute and the masturbator to confirm their sexual identity as the norm, so too, contemporary Swedes require the modern-day deviants to help establish what constitutes the boundaries of good sexual citizenship.

9 This includes activities such as solitary sex; anal sex; boys coercing girls into having sex; sexual activities; and rights of people with severe disabilities and commercial sex. None of these activities is the same as another and neither do they follow the same process of problematisation. They are, as Kulick notes: 'Disparate images, not exactly coherent or about the same topic or concern, and not all animated by the same kinds of relationships or power . . . [but make sense in] the larger context in which the discursive management of sexuality occurs' (Kulick 2008: 2–3). What connects these disparate forms of sexual activity is the fact that they all struggle to fit an increasingly restrictive normative framework and when judged according to the official norm of 'good sex', as they increasingly are, they are found deficient.

united in its approach to the issue. Such solidarity is very unusual and much less likely in countries in which prostitute women are organised or unionised as sex workers. In contrast to other countries, sex workers in Sweden are not represented politically. Indeed, there have been moves to stop sex workers entering unions, membership of which is a crucial factor in ensuring political recognition in Sweden. This has meant that those who actually sell sex were excluded from the mainstream political process and dialogue. By contrast, the women's movement was firmly embedded in the Swedish political process, in a large part, due to the established popular movement tradition in Sweden or *folkrorelser*, which has a history of recognition in political matters. The parliamentary motion to criminalise prostitution came from *S-kvinnor* (the Association of Social Democratic Women, the women's branch of the Swedish Social Democratic Party, which represents 120 women's associations from across the country) in 1998 and from that point on, as Gould notes from interviews with those involved: '[I]t was universally thought that once the Congress decision had been made, the government – with 50 per cent of ministers being women, many of whom were members of *S-kvinnor* – had no alternative but to bring in the legislation' (2001: 450).[10]

The law that criminalises purchasing sex has been described by one of Sweden's leading commentators, Sven-Axel Månsson, as being 'located . . . within an explicit pro-feminist ideological framework' (Månsson 2001: 135). Yet, it is important to note at the outset that feminism contains a number of competing theories on prostitution. However, within the Swedish feminist movement, a radical feminist view[11] – a belief that prostitution symbolises women's oppression and is, therefore, incompatible with women's equality and must be outlawed – has become *the* accepted view. Commercial sex occupies a pivotal place in the radical feminist imaginary; inherently degrading, it is frequently cited, alongside pornography, as the epitome of the female condition under patriarchy. As Pateman

10 The high representation of women and cooperation between women in parliament (over 40 per cent of the Riksdag and 50 per cent of government ministers were women who had strong connections to women's organisations (Svanström 2004)) meant that any public opposition to the law was scarce, voiced only in the press and rarely via the political process (Andersson and Östergren 1998a, 1998b).

11 In this schema, prostitution is not simply an example of women's oppression or a context in which women may experience harm, but is regarded as 'a foundational idea that pre-determines it' (Scoular 2004a). It is a 'class condition' that impacts on all women and society and can therefore be framed as a barrier to equality. This reasoning is used to garner the support of all women in Sweden for the new law. For example, in an article in the leading Swedish newspaper *Expressen*, entitled 'Men, Power, and Contempt', the authors (the minister for gender equality at that time, Margareta Winberg, and anti-prostitution activist Louise Eek) note:

> In a society with prostitution *all* women suffer from the view that women can be bought. Between the man who buys and the woman who is bought there is a relation of subordination and domination that cannot be ignored. Every 'purchase' reproduces this power structure and in that way legitimates the general patriarchal structures in society.
>
> (Kulick 2005: 232, fn 42, emphasis added)

notes: 'Prostitution remains morally undesirable . . . because it is one of those most graphic examples of men's domination over women' (Pateman 1983: 56).

Within this schema, sexuality is considered to be the primary dynamic in the ordering of society and the primary determinant of women's subordination.[12] Abolitionism is their goal and the role of law has a vital role to play in making incursions into this supply/demand dynamic by criminalising the purchasers of sex and by dealing with women as victims of what is regarded as a contemporary form of sexual slavery. Law becomes *the* medium for this political campaign. 'Choice' is a misnomer as radical feminists dispute that autonomy can be exercised in a system that is fundamentally oppressive (Jeffreys 1997a; Raymond 2004). The notion of slavery, first coined by Barry in her 1979 book *Female Sexual Slavery* and the figure of the sex slave are used to justify abolitionism and challenge the apparent naturalness of legalisation. Radical feminists seek to challenge the apparent reification of prostitution and to highlight the prevalence of a political economy of sex in which 'Men create the demand and women are the supply' (Hughes 2000: 635).

Prostitution represents such a violation of personhood that no one can consent to it. Campaigns, often taken on behalf of others, centre around the slogan that women are 'not for sale' (Stark and Whisnant 2004).[13] By rendering agency as irrelevant, radical feminists unapologetically render themselves antithetical to rights discourses or to the regulation of the sex industry. *Any* political or legal recognition of 'sex work' (via decriminalisation or legalisation) is thought to both sanction a culture in which men purchase women for sexual gratification and to normalise violence and sexual abuse. Instead, their focus is on reforming the law to promote the abolition of all forms of prostitution.

Yet the radical feminist approach to prostitution has a number of limitations, such as essentialism, gender myopia and a limited political vision, which I have discussed at some length in my previous work (see Scoular 2004a, 2004b; Scoular and O'Neill 2007). That prostitution is currently structured according to social inequalities, which are frequently fortified by violence and coercion, is not in dispute, and radical feminist work in this area has made an important contribution in highlighting the relationship between commercial sex and patriarchy. However, the construction of

12 As MacKinnon famously explains 'sex is to radical feminism what work is to Marxism' (MacKinnon 1982: 515) and prostitution, by analogy, is frequently cited as a 'class condition':

> My study of sex as power . . . inevitably, continually, unrelentingly returns me to prostitution . . . one cannot mobilize against a class condition of oppression unless one knows its fullest dimensions. Thus my work has been to study and expose sexual power in its most severe, global, institutionalised, and crystallized forms . . . Prostitution – the cornerstone of all sexual exploitation.
>
> (MacKinnon 1982: 515)

13 It is interesting that this slogan 'Not for Sale' is also used in some religious groups campaigns against human trafficking. See, for example, the Not for Sale campaign by Chaste – Churches Alert to Sex Trafficking Across Europe (http://www.notforsalecampaign.org/). See Bernstein (2010) on the relationship between feminism and religious discourse in contemporary anti-trafficking campaigns.

prostitution as violence against women and the way in which gender relations are inscribed in law, with women appearing as 'victims' seeking state protection from the actions of individual men, is a perspective that has created considerable unease within feminist circles, and is resisted by those who recognise agency or certainly ambivalence in the discourses of sex workers (Bell 1994; Kempadoo and Doezema 1998; Scoular 2004b). Viewing prostitution as the epitome of gender violence obscures the contingencies and diversity of the structures under which it is constituted (Scoular 2004b), it also makes a problematic distinction between commercial and apparently non-commercial relationships. The Swedish law criminalises 'casual sexual relations for payment'. This raises the issue not only of how we define what a casual relationship is,[14] but also the normative point about why casual encounters have been problematised and not long-term relationships, where we know that economic dependence and violence is commonplace. By defining prostitution as inherently abusive (across both time and space), some radical scholars attribute a particular value to sex, which is then used to argue against its commodification (Phoenix and Oerton 2005: 387). By problematising commercial sexual relations, the official state feminism of Sweden promotes the legal fiction that marriage and long-term partnerships are always consensual and equal. This obscures the continuities in power dynamics and reifies love and the dominant norms of sex that they seek to destabilise. In many radical critiques of prostitution, Pateman, for example, defines the difference between paid sex and loving sex as:

> [The] difference between the reciprocal expression of desire and unilateral subjection to sexual acts with the consolation of payment, it is the difference for women between freedom and subjection.
>
> (Pateman 1983: 204)

Barry echoes this when she notes that 'when sex is not explicitly treated as genuine human interaction, it dehumanises the experience and thereby dominates women' (1995: 28). This fails to recognise the contested nature of sex itself and confirms current normative understandings of 'genuine' sex as in some way outside power.

As I have discussed in earlier work (Scoular 2004a; Scoular and O'Neill 2007), by singling prostitution out for special attention, radical feminists accept culturally specific processes that separate work from relationships of intimacy (Olsen 1983: 1497; Zatz 1997: 303), missing the more complex and potentially challenging relationship that sex work has to gender hierarchy. Described by Zatz as a 'bifurcated event', prostitution is an act that cannot be identified as singularly a

14 In their evaluation of the law, BRÅ considered the phrase 'casual sexual relation' as vague. This was evidenced by the fact that 50% of the prosecutors interviewed considered that frequent and regular clients could be charged under the new law, while 50% did not regard this relationship as casual (BRÅ 2000: 40). This is not fundamentally addressed by current amendments (which include outlawing regular meetings with the same prostitute, escort services and buying sex for someone else, e.g., a stag night).

market transaction or the realisation of private desire (1997: 303). The fact that sex work does not neatly adhere to one of these realms fuels the whore stigma (Pheterson 1989), which can be read as an expression of deeply felt anxieties about women trespassing the boundaries between private and public (McClintock 1992: 73). This also motivates criminalisation, which attempts to force back public elements of prostitution into the realm of private sexuality, thus keeping the economy and sexuality 'symbolically separated', maintaining the boundary between the forms of affective labour, routinely assigned to and expected of women and those practices recognised as work (Zatz 1997: 287).

Radical feminist problematisations of prostitution fail to recognise these more complex relations. Yet despite, or perhaps by virtue of, its shortcomings, radical feminism has become very influential in campaigning where it provides a useful ally for a linear politics, which seeks to use law to magnify vice and virtue. The collapsing of complex social issues into an accessible and linear story of good and bad sex, of victimised, docile women and bad men with evil intentions appeals to policymakers who seek to simplify complex social issues, in particular those that are increasingly defined as issues of equality and gender-based violence, and graft criminal justice solutions onto them. Indeed, this connection was bolstered by the new law's positioning as part of a package of measures to counteract violence against women, entitled *kvinnofrid*, which roughly translates as women's peace and includes legislation on rape, domestic violence and sexual harassment. The law:

> [P]resuppos[es] that a real change in gender relations calls for a radical reconsideration of men's responsibility in prostitution. The basis of such a reconsideration is that prostitution must be defined as a male issue; that prostitution is about men's sexuality, not women's.
>
> (Månsson 2001: 135)

Yet, as powerful as feminist discourse in Sweden may be, it did not achieve this 'radical reconsideration' on its own. For such a stark reversal to take place, and men's responsibility even to be considered as an issue, certain constructive work had to already be underway, not only to problematise purchasing, but also to identify a target for such responsibility to be transferred. The move to criminalise purchasers, an incursion into what had previously been perceived as a male sex right, would not have been possible were it not for two decades' worth of social science work, and psychological studies which, alongside radical feminist doctrine, coalesced to *constitute* the client as a modern objectified subject in the late twenty-first century, providing a target for subsequent criminal and social intervention.

The client as deviant: the original of the species

Since the 1970s, Sven-Axel Månsson, commonly described as the 'Swedish grand old man in research on gender, violence, sexuality and prostitution' (Jacobson 2002: 23), has sought to reverse the tradition in scholarship, to move it away from an exclusive focus on women selling sex and to turn the spotlight onto men. He explains:

> From an historical point of view, focusing on the clients both in research and in social and penal practices, constitutes a major shift in perspective. The fact is that the client's role in the sex trade has rarely been challenged . . . Around the man as a consumer there has been no such emotionally charged images. He has been anonymous or entirely invisible.
>
> (Månsson 2005a: 9)

However, the activities of clients do not just become 'visible' through this process of illumination, rather in a process similar to the creation of the homosexual identity and the 'female prostitute' subject in the nineteenth century, the client is constituted as a new life form, and is 'fleshed out' through a series of government-funded, socio-scientific and psychological studies and media reports produced in the two decades before the new law was introduced.

Origin of the species: the constitution of the client

> In the same way that the sodomite, in Foucault's famous formulation, became transformed from 'temporary aberration' to 'a personage, a past, a case history, and a childhood, in addition to being a type of life, a life form' by 19th century doctors, so is the act of paying for sex currently becoming transformed by 21st century social workers, journalists and others from being an activity to a symptom that one has 'a personage, a past, a case history, and a childhood, in addition to being a type of life, a life form'.
>
> (Kulick 2008: 12)

The client first emerges in a 1981 report, co-authored by Månsson (Borg et al. 1981), which offers an early typology of apparently two distinct client personality types: 'I Buy what I Want': men who can form relationships with women but want sex without a relationship, are distinguished from the unfortunate: 'There are no Other Women', a category used to describe those who cannot, due to 'their shyness, fear, age, physical or mental handicap or isolation' find a sexual partner without paying (Kulick 2005: 214).

The 1984 report *Sexualitet Utan Ansikte: Könsköparna*, by Sven-Axel Månsson and Annulla Linders translates as *Sexuality without a Face*, which provides a telling insight into the dehumanising process as the client is increasingly pathologised as outside the norms of acceptable human sexuality. In this study, 61 interviews with men attending a VD clinic are analysed using a psychoanalytic framework, drawn from a mish-mash of the theories of Jung, Marcuse and Chodorow. This centres around a male/female psychological binary that casts male sexuality as being preoccupied by objectification and detachment and female sexuality as centring around connectedness, closeness and emotion. According to this model, those who purchase sex, perform an exaggerated version of a more general patriarchal sexuality. They take on masculine values (detachment) 'too well' and fail to adopt womanly qualities of 'closeness and nearness' and, instead, objectify sex. This aberration, which according to the authors, 'obstructs' their capacity for 'a genuine encounter with a woman' can be 'cured' by therapised interventions and specialist services for a group who are increasingly being viewed not simply as 'unenlightened' but as psychologically disturbed and dangerous (Månsson and Linders 1984: 27, quoted in Kulick 2005: 215).[15] As Kulick further notes:

> Buying sex in Sweden is rapidly coming to signify not merely a politically unenlightened male but a disturbed male, a deviant male, an unintelligible male. And that very deviance and unintelligibility is, predictably, paving the way . . . for demonization, criminalization, and punishment.
>
> (Kulick 2005: 219)

Indeed, a 1996 government-funded report (Sandell et al. 1996), widely cited as providing the impetus for the legal change that follows a few years later, casts purchasing sex as symptomatic of a deeper, more serious psychological problem, a diagnosis confirmed via statements by psychoanalysts and sexologists cited with authority throughout the report:

> When a person has sex without love, or sex just for the sake of experiencing sex, I see that as a serious psychological defect . . . For reasonably normal people, love and sex go together.
>
> (Sandell et al. 1996: 164)

The 'unhealthy separation' of love and sex is increasingly pathologised as a psychological defect, and linked to other sexually deviant behaviours. It has become a perversion:

> All sexually deviant behaviours have a dehumanised object, there is an inability to feel empathy, an inability to love. The more love there is in a relationship, the less perversion there is. In its compulsive form, buying sex can also be characterized as a perversion.
>
> (Sandell et al. 1996: 16)

Having established the pervert normatively, in a move that both echoes the work of writers such as Parent-Duchâtelet and Acton, and invokes Foucault's earlier insights, the authors then ask themselves, 'Who is that man who buys sexual services? What does he look like? Why does he buy sex? What lies behind the buying?' (Sandell et al. 1996: 89) (see Table 3.1). The authors then set out to answer their own rhetorical question with data gleaned from 40 interviews, which

15 These encounters can be interpreted in different ways of course, see, for example, Bernstein's idea of 'bounded intimacy', which describes a change in sexual ethics – of temporally mediated sexual intimacy – not the absence of ethics (Bernstein 2007a).

Table 3.1 Types of client

	Omnivorous consumer	*Relationship avoider*	*Supplement buyer*	*Relationship seeker*	*Refused*
Personality	Positive self-image; radiates authority, self-confidence Does not have a bad conscience about buying sex Unconsciously afraid of impotence	Terrified of close, long-term relationships with women Buys sex to avoid demands in a relationship; sees nothing wrong with this	Has difficulty talking about feelings; empathetic but lacks understanding of the 'mutual play of the relation between the sexes' Prostitution leaves his real needs unfulfilled	Low self-confidence; has difficulty establishing social contacts	No self-confidence, few friends; desperately wants a relationship with a woman but feels unworthy and ugly
Relationships	In a stable heterosexual relationship; has others on the side; consumes pornography	Has no stable relationships with women but many temporary ones; consumes pornography	In a traditional heterosexual relationship Values the relationship but is unhappy with the sex	Few relationships with women; buys sex in between these relationships	Only relationships with women are prostitutes; consumes a lot of pornography
Childhood	Happy childhood characterised by love and affection but too few limits	Disturbed relations with mother and other women during childhood have resulted in fear of dependency and closeness	Happy childhood; no particular problems during childhood or puberty	Disturbed relationship with mother	'Cold' upbringing
Cure	Needs therapy to get in touch with his true feelings, and 'training in maleness' to understand that 'real men are not just hard, but also sensitive and soft'	Needs therapy to get in touch with his true feelings, and 'training in maleness' to understand that 'real men are not just hard, but also sensitive and soft'	Needs therapy, both individually and with his partner; needs contact with social workers and men's support group	Needs therapy and contact with social workers and men's support group to 'provide him with the opportunity to acquire a clearer role of as a man'	Needs therapy and contact with social workers and men's support group to 'provide him with the opportunity to acquire a clearer role of as a man'

Source: Sandell et al. (1996)

operate to furnish the sex buyer with 'a personage, a past, a case history and a childhood' (Foucault 1980: 43)[16] and even a cure.

The typology developed via social science methodology functions both as a mode of classification and as a diagnostic epidemiology. A form of therapeutic intervention is matched to each category of buyer/pervert. Therapy helps men reconstruct themselves and their sexual preferences towards good sex with *socially equivalent* partners. The implication being of course that sex workers are not 'real women' – a sentiment repeated throughout the Swedish normative project. Månsson claims that:

> Confrontations provoking men's consciousness about the implications of their purchase of prostitutes may actually mean freedom for the man to choose the challenges which lie in a relationship between 'socially equivalent partners' joining those men already 'engaged in developing a broader repertoire of male lives – socially, emotionally and sexually'.
>
> (Månsson 2001: 145)

'Confronting' these men in therapy is an interesting mix of words – it gives a great insight into the 'loving force of the bio-power' (Tadros 1998: 103). Counselling operates a form of normative reconstruction, instituted for the subjects' own good. What is interesting is that these interventions operate in advance of legal power as purchasing sex is *not yet* sanctioned by law, although the process of pathologisation makes criminalisation almost inevitable.

Four hundred thousand Swedish perverts

The final step on the path to criminalisation comes when the 1996 *Sex in Sweden* survey results (Lewin 1998) (again co-authored by Sven-Axel Månsson) provides actuarial evidence of the scale of the problem. Out of the 2,810 respondents, 187 (12.7 per cent of the general population) answered yes to the question: 'Have you ever, with money or other remuneration, paid to be together sexually with someone else?' From this, Kulick playfully suggests that through 'a process of discursive construction and actuarial measurement 400,000 Swedish perverts were effectively created' (Kulick 2005: 205–206). This may appear flippant or an exaggeration but it is indeed the implication of the process of pathologising the client.[17] It is against this context, of epidemic levels of perversion, that the Swedish parliament, for the first time in history, criminalised only the purchase of sex.

16 The four social workers who co-authored the book claim: '[I]f one wants to understand the male buyer of prostitutes, one has to get behind the myths and the stereotypes and see him both from his personal perspective, his childhood and family situation, and in a societal, historical, and cultural perspective' (Sandell et al. 1996: 53, quotation and translation Kulick 2005: 215).

17 The figure of one in eight men purchasing sex is later used to publicise and legitimate the new law in a series of poster campaigns (see Figure 3.3 in text).

Assessing abolitionism

A constitutive approach is invaluable in developing a critical appreciation of contemporary prostitution reform such as neo-abolitionism. A governmental approach has a crucial bearing on how we should evaluate a model that is gaining in influence in many jurisdictions in the EU and beyond, helping us understand the *social* (not ideological or even 'legal') processes of policy formation and transfer, as other jurisdictions more or less successfully attempt to follow suit. A governance apporach provides a more nuanced analytical framework from which to analyse these models, which goes beyond the typical binary debate between repressive vs. liberal law making.

Exporting abolitionism: understanding policy transfers

While the rhetoric of abolitionism is currently very strong internationally and there is much pressure from various constituencies at a local and international level to 'go Swedish' (Osbourne 2014), policies do not simply jump across borders. Rather the process of policy transfer involves particular governmental processes, which operate in distinctive regulatory cultures. Few states will be able to achieve as complete a problematisation as Sweden, where a distinctive combination of ideas, alliances and actions *produced* the Swedish abolitionist model.

Even in Sweden's neighbour countries, which have enacted similar laws (such as Norway, Iceland and Finland, which enacted only partial bans) and share similar political traditions, *empirical* researchers highlight significant differences, putting paid to any notion of a universal 'Nordic model' (Skilbrei and Holmström 2011). Such variation is even more pronounced in countries with a different political culture, greater diversity in feminist thinking and where sex worker rights organisations are more established and better represented in the political discourse.

For example, in the legal systems of the UK (with which I am more familiar), while abolitionism has had a noticeable impact on prostitution policy and practice over the last decade, in my work with colleagues documenting this process, I have been at pains to highlight and explain the peculiarities of this 'creeping abolitionism' (Scoular and O'Neill 2007; Scoular and Carline 2014, 2015). While some states have criminalised purchasing, notably Northern Ireland, governments in mainland UK have thus far not followed suit. Legislative amendments have also been proposed in both UK parliaments to criminalise clients but they have not been successful thus far.[18] Most recently, a self-appointed All Party Parliamentary Group

18 In England and Wales in November 2014 an amendment was proposed to the Modern Slavery Bill by Fiona Mactaggart MP to criminalise the purchase of sex but it was defeated and does not, at time of print, form part of the Bill. Similar attempts have been made in Scotland. In 2010 an amendment to the Criminal Justice and Licensing (Scotland) Bill was tabled by Trish Godman MSP to criminalise the purchase of sex but rejected by the Justice Committee. A further attempt was made in June 2015 by Rhoda Grant MSP to amend the Human Trafficking and Exploitation

on Prostitution and the Global Sex Trade (hereafter APPG) recommended that the purchase of sexual services becomes a general offence in the UK (APPG 2014). Like the European Parliament, this body has no legislative power but both offer important symbolic weight to a neo-abolitionist trend that is spreading across Europe and much is being made of their pronouncements by supporters of the Swedish model (Honeyball 2014: Oppenheim 2014; Osbourne 2014; Smith and Honeyball 2014).

While the Swedish approach has yet to take hold in mainland Britain, law and practice *have* changed as the purchase of sex has been increasingly understood as an issue of sexual exploitation, a problematisation that has been increasingly grafted onto an existing 'liberal' model, which prioritises public nuisance. This has led to what I have called a 'very British abolitionism'[19] (Scoular and Carline 2014, 2015), a term I use to describe a fragmented process of problematisation, whereby prostitution is both a public nuisance and sexual offence. Only some forms of sex purchasing are illegal but the activity as a whole is increasingly pathologised, and prostitutes, represented universally in policy discourse as women, oscillate between being both victim and offender.

'Creeping abolitionism in the UK'

While the subject of male licentiousness, sexual slavery and abolitionism have certainly been on the campaigning agenda since the Victorian era, such issues have never really taken centre stage in UK policy circles until relatively recently. Rather a system of liberal governance, with a focus on prostitution as a public nuisance, famously espoused by the Wolfenden Committee of 1957,[20] has characterised the British approach for almost a century.

This approach confines state intervention to the public aspects of prostitution, imposing a punitive regime on the public acts of soliciting.[21] This established and

(Scotland) Bill both to criminalise the purchase of sex and also to repeal soliciting laws. This too was defeated and, at time of print, does not form part of the Bill.

19 The criminalisation of the purchase of sex was introduced into Northern Irish law through section 15 of the Human Trafficking and Exploitation (Criminal Justice and Support for Victims) Act 2015. The Act came into force on 1 June 2015. In the Republic of Ireland the Criminal Law (Sexual Offences) Bill 2014 was introduced into the Oireachtas in November 2014 and it includes a provision to criminalise the purchase of sex. At time of publication, the Bill was still making its way through parliament and had not yet become law.

20 The Wolfenden Committee Report 1957 famously advanced a liberal mode of governance in which 'it is the function of the law to preserve public order and decency, to protect the citizen from what is offensive or injurious and to provide sufficient safeguards against exploitation and corruption of others' (para. 13) and 'there must remain a sphere of private morality and immorality which is, in brief and crude terms, not the law's business' (para. 60).

21 The 1956 Sexual Offence Act and the 1959 Street Offences Act in England and Wales operated to discipline all women who solicited on the streets, irrespective of whether any complaint had been made against them as those identified as a 'common prostitute' would be charged without caution. In Scotland, soliciting or loitering in a public place for the purposes of prostitution is criminalised under the Civic Government (Scotland) Act 1982.

maintained a gender asymmetry – with the woman who sells sex, rather than her male client, being the main focus of attention. Meanwhile the liberal approach delineates a private sphere of non-intervention, creating an unregulated market in which private forms of commercial sex are, by omission, sanctioned and as such have very much proliferated (Matthews 1986; Hubbard and Scoular 2009: 135–153).

This approach has come under some strain, and efforts have been made, as in Sweden, to achieve some gender balance and bring men into the spotlight.[22] Since the 1980s male street clients have been increasingly seen as dangerous in the British context. Media anxiety surrounding the multiple murders of women by the 'Yorkshire Ripper' (Jouve 1986; Smith 1989; Segal 1994) in particular, created considerable fear and anger, which Walkowitz (1982) argues fuelled an anti-violence campaign and set the scene for increased legal surveillance and criminal penalties to be attached to certain purchasers. Thus the Sexual Offences Act 1985 created the offence of kerb crawling,[23] which although never enforced to great extent (in contrast to soliciting by females), created a new category of offender (who lies somewhere between a sex offender and public nuisance), a target for new interventions (such as the experiments with kerb-crawler rehabilitation schemes for clients[24] (Bindel 1998) and further criminal sanction.

A series of reviews of prostitution took place in the early part of the twenty-first century[25] (UK Home Office 2004, 2006, 2008). While these reviews provided an opportunity to consider different conceptualisations of the problem, beyond its current confines, this was not grasped and an understanding of prostitution as a

22 The pathologisation of the client has not thus far been as extensive in the UK as it was in Sweden. Social science literature is not as developed, however, radical feminist researchers have been increasingly involved in producing 'research' to provide 'evidence' of sex purchasing as a form of abuse (Coy et al. 2007; Bindel and Atkins 2008; MacLeod et al. 2008).

23 It is an offence that any man 'solicits a woman for the purposes of prostitution from or near a motor vehicle, persistently or in such a manner likely to cause annoyance to the woman solicited, or nuisance to other persons in the neighbourhood' (s.1); or, in a street or public place 'persistently solicits a woman for the purpose of prostitution' (s.2).

24 These schemes were piloted in some areas as the way to challenge male purchasing behaviour (Bindel 1998), although they have been met with considerable criticism (Self 1999; Kinnell 2000; Campbell and Storr 2001). Research highlights that such schemes feature an overrepresentation of lower socioeconomic classes and questions the purported 'educational claims' of the programmes, noting more ambiguous objectives with punitive qualities tending to emerge in practice, which focus on 'moralizing, blaming and shaming' (Fischer et al. 2002: 396) the individual client (ibid.; Cook 2015).

25 This followed on from a dedicated review of sexual offences in England and Wales initiated by the UK Home Office (2000). While the remit of the review originally extended to prostitution, it was subsequently decided that bar the introduction of a new anti-sex-trafficking offence and redefining of some soliciting offences as non-gender specific in the Sexual Offences Act 2003, this issue required further, and distinct, consideration. This was subsequently undertaken in a number of reviews that followed (Home Office 2004, 2006, 2008) and formalised in a number of proposals in England and Wales via the Policing and Crime Act 2009.

species of sexual offence was grafted onto the previous policy edifice of public nuisance.

Sex workers were not consulted during the reform process and the rich body of empirical data on the diverse experiences of both men and women working in the intersections between commerce and sex was side-lined, as a criminal justice approach dominated. This was informed by a more limited research base drawing on the work of those experienced in the field of violence against women (see, e.g., Hester and Westmarland 2004). This meant that focus was narrowed on sex work as heterosexual street-based prostitution, which was considered to be inherently abusive. For example, in the foreword to the 'Paying the Price Consultation' (PTP), then Home Secretary David Blunkett stated:

> Prostitution can have devastating consequences for the individuals involved and for the wider community. It involves the abuse of children and the serious exploitation of adults – many of whom are trafficked into and around the UK for this purpose.
>
> (Home Office 2004)

The imagery that was chosen to accompany this consultation paper is also interesting. It features a fractured image of a child standing in front of a shattered pane of glass. The juxtaposition of broken windows and a 'broken child' is utilised to represent the subject of prostitution's need for protection and connotes a risk of contagion if left unaddressed. The use of a child usefully side-steps the contradictions and complexities of adult women engaged in prostitution. They are in effect infantilised as they become the consultation's primary focus for surveillance, control, intervention and rehabilitation.

The influence of radical feminism in this process of policing information is clear. The phrase 'commercial sexual exploitation' proliferated in policy documents and has increasingly become a synonym for prostitution. NGOs experienced in the field of gendered violence became experts and the role of law and state agencies was increasingly focused on 'shift[ing] the burden' of criminal justice interventions from sellers onto buyers (Home Office 2007a) and reducing both demand and supply.

This excluded various forms of regulation that could support individuals to work more safely and experience less exploitation (whether physical, economic or social) (see Sanders 2005; Sanders and Campbell 2007; Sullivan 2010), such as allowing women in off-street locations to work together in order to increase safety[26] or the use of managed zones, both of which were rejected without discussion (Home Office 2006), as they were seen as antithetical to increasing zero-tolerance approach to the industry. In line with this policy, there

26 Managed zones were, at that time, being explored in Liverpool (see Clark et al. 2004). They had also operated informally in Edinburgh but this policy became strained to breaking point via the combination of gentrification and the increasing influence of abolitionism in Scots prostitution policy.

has been a further increased stigmatising, policing and criminalisation of purchasers (Sanders 2005; Sanders and Campbell 2008; Sanders 2009; Brooks-Gordon 2010) which has tended to attach to public aspects of purchasing sex and the existing category of kerb crawler. Kerb crawling was made a criminal offence in Scotland (Prostitution (Public Places) (Scotland) Act 2007) despite adequate common law provision. In England and Wales, kerb crawling has steadily become a summary offence (see s.51A of the Sexual Offences Act 2003), tariffs have increased and prosecutors can order the seizure of vehicles or disqualify persons from driving under ancillary powers (Brooks-Gordon 2010). As a result of section 19 Policing and Crime Act 2009, there is no longer a requirement of persistence, as kerb crawling is increasingly becoming a status-, as opposed to a nuisance-, based crime. More recently, as a result of s.14 of Policing and Crime Act 2009, it has become an offence to make or promise payment for the sexual services of a prostitute who has been subjected to exploitative conduct by a third party.[27] Significantly, this is a strict liability crime – a buyer's knowledge or otherwise of the exploitation is irrelevant. 'Naming and shaming' policies have also been promoted, by local and central governments against this 'group' (Home Office 2007b).

These campaigns demonstrate that the basis of the offence of kerb crawling is 'productively' unclear – what is in law a nuisance-based public order offence is simultaneously represented as a sexual offence in governmental discourses, as Figures 3.1 and 3.2 vividly illustrate.

Protecting women

Alongside the increasing problematisation, responsibilisation and criminalisation of 'some' purchasers, there has been a greater emphasis on women involved in sex work as victims and on supporting women in their exit from the evil grip of the sex industry. This characterisation of women as uniform victims, in turn, helps to add support for the increased demonisation and criminalisation of clients. However, in contrast to Sweden, where exiting is supported by social service interventions and soliciting by sex workers is decriminalised, there has been little political will to abolish offences relating to those who sell sex. Instead, governments in both the UK and the Republic of Ireland have persisted with a criminal justice approach, with increased enforcement (including the use of anti-social behaviour orders (ASBOs)) for street sex work in particular, raids on indoor establishments under the guise of tackling trafficking and exploitation and the tightening of restrictions on licences for sexual entertainment venues (Hubbard 2015) operating *alongside* interventions that promote prevention and support for women to exit prostitution. A prime example of this twin-track approach is the enforcement and support orders (ESOs) introduced in England and Wales by the Policing and Crime Act

27 This was implemented ostensibly in order to address international obligations relating to trafficking, in particular the Council of Europe Convention on Action against Trafficking in Human Beings 2005. See *Tackling the Demand* (Home Office 2008).

Figure 3.1 'Special Offers for Kerb Crawlers' campaign poster
Image courtesy of Community Protection in Nottingham

2009. These orders replace the previous system of fines for those convicted of soliciting in a street or public place for the purposes of prostitution and require an 'offender' to attend three meetings with an 'appropriate person', during which they must 'address the causes of the conduct constituting the offence' and 'find ways to cease engaging in such conduct in the future'.[28]

28 Meetings must be conducted within six months and a failure to attend without a reasonable excuse will result in breach. On breach, the magistrate may revoke an order and resentence accordingly, by imposing either a fine or another order. If following a breach an offender is summoned to court

Figure 3.2 'Kerb Crawlers End up behind Bars' campaign poster

Image courtesy of Wolverhampton City Council

As with kerb crawling, the legal basis of the new order is productively unclear. The offending conduct that triggers the order is soliciting in a public place. Thus, in theory, 'ceasing to engage in such conduct' could be achieved by working indoors or in ways that do not constitute a nuisance. However, it appears, from policy guidance and from practice (see Carline and Scoular 2014, 2015), that it is prostitution per se that is considered, by law makers and officials, to be the offence, although this is not by virtue of formal law. This slippage is similar to that experienced by kerb crawlers; the increasing problematisation of commercial sex gives the impression of legal sanction.

Analysing abolitionism: beyond binaries/good vs. bad

The advent of the Swedish law and its adoption in other jurisdictions has inevitably inspired strong binary reactions. Supporters of the law talk of the move as a positive extension of the Scandinavian democratic tradition and see it as a

and she fails to attend, a warrant for her arrest may be issued. If arrested, she may potentially be detained for up to 72 hours before her court appearance (Policing and Crime Act 2009: sch. 1).

progressive approach to gender equality (Jeffreys 2007a; Honeyball 2014) and as signalling a welcomed and 'renewed welfare approach' (Matthews 2005), while critics denounce these reforms as draconian and paternalistic, a 'return to a much more conservative sexual morality' (Kulick 2008: 3) and oppose the criminalising of consensual sexual activity on classic civil liberty grounds. Yet these analyses take too narrow a view of power that does not simply operate via censure, but operates productively.

Law's increasing involvement with bio-power has radically altered how legal power works and relatedly the questions we can ask of it. Recognising this more expansive site of power means we need to ask more than simply whether the law on purchasing sex is good or bad or highlight implementation gaps in formal law but instead probe more deeply on what these extended forms of governance mean for men and women, and for sexual relations in the twenty-first century.

Punishing bad men in the name of gender equality?

> There is a question which is essential in the Modern Tribunal, but which would have had a strange ring to it 150 years previously: 'Who are You'.
>
> (Tadros 1998: 102, paraphrasing Foucault 1978: 1)

Foucault's observation in his work *The Dangerous Individual* is that law in normalising societies is increasingly concerned with lives rather than with acts. As I have previously shown, through a series of social science studies, media campaigns and law reforms, the Swedish buyer of sexual services is being transformed from someone who *does* something to someone who *is* something. This process is captured in a series of poster campaigns, which accompanied a recent UK government's campaign against kerb crawlers (see Figure 3.3). It vividly captures the processes of pathologisation, in which the client is reduced to a spoiled identity – his life, his job, even his family is wiped and only his perversion remains – it defines him. What he does becomes what he is.

Legal measures are no longer concerned with harm created by client's violence (or nuisance) but rather their very being is presumed to be harmful. In strict liability cases, it is no longer necessary to *prove* harm – a cornerstone of criminal process in liberal systems. The mere identity of being a sex purchaser means certain individuals can be punished.

Civil liberties, while, of course, a relevant consideration (as the previous discussion of kerb crawlers and s.14 attests)[29] arise not simply from the operation of repressive state power. The law is not simply repressive neither is it simply the culmination of a social process of problematisation but is a vital part of it. The law punishes bad men but it also instantiates the construction of client as a pervert

29 So far there have been no reported cases of s.14 offence; see, e.g., Post-legislative Scrutiny of the Policing and Crime Act 2009 (https://www.gov.uk/government/uploads/system/uploads/attachment_data/file/389017/45657_Cm_8987_accessible__2_.pdf).

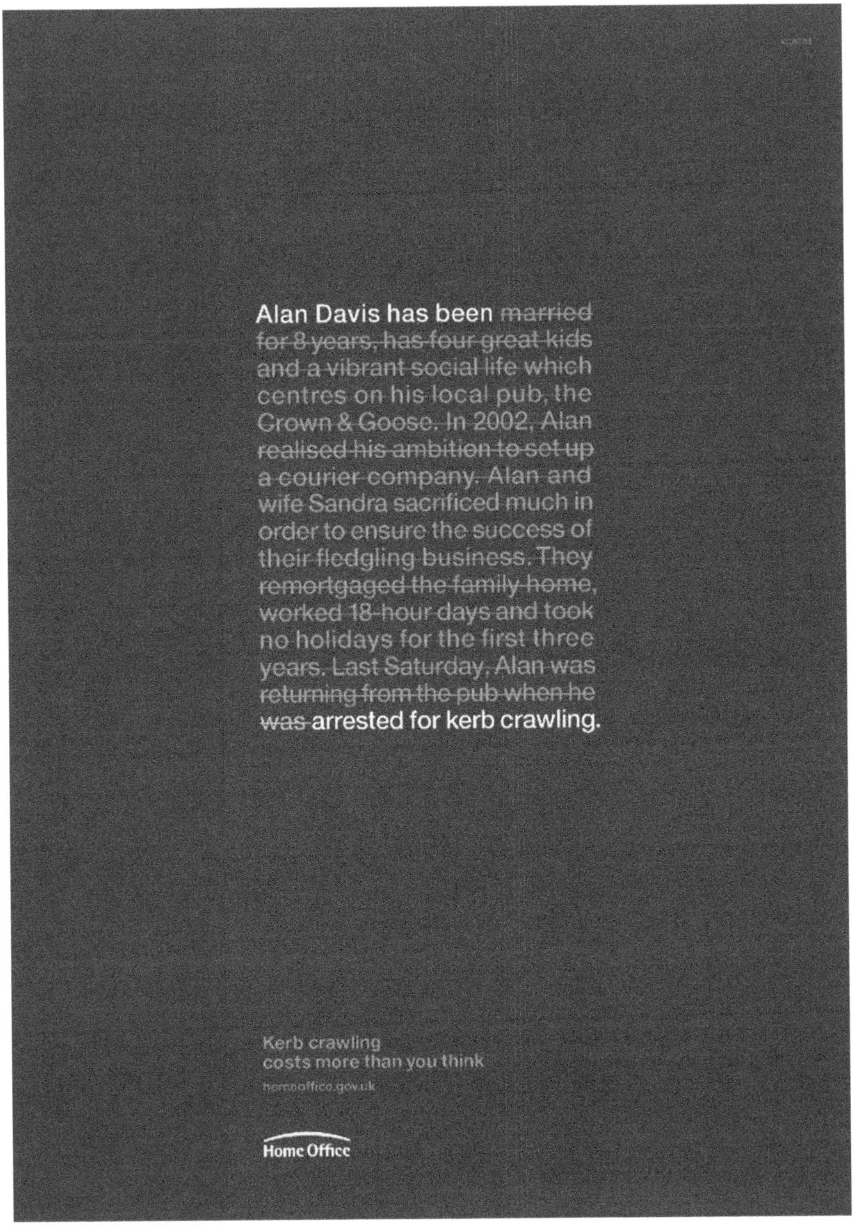

Figure 3.3 Home Office 'Kerb Crawling Costs More than You Think' campaign poster
Image courtesy of the Home Office

created by the previous research studies. The governance processes that should concern us take place over a much more diffuse site, and extend to a much wider range of actors, than the simple exercise of formal police powers – the consequences of which are much more wide ranging than the criminalisation of a relatively limited group of men. Arrest figures are simply the tip of the iceberg as much wider processes are involved in reframing prostitution as a form of sexual exploitation and reconstructing prostitutes and clients as victims and abusers. Processes of responsibilisation or self-governance are encouraged across a number of quasi-legal forums and techniques, from John Schools, exiting programmes, rehabilitation programmes, psychologist sessions to men's groups. These forums feature a hybridisation of legal and non-legal authority, whereby normative control is exercised by a wider range of mechanisms and forms of professional intervention. Far from appearing as coercive, these forms of extended governance are instituted for the subjects' own good. Therapised interventions, rather than appearing as social engineering, are instead presented as being for the subjects' own good, offering liberation from a negative male role and as support to get back onto the correct normative path (Månsson and Linders 1984), that is to 'proper' state-sanctioned intimacy. These modes of self-governance may be more adept than sovereign power[30] as they can be deployed economically – only if they fail will criminal sanctions be necessary.

Thus while rates of arrest may be low this does not necessarily demonstrate a weakness in the law, as the law is only one part of a much wider process of normative reconstruction, which only relies on sovereign power as a last resort.

Equality and punishing bad men? Making women safer?

Law and policy in prostitution have, of course, for centuries been discriminatory, focusing almost exclusively on the female role while largely ignoring the position

30 A prime example is the narratives that are used in the media to discipline. For example, Kulick recounts 'Pete's Story' an account of a 30-year-old 'in recovery' from buying sex, which featured in *Dagens Nyheter* (Sweden's largest daily newspaper) in October 2003, a few years after the new law was enacted. Under the heading 'Now I can Stop This Filth', it documents a 'troubled' family background (this includes adoption, a father who 'drinks a lot at weekends' and a rather enigmatic mother described as 'both distant and close'), suggesting the roots of his destructive behaviour. A 'destructive lifestyle' seeking out pornography, strip clubs and prostitutes is described and diagnosed via Månsson's typology as symptomatic of 'hyper-manliness'. Ensuing guilt compels Pete to call a men's hotline, which, in turn, refers him onto specialist therapy to cure his addiction. His road to recovery is then documented. In his confessional, Pete says he is now in a stable relationship and has only had a few 'relapses' into pornography during the past five years. In a phrase that appears to mirror the sexologists of Sex Buyers, he notes: 'For normal people, you know, lust and sex go together with love and warm, intimate moments. I hope I can get there one day' (Pete, quoted in Kulick 2005: 218–219).

Pete's story reads like a case history, one that Foucault would relish. It also demonstrates that he has internalised and responsibilised according to the Swedish norms of good sex.

of the male client. However, we must also ask: what does turning the spotlight on men in this way do? Does this pathologising process make women any safer, any more equal? By asking these questions, it immediately becomes apparent that that we cannot talk in such aggregate terms about the sexes and their experience of law. It is clear that the symbolism of the law may provide reassurance for some, maybe even providing a foothold in politics. For others, it has very negative effects.

Despite promising to offer a gendered analysis of global market forces, these approaches individualise the problem by focusing on the personalities of men who seek out prostitutes and simply shift the whore stigma to a new deviant group.

The complex aetiology that explains the purchase of sex within a cultural, gendered and economic context (Brooks-Gordon and Gelsthorpe 2003: 438) is brutally simplified in the necessarily rigid definition of criminal responsibility which 'divides the world into victims and victimizers' (Bernstein 2001: 389). Deviant identities are 'produced' and become the focus for law reform, while the social factors that construct these identities in the first place are ignored. As O'Connell Davidson notes, the abolitionist-inspired models that have emerged seek to tackle demand via criminalisation: 'abstract prostitution from its systemic and structural roots and treat it merely as a question of individual morality' (1998: 199). Responsibility becomes increasingly narrowed to client motives and individual sexual ethics, which are pathologised rather than explained in relation to their historical specificity and to the social and economic institutions that themselves structure the relations of gender domination (Scoular 2004b).

The message that men who pay for sex are incapable of appropriate conduct as free individuals (as they are increasingly a pathological species) invalidates any measures that may seek to engage with clients and sex workers as rational sentient actors.[31] Sex buyers are increasingly constructed as being psychologically disturbed – the possibility of acting ethically is impossible. Law and policy, rather than engage with those who buy and sell sex, simply banishes them. This process has implications for those whom are to be protected from these monsters as they too become excluded from reasoned discourse.

Being outside

There have been a number of evaluations of the law since its inception, although none features a straightforward comparison of the situation before and after the legislation. The government is keen to stress the ideological feel-good factor of the law, however, empirical study is more circumspect. In terms of the practical effects

31 The strict liability offence is a good example, where clients are criminalised regardless of knowledge, creating no incentive to report conditions of force or to act to reduce harm in the activity. Moreover, if the law were serious and wanted to address those who have sex regardless of consent, the charge of rape may be more appropriate.

of the new law, the consistent message across a number of evaluations and sources, including those conducted by governmental departments, is that conviction rates have been low (relative to the apparently epidemic figures of sex purchasing), amounting to around 500 in the first ten years. Early research noted that, of the cases filed by the police, the majority of investigations were discontinued due to insufficient evidence and few proceeded to court. Figures from the Swedish National Council for Crime Prevention (see Table 3.2) reveal numbers of reported cases (in the middle column) and the number of convictions, summary prosecutions and 'waivers of prosecution' (in the right-hand column) for the offence of 'purchase of sexual services'.

These figures, of course, tell us little about the deterrent effect of law, simply the rate which law is enforced and its increasing may even question the assumed impact of the ban on purchasing (see http://factsaresacred.ie/wp-content/uploads/2013/07/ JPG1.jpg). Moreover, academic research has shown, when action is taken through criminalisation, or via the quasi-legal forums of John Schools and naming and shaming campaigns, evidence from Sweden, and indeed internationally, is that it typically operates on 'a lower tier of male heterosexual practices' or to 're-gender sexual stigma in certain middle-class factions'. Work on the legal geography of sex work in Sweden shows how sophisticated forms of spatial governance operated to produce geographies of legitimate and illegitimate sex, with safe spaces for consumption and civility coded as indoor and the street increasingly denigrated and most heavily surveilled, leaving the more mainstream corporate and private market untouched (Hubbard et al. 2007).

Reports also note a temporary reduction in street sex work, leading to the displacement and worsening conditions. Research by Kulick and

Table 3.2 Figures for the Swedish offence of 'purchase of sexual services', 1999–2011

Year	*Numbers of reported cases*	*Numbers of convictions, summary prosecutions and waivers of prosecution*
1999	94	11
2000	92	29
2001	86	38
2002	110	37
2003	300[1]	72
2004	156	48
2005	460[2]	94
2006	163	108
2007	189	85
2008	187	69
2009	352	107
2010	1,277	336
2011	765	450

Source: Swedish National Police (2013)
The notes attached to the figures in 2003 and 2005 explain that numbers were higher in these year as a result of specific police operations.

Jacobson[32] has highlighted that the law has negatively affected *some* women's safety: that criminalising the purchase of sex in order to provide greater protection for women has had the paradoxical effect of generating higher levels of risk and danger to those most vulnerable – street-based sex workers – yet this is incidental to the larger normative message.[33] Police time and resources are directed towards prostitution rather than rape and other violent crimes.For those on the streets, already working under the harshest environments, conditions have worsened, due to greater policing, a drop in custom leading to lower prices, less choice of clients, quick transactions and consequently greater risk taking (Nord and Rosenberg 2001). These findings were echoed in Östergren's interviews with women, who reported experiencing greater stress and danger on the streets, with many forced to move into illegal brothels or to work alone from indoor locations, leaving them more isolated than before which arguably exposes them to greater risks of violence and open to greater exploitation behind closed doors (Östergren 2003).

Victims

Yet, despite these consistent reports about the negative effects of the law, it seems to have little resonance with policymakers.[34] It is difficult to raise the issues of sex worker wellbeing in the Swedish context. Sex work is said to undermine women's

32 In Sweden, despite the fact that purchasing sex was criminalised irrespective of location our work found that the law has been selectively enforced; with the main focus being on the highly visible spaces of street prostitution. Although relatively small by international comparison, street sex work became 'the' overwhelming target of media attention, public expenditure and police efforts, with 7 million kronor (over £500,000) initially been given to the police to enforce the law, leading to an initial, but probably only temporary, reduction in its activity as a result of targeted enforcement. This led to a classic displacement with a concomitant rise in 'hidden' forms of prostitution evidenced by the increase in an already expanding, yet little regulated, market in sex accessed via the internet, in pornographic magazines, and via informal networks (Hubbard et al. 2007).

33 Kulick notes the consequences of the law for street prostitutes in Sweden are that sex workers are driven to accepting more clients and more unstable and dangerous clients; have strong incentives not to carry or use condoms; increased risk of venereal diseases and HIV; are increasingly out of touch with social workers; subject to increased police harassment; are arrested and immediately deported if undocumented; are unwilling to report violent clients or pimps (especially if undocumented); the number of sex ads on the internet on the rise and clients no longer willing to provide evidence against violent or exploitative profiteers (Kulick 2003).

34 The response to this more complex experience by supporters of the law is in keeping with the symbolic nature of the reform, in that it dismisses these practical effects and turns attention to changes in public opinion which presents high levels of satisfaction with the law. A recent public attitudes survey in Sweden conducted in 2014 showed that 72 per cent of those surveyed were in favour of the sex purchase law, 85 per cent of women and 60 per cent of men (Länsstyrelsen Stockholm 2015). Public opinion polls are not, of course, in any sense direct indicators of behaviour, but they are, it must be recognised, consistent with ideological aims of the law. This leads to opposing sides consistently speaking across each other, with critics of the law highlighting, via social science, the negative effects of the law and its supporters focusing instead on ensuring the coherence, integrity and success of its central message.

equality and social inclusion is only possible via exiting. For those who remain the situation is close to the incomprehensibility of the clients. The flipside of a normative order that defines good sex as a non-commercial exchange between 'social equals' (real women and reconstructed men) is that those involved in sex work are in effect socially dead. They are not 'real women' as the previous studies claim and their struggles for recognition while in situ go unrecognized.

This acts to undermine efforts to reduce the sexual violence and exploitation *in* the context of sex work (and not simply at an ideological level) or create more egalitarian conditions for sex work. Assuming that all clients are violent, makes the distinction that sex workers have to make (and do make every day) between good and bad clients irrelevant, and puts paid to efforts which seek to encourage increased reporting of rape and violence in sex work (see discussion in Chapter 5). Efforts to achieve a fairer distribution of power and money, and to improve workplace conditions, are not possible as women in sex work, and any notion of their in situ rights or in situ safety needs, are invisible and incomprehensible, in a normative framework that can only accommodate victimhood.

Exiting

In this schema, those engaged in sex work are outwith protection of law. Only exiting is considered to make women safer, despite evidence that women's experience of leaving sex work is as varied as their experience inside (Scoular and O'Neill 2007). Contrary to the rhetoric, exiting does not uniformly serve women. According to the very studies that are relied on by governments to promote such schemes (Månsson and Hedin 1999) while exiting represents a positive step for some, for others it is described as a social death and all of these trajectories are very much dependent on economics.[35] These more mixed findings do not stop the uncritical and indeed

35 Månsson and Hedin's study of women leaving prostitution in Sweden (Månsson and Hedin 1999) is used by governments who seek to promote exiting as a universal good (see, e.g., UK Home Office 2004, 2006). Yet the research is used in a very selective manner and the different trajectories of the women's lived experiences presented in the original study are overlooked, as attention is focused on those 'trapped in prostitution and their successful exit'. Yet Månsson and Hedin's sample of 25 women showed considerable variation in terms of exit experiences: for those who were loosely integrated into the milieu, exit was quick and executed primarily by the women themselves; others, however, 'who had for many years been exploited in prostitution', had reached the limits of what was existentially bearable (Månsson and Hedin 1999: 67). The specific outcomes for this latter group (who received considerable assistance to exit) were also variable; a third had found it relatively easy to make the transition to study and 'work', a third remained in treatment and a final third remained unemployed several years later, described as having 'long vacillated between temporary employment, vocational training, welfare dependency and periodic relapses into prostitution' (Månsson and Hedin 1999: 73). This led the authors of the study to conclude that for

compulsory promotion of exiting by governments, which, as I have previously argued should be viewed as a benign form of welfarism, and more as a form of governance via responsibilisation (Scoular and O'Neill 2007).[36]

Governance feminism: the politics of protectionism

> People know what they do; frequently they know why they do what they do; but what they don't know is what what they do does.
>
> (Foucault 1982a: 187)

Literally, figuratively and politically space has been constricted for sex-working women as a result of abolitionist discourse and a responsibilisation agenda. Those involved in prostitution are excluded from reasoned discourse. Their presence across media reports, in campaigns and in political debate is only to confirm 'the victim-oriented mainstream discourse' (Gould 2001: 452). They are, in effect, vessels of symbolism. A number of feminist writers are critical of the use of a victim in abolitionist campaigns to counter prostitution and trafficking for similar reasons. Andrijasevic, for example, uses the image of a docile female subject, suspended, like a puppet on a string, to powerfully critique trafficking discourse (see Figure 3.4).[37] The representation of violence in such accounts is, she claims:

> [V]iolent itself since it confirms the stereotypes about eastern European women, equates the feminine with the passive object, severs the body from its

some women, exiting represented a positive step, but, for others, 'exiting' prostitution signified a 'social death' (Månsson and Hedin 1999: 129).

Also notable is the fact the study mentions structural factors, most importantly, the difficulties for those leaving in the 1990s due to the recession and the flexibilisation of the labour market. Yet when the research is mentioned to support policy interventions, these factors are ignored or rendered subsidiary to the individual aspects of role ascription, appearing as individualized risks rather than as structural forces beyond individual control.

36 The trigger for the orders is 'soliciting in a street or public place for the purposes of prostitution', which is now defined as on two or more occasions over a period of three months, a significant extension from the previous requirement of two or more occasions in one day. The new orders require an 'offender' to attend three meetings with an 'appropriate person', during which they must 'address the causes of the conduct constituting the offence' and 'find ways to cease engaging in such conduct in the future'. Meetings must be conducted within six months and a failure to attend without a reasonable excuse will result in breach. Described as an 'enforcement plus support' model (Phoenix 2009), failure to engage in meetings can result in a court order and possible imprisonment if breached. Thus in order to 'protect', the net of control has been widened to include a larger group of women who are now subject to compulsory rehabilitation.

37 There are many analogous images, e.g., a group of young naked women in shrink-wrapped meat packaging labelled 'fresh meat', women pictured with barcodes on varying parts of their body, and images of a naked woman handcuffed to a shopping trolley.

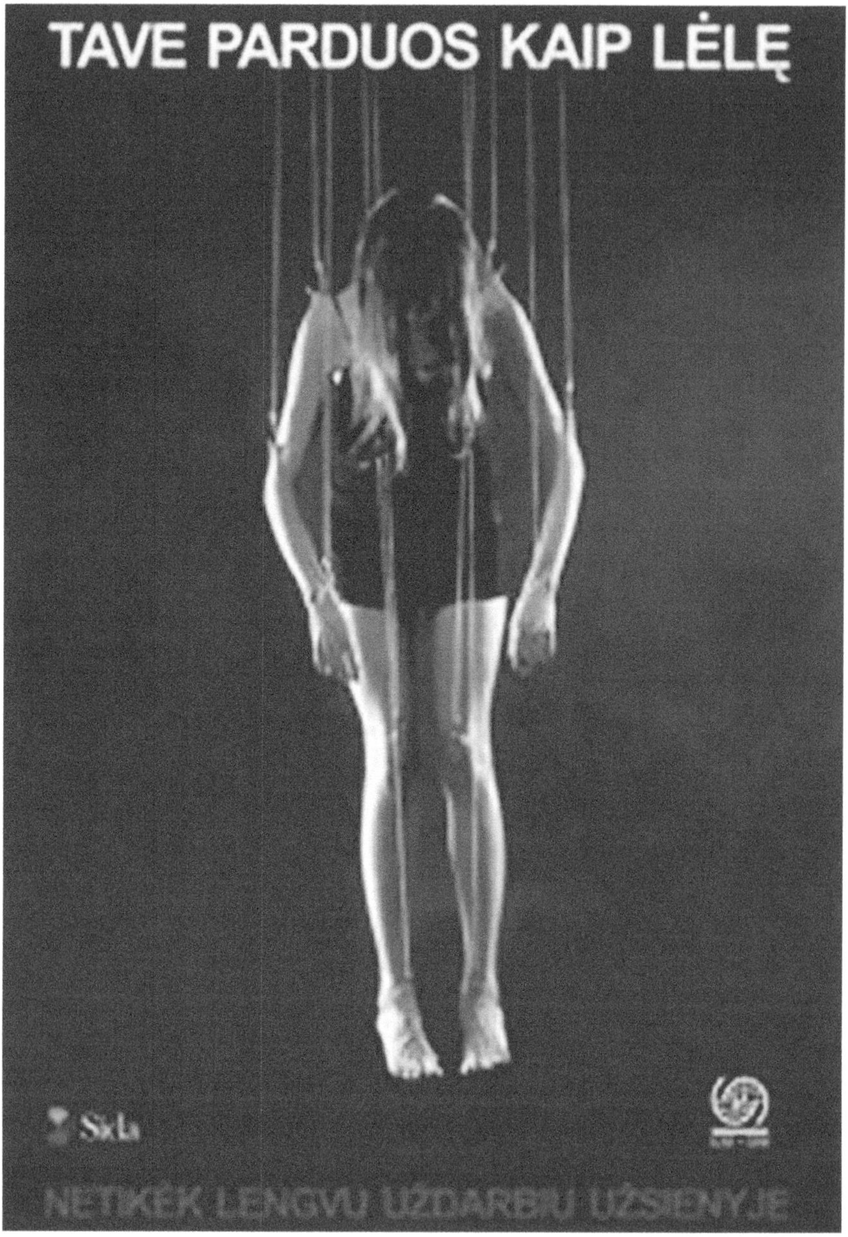

Figure 3.4 Baltic states' anti-trafficking in women campaign poster, 2001–2002
Image courtesy of International Organization against Migration (IMO)

> materiality and from the historical context in which trafficking occurs, and finally confines women within the highly disabling symbolic register of 'Woman' as to maintain an imaginary social order in Europe.
>
> (Andrijasevic 2007)

Similarly, Östergren's (2003) interviews with sex workers in Sweden reveal feelings of only being heard as victims, expressing gratitude for the law. Their more critical perspectives of being 'incapacitated by the state', discriminated against [and] endangered by the very law that seeks to protect them have not been represented in mainstream discourse.

These strategies are based on what Wendy Brown (1995) calls *ressentiment*, an appeal to the state for redress for an injured identity, which ends up re-inscribing, rather than neutralizing, the injured identity, leaving little space for agency and more complex accounts of the subject/power nexus. She notes:

> [S]eeking protection from masculinist institution against men [is] a move more in keeping with the politics of feudalism than freedom. Indeed, to be 'protected' by the same power whose violation one fears perpetuates the very modality of dependence and powerlessness marking much of women's experience across widely diverse cultures and epochs.
>
> (1995: 65)[38]

As I have argued with O'Neill, the subject is conflated with her oppression. Like the client, what she does becomes who she is; her identity is fixed along a victim trajectory that has little room for her agency and more complex account of identities and subjecthood (O'Neill 2001). Not only does this reify an image of the prostitute as a sexual subordinate, it also sustains the myths and norms of the sex industry – of potent men and submissive women – rather than transforming them (Shrage 1994: 134).

This is the great irony of systems of liberal equality, that paradoxically, 'to eliminate gender imbalance in society, [they] continually reinforce the idea that women and men differ from one another' (Kulick 2005: 212), fuelling rather than challenging the more problematic dynamics of the sex industry that eroticises such binary and gendered power differentials.

At the same time romantic love is being valorised. Ironically this is happening precisely at the historical moment that sexuality has become more 'liquid', more diverse, loosened from its tie to social obligations and recognised as a means

38 For these reasons we should be cautious about attempts to protect women sexually. As Cornell notes:

> Feminism must not focus *solely* on what men have done to women. [It] must continuously seek ways in which women can unleash their own imaginary from the constraints that have been imposed upon them through rigid definitions of femininity.
>
> (Cornell 1995: 104, emphasis in original)

to satisfy desire. These same strands of feminism have colluded with conservative forces to sanction forms of sexuality and to re-chain sexuality to love (Kulick 2008: 18). As Kulick notes:

> Under the guise of gender parity, progressive feminism, individual fulfillment, and the social good, sex is once again becoming harnessed to love in ways that may seem benign but may actually undermine feminist futures.
>
> (Kulick 2005: 221)

This is not to argue that prostitution as it currently operates is not oppressive and often violent. That prostitution is currently structured according to social inequalities which are frequently fortified by violence and coercion is not in dispute, and radical and other feminist work in this area has made an important contribution to highlighting the relationship between commercial sex and gender inequality. However, this stems not from any inherent meaning but from the structures under which sex work is constituted. This understanding, however, calls for a radical shift in law and policy away from viewing prostitution as an 'evil' produced by abject morals, by capitalism or patriarchy or even neoliberalism, to seeing 'the evil in the way sex commerce is produced and shaped in classist, sexist, and racist [and neoliberal] society' (Shrage 1994: 161). As Davis notes:

> [T]he more attention given to prostitution as a 'significant' and 'special' problem requiring extraordinary measures, the less we see the ordinariness of prostitution as a normal response to gender distinctions and market and political inequalities.
>
> (1993: 9)

Indeed, it is somewhat ironic that Sweden's traditionally superior welfare state, which has provided an important buffer to market inequalities, assisted in achieving greater levels of gender equality and (alongside there being relatively low urban conurbations) is largely responsible for Sweden having one of the lowest rates of prostitution in Europe in the first place,[39] has been overlooked in favour of individualised interventions.

Conclusion

In this chapter, I have provided a critical account of the very specific process of problematisation that have resulted in the purchase of sex becoming increasingly

39 Much energy has been spent in devising, implementing, defending and exporting the law. Yet it is less incongruous if we see it as exporting 'a way of life'. I have always thought that the numbers involved in prostitution owe more to the relatively low urban numbers and the tradition of robust welfare support, a policy that is becoming increasingly untenable and that many politicians seem unlikely to want to emulate.

or indeed fully criminalised in parts of the Western world in the twenty-first century – a radical incursion into an assumed male sexual licence that would not have been possible, or indeed contemplated, in earlier periods.

The coherence of the Swedish law and message is a key factor in its success. Yet the political consensus offered by the construction of the prostitute subject as a victim of gendered power, is achieved by overlooking the complexities and contradictions inherent in prostitution that point to wider structures, beyond narrow male medical pathology including law, which intersect to create its marginal status.

This account recognises that feminism is a discourse that does not stand outside of political processes but rather operates to shape and develop 'issues' and lodge them in 'administrative procedures for ordering, organizing and ruling contemporary society' (Walker 1990: 16).

Feminists have gained political voice by casting prostitution as a special problem that they are uniquely qualified to address. In doing so, they have silenced other interpretations and experiences in favour of advancing a problematisation that individualises responsibility and leaves many material factors untouched and supports rather than challenges certain forms of neoliberal governance. The rhetoric of victimhood consolidates and legitimises law's power over women's bodies, foreclosing any possibility of law, legal processes and norms having a more productive role as part of a wider politics recognition, empowerment and support. Legal interventions, which could support a much broader-based politics of social justice, instead become narrowed into a reductive criminal justice framework.

My point is not simply to dismiss feminist analysis or legal interventions altogether but rather:

> [T]o creatively engage with, deploy and extend feminism *and 'law' [i.e., legal processes, institutions, discourses and actors]*, in ways that address the kinds of concerns that motivate feminist interventions into sexual practice, but that generate and support a social politics of recognition, empowerment and support, not incomprehensibility, pathologization and criminalization.
>
> (Kulick 2005: 19, emphasis added)

The experiment in outlawing sex is not, I argue, a legal intervention conducive to a politics of recognition, empowerment and support. In my next chapter, I consider whether sex workers' engagement with rights fares any better.

Chapter 4

The prostitute as a rights-bearing subject

Introduction

Sex workers' rights offer much promise. They tap into a contemporary legal and political discourse and language and seem to offer a dynamic alternative to the strictures of abolitionist protection and control. By stressing agency and seeking recognition through increased access to norms and privileges of universal

Figure 4.1 Prostitutes demonstrating for their rights

Image courtesy of PJ Starr

citizenship, rights utilise a comprehensible and current political vocabulary to leverage inclusion for those currently denied access to the polity via regimes of criminalisation and related discourses of moralism and victimhood. Furthermore, there is something potentially groundbreaking about the very invocation of rights by this formerly excluded group, when subjects traditionally excluded from a dominant order, seek entry in the (master) discourse, by making (liberal) political demands via the assertion of rights claims, they threaten to unsettle 'the order of things' (Foucault 2001) as the image in Figure 4.2, used by the International Union of Sex Workers (IUSW), provocatively and graphically depicts[1].

Figure 4.2 International Union of Sex Workers silhouette

Yet, while recognising this undoubted potential, I also seek to interrogate the extent to which contemporary sex workers' rights, as they are currently configured, can fulfil their promise and whether in practice they can overcome the modernist shackles that have ensnared other political and legal campaigning in this area (for example, in the abolitionist/victim centred approach outlined in the previous chapter) and which plague contemporary citizenship norms more generally.

I begin by offering a brief history of the movement for sex workers' rights. Acknowledging a great breadth and diversity of activities that fall under this heading (which range from uncoordinated and sporadic acts of resistance, grassroots movements to international organisations with covenants, constitutions and manifestos), I focus my attention on the way in which sex workers' rights struggles have emerged and are expressed

1 I had hoped to use the picture 'I've Got it All' by the artist Tracey Emin in this context but the artist did not grant permission. The image features the artist's legs splayed, holding handfuls of cash in between her legs. The image is currently curated by the Saatchi Gallery where the picture can be viewed (http://www.saatchi-gallery.co.uk/artists/artpages/tracey_emin_i_got_all.htm) and is described as a 'shameless, 2 fingers up to her critics. She triumphed and has money "up to the whazoo" to boot'. I think the picture conveys something more interesting about the artist's work, which breaks many taboos by bringing subject matters such as abortion, female desire, childlessness into the artistic domain. In 'I've Got it All', the artist is both subject and object of her art and she

in the context of particular liberal democracies, examining the way in which political aspirations have translated into legal claims that express demands for 'sexual minority rights' and 'workers' rights'. I highlight the potential problems that may arise from this particular construction and its attendant modes of mobilisation, as they tend to individualise claims and to serve, rather than disrupt, programmes of governance.

Rights are, after all, the lingua franca of liberalism, and as any good critical scholar knows, their realisation risks incorporation into and dependence upon the very structures that they are intended to challenge. The history of engaging with liberal legal rights discourses reveals their tendency to neutralise and limit the more radical challenges of broader social justice movements.

These contradictory features of rights are evidenced by the findings of a number of empirical studies on sex work regulation in late modern states. By reflecting on my own and others' work, I demonstrate that rights' claims and models that rely on the notion of a stable, universal, modernist voluntary subject, have a tendency to individualise, to exclude many, and to act to support, rather than to challenge, regulatory modes of governance. This account of the promise and paradoxes of sex workers' rights in late modern liberal societies, provides important groundwork for the subsequent chapter, which goes on to consider how we may critically embrace rights as part of a post-structural approach to law.

The emergence of sex worker discourse: or a brief and selective history of sex workers' rights

It is impossible to reduce the emergence of sex workers' rights into a single event, location or even idea. Just as the activity itself is not a modern phenomenon, expressions of solidarity, self-organisation and political action by those involved in selling sex are not new.

Those involved in sex work have participated in forms of political resistance throughout history. Specific prostitutes' protests have been recorded as far back as 1790 in Paris, where 2,000 women marched against their treatment by Parisian police (Bassermann 1993) and Oldenburg describes the role of courtesans in Lucknow's efforts to resist British rule (Oldenburg 1990) while Louise White offers a captivating ethnography of prostitutes' struggles in the context of colonial rule in Kenya (1990).

While much of the early writing on the movement of sex worker activism is, of course, by no means unique to the West, neither is it restricted to liberal democracies. The last 20 years have witnessed an increased recognition of struggles in different social and cultural contexts, recognising the diversity and vibrancy of

holds the wealth. For me, this evokes something pertinent to the sex workers' rights' movement where there is something similarly challenging about the juxtaposition of money and sex, where women can call the price and seek to hold rights.

the contemporary movement for sex workers' rights, which extends well beyond Western democracies and the global North (Kempadoo and Doezema 1998).

Recent areas of activism include the incredible efforts of the Durbar Mahila Samanwaya Committee (DMSC). This Kolkata-based union represents 65,000 members and has campaigned for recognition of sex work as work and for decriminalisation. As well as political campaigning DMSC operates social services including peer-run HIV prevention, schools for sex workers' children and their own banking and credit facility – Usha Cooperative Ltd. They are also represented on 'self-regulatory boards' in Kolkata's red light districts where along with local government representatives, lawyers, doctors and social workers, they are responsible for identifying and assisting 'trafficked, forced and minor sex workers' (Kotiswaran 2014a: 400) as well as offering support to women working voluntarily on 'what to expect in sex work' (ibid.) (see Agustín 2008; Kotiswawaran 2011, 2014a).

SWEAT (Sex Workers Education and Advocacy Taskforce) was formed in the early 1990s in Cape Town. Recently it has been working with the Women's Legal Centre and Sisonke, another South African sex worker rights' organisation, to train a number of current and former sex workers as peer paralegals to advise and represent sex workers against harassment and abuse at the hands of clients and the police.

Also notable is the 2007 strike in Bolivia by 35,000 women who refused to report for mandatory medical examinations, who took part in hunger strikes and some even stitched up their lips in 'silent' protest against laws and state brutality to eradicate prostitution, which included burning brothels, assaults and forcible removal in the city of El Alto (La Paz 2007).

Similarly harrowing are the protests by sex workers in South Korea in 2011, whereby hundreds of sex workers took to the streets of Seoul, with some reportedly dousing themselves in petrol, in protest against strict anti-prostitution laws and crack downs on brothels (Kim 2011).

In Argentina, the Asociación de Mujeres Meretrices de Argentina (AMMAR) has been successful in bringing about legal change for sex workers at a local level as well as establishing health and educational and social care services, for sex workers and their children (Hardy 2010).

While recognising this larger context, the current chapter chooses to focus on liberal democracies. However, rather than present this experience as a universal account, I offer this only as an example, as a case study of a *particular* culture of sex workers' rights. The focus of my work is less on providing a history of sex workers as social movement, and more on the socio-legal and cultural invocation of sex workers' rights, as liberal artefacts, and what this may mean in terms of particular ways of understanding the subject of law and prostitution and possibilities for justice that arises from their interaction.

The origins of 'liberal' sex workers' rights

The 1975 occupation by prostitutes of a church in Lyon is widely cited as the genesis of the movement of sex workers' rights in Europe. Described by some activists as 'our stonewall' (Quan 1990: 3), it began when 150 women occupied the main church in Lyon to protest about their treatment by the authorities, in particular, police failure to attend to the unsolved murders of local prostitutes amid increased harassment, fines and arrests. This blatant, yet sadly oft-repeated injustice, sparked similar church occupations, or 'strikes' as they were termed, across France by fellow prostitutes demanding equal treatment to other French citizens. In Paris, sex workers made a list of demands which included: full rights as citizens, a non-punitive tax system, pensions and welfare rights akin to 'any other French woman'. Despite the brevity of the strikes (they lasted a week, ending when police invaded churches (see Mathieu 2001)),[2] they were a defining moment in the sex workers' movement, helping to launch the French Collective of Prostitutes and similar groups such as the English Collective of Prostitutes (ECP) in England, HYDRA in Germany, De Rode Draad in the Netherlands among others, and also in Australia, Italy, Denmark, over the next decade (see Sanders et al. 2009: 96).

The activities of the San Francisco-based interest group COYOTE (Call Off Your Tired Old Ethics) is also often cited as the inspiration behind the modern sex workers' movements in the global North (see Jenness 1990: 3). Having been formed in 1973 under the leadership of Margo St James, COYOTE sought to challenge dominant associations of prostitutes with deviancy, victimisation and disease, all prevalent in legal, feminist and public health discourses at the time. The group's pioneering work in challenging stigma and discrimination and its efforts to develop a counter-discourse of sex workers' rights influenced other notable prostitute organisations in North America such as Prostitutes of New York (PONY) and Prostitutes Education Project (PEP) in Michigan and continues to inspire contemporary campaigns for labour rights (Jenness 1990; Weitzer 1991; Bell 1994).

COYOTE was involved in the organisation of two 'World Whores' Congresses' in Amsterdam in 1985 and in Brussels in 1986 and in an intervening Whores' Summit held in San Francisco in 1989. Describing themselves as 'feminists in exile', activists organised these congresses to campaign against not only legal discrimination, but also their exclusion from what they regarded as 'their rightful place in the feminist movement' (Pheterson 1989:17).

These meetings led to the establishment of an executive body, known as the International Committee for Prostitutes' Rights (ICPR)[3] and the creation of the first international instrument for sex workers, the World Charter for Prostitutes' Rights, described in Table 4.1. This and associated charters are important elements in the process of translating sex workers' needs and interests into the universal liberal framework and language of rights. Through these activities, sex workers appear as a distinctive social movement, claiming rights on behalf of a defined constituency.

2 For more on this issue, see Kurbanoglu 2011.

3 Since 1992 this now comes under auspices of the Network of Sex Worker Projects (NSP).

Table 4.1 World Charter for Prostitutes' Rights, International Committee for Prostitutes' Rights (1985), Amsterdam 1985

Laws

Decriminalise all aspects of adult prostitution resulting from individual decision

Decriminalise prostitution and regulate third parties according to standard business codes. It must be noted that existing standard business codes allow abuse of prostitutes. Therefore special clauses must be included to prevent the abuse and stigmatisation of prostitutes (self-employed and others)

Enforce criminal laws against fraud, coercion, violence, child sexual abuse, child labour, rape, racism everywhere and across national boundaries, whether or not in the context of prostitution

Eradicate laws that can be interpreted to deny freedom of association, or freedom to travel, to prostitutes within and between countries. Prostitutes have rights to a private life

Human rights

Guarantee prostitutes all human rights and civil liberties, including the freedom of speech, travel, immigration, work, marriage, and motherhood and the right to unemployment insurance, health insurance and housing

Grant asylum to anyone denied human rights on the basis of a 'crime of status', be it prostitution or homosexuality

Working conditions

There should be no law that implies systematic zoning of prostitution. Prostitutes should have the freedom to choose their place of work and residence. It is essential that prostitutes can provide their services under the conditions that are absolutely determined by themselves and no one else

There should be a committee to insure the protection of the rights of the prostitutes and to whom prostitutes can address their complaints. This committee must be comprised of prostitutes and other professionals such as lawyers and supporters

There should be no law discriminating against prostitutes associating and working collectively in order to acquire a high degree of personal security

Health

All women and men should be educated to periodical health screening for sexually transmitted diseases. Since health checks have historically been used to control and stigmatise prostitutes, and since adult prostitutes are generally even more aware of sexual health than others, mandatory checks for prostitutes are unacceptable unless they are mandatory for all sexually active people

Services

Employment, counselling, legal, and housing services for runaway children should be funded in order to prevent child prostitution and to promote child well-being and opportunity

Prostitutes must have the same social benefits as all other citizens according to the different regulations in different countries

Shelters and services for working prostitutes and retraining programmes for prostitutes wishing to leave the life should be funded

(Continued)

Table 4.1 (Continued)

Taxes
No special taxes should be levied on prostitutes or prostitute businesses
Prostitutes should pay regular taxes on the same basis as other independent contractors and employees and should receive the same benefits
Public opinion
Support educational programmes to change social attitudes that stigmatise and discriminate against prostitutes and ex-prostitutes of any race, gender or nationality
Develop educational programmes that help the public to understand that the customer plays a crucial role in the prostitution phenomenon, this role being generally ignored. The customer, like the prostitute, should not, however, be criminalised or condemned on a moral basis
We are in solidarity with workers in the sex industry
Organisation
Organisations of prostitutes and ex-prostitutes should be supported to further implementation of the above charter

Source: Pheterson (1989)

Unionisation

Figure 4.3 SEX WORKERS OF THE WORLD UNITE!

Source: Lopes (2001)

Alongside organising as pressure groups, there has been a move across prostitutes' rights groups internationally towards increased involvement in the trade union movement.

Sex worker unionisation seeks to harness the solidarity of fellow workers and access protections and support from the wider labour movement to fight exploitation. As Gall notes, this has involved a move away from civil and human rights towards economic, labour and workers' rights. This imperative is facilitated by refiguring the selling of sex and sexual services as a form of emotional or erotic labour and therefore as deserving of rights under legal models (Gall 2007: 70). The use of the category 'work' aims to de-exceptionalise the sex in sex work and pushes for it to be viewed and treated as a form of service work, as 'work like any other' (Pheterson 1989). This change in terminology opens up the possibility of individuals and groups establishing, instituting and enforcing labour entitlements as a means of seeking increased recognition and rights (Gall 2007).

Sex workers were first accepted as official members of a trade union in 1996 when a number of Australian sex workers joined the Liquor, Hospitality and Miscellaneous Workers Union (now called United Voice), drafting their own terms and conditions (see Chapter 5). Sex workers' unions are now present in many parts of the world, although their mode of constitution differs greatly. While many sex workers have formed dedicated sex worker unions such as Ver.di in Hamburg, Germany, and the independent union STRASS (Syndicat du Travail Sexuel) in France, others have sought affiliation with established unions. For example, AMMAR, in Argentina, is affiliated to the CTA (Central de Trabajadores Argentinos), a national trade union confederation[4] (Hardy 2010). The Karnataka Sex Workers' Union, based in Bangalore, India, has established itself as a workers' union and affiliated to the New Trade Union Initiative (NTUI),[5] and De Rode Draad (Red Thread) in the Netherlands is affiliated to the Federatie Nederlandse Vakbeweging (Dutch Union Federation-FNV). The large union in Barcelona, Comisiones Obreras, with communist origins, also includes sex workers and since 2002 those working in the 'adult entertainment' industry in the UK have been able to join the General and Municipal Union.[6]

4 AMMAR began through the informal organisation of women who worked on the streets of Buenos Aires in 1994. By 1995 they were informally affiliated with the CTA and by 2001 were formal members of the national confederation.

5 An article from 9 March 2011 states that: 'The union formed in 2006 consists of about 1,000 registered members across the state' (http://www.dnaindia.com/bangalore/report-karnataka-sex-workers-want-right-to-work-1517602). Another written in 2012 that 'the union started in 2006 with around sixty members. Comprising nearly six hundred full-time, part-time and seasonal sex workers presently, most are women living in Bangalore and nearby districts. KSWU is India's first sex workers' trade union' (http://www.thealternative.in/society/redrawing-margins/).

6 The GMB is the general Trade Union in UK and the third largest. At the time of writing there are thought to be approximately 200 members in the adult entertainment branch, although some difficulties are reported and there are fears that it may be closing (see Lopes and Webber 2013).

Figure 4.4 Sex workers' rights = human rights

Building on these developments, the International Committee on the Rights of Sex Workers in Europe (ICRSE)[7] organised a meeting in Brussels, Belgium, around the theme of 'Sex Work, Human Rights, Labour and Migration'. This conference attracted almost 200 participants and ended with a march to the European Parliament, to present a manifesto: 'The Declaration of the Rights of Sex Workers in Europe' (http://resources.tampep.eu/documents/Declaration_booklet_colour.pdf), endorsed by 120 sex workers and 80 allies from 30 countries. This declaration outlines a system of positive civil, political and labour rights for sex workers which the ICRSE calls to be universally adopted (see Figure 4.4; see also Table 4.2).

This instrument mimics the European Convention on Human Rights, and in so doing highlights sex work's exclusion from what is considered to be the mainstay of universal citizenship. Like the earlier 'manifestos', this declaration offers a platform for legal and political recognition, acting as a lever for inclusion into the political community. However imperfect their realisation may be (as we shall see in the course of the chapter), the rights claims made in these documents can be said to operate as 'performative mechanisms of community' (Golder 2011) and speak to the promise of rights discourse.

7 The ICRSE have adopted the red umbrella as a symbol of resistance to discrimination.

Table 4.2 Declaration of the Rights of Sex Workers in Europe, 2005, International Committee for Prostitutes' Rights

The Declaration

All individuals within Europe, including sex workers, are entitled to the following rights under international human law. All European governments are obliged to respect and fulfil:

I The right to life, liberty and security of person
II The right to be free from arbitrary interference with one's private and family life, home or correspondence and from attacks on honour reputation
III The right to the highest attainable standard physical and mental health
IV The right to freedom of movement and residence
V The right to be free from slavery, forced labour servitude
VI The right to equal protection of the law and protection against discrimination and any incitement to discrimination under any of the varied intersecting status of gender, race, citizenship, sexual orientation etc.
VII The right to marry and found a family
VIII The right to work, to free choice of employment and to just and favourable conditions of work
IX The right to peaceful assembly and association
X The right to leave any country, including one's own, and to return to one's own country
XI The right to seek asylum and to non-refoulement
XII The right to participate in the cultural and public life of society

The promises of sex workers' rights

These developments describe a growing internationalisation of sex worker movements and an increasing reliance on and appeal to legal rights discourse. Evidence from the various campaigns suggest that rights can play a role in achieving local change and provide solidarity across a number of levels (transcending international, sexual and workplace boundaries) to challenge injustice.

Capitalising on the contemporary currency of human rights discourse, rights draw upon the emancipatory tactics and language of other social movements and appeal to a universal language of citizenship, connecting local struggles with a wider movement across the globe and forming coalitions with other groups campaigning for sexual minorities and labour rights.

Sex worker rights' campaigners seek to move beyond images of disease, deviancy and even victimhood and replace it with a discourse of recognition, as citizens who experience discrimination and are holders of human rights.

Rights' challenge stigma

Framing issues around 'rights' has helped campaigners challenge the constructions of the prostitute as a marginal social identity and offers an alternative to dominant discourses of morality, disease and criminality.

One of the real successes of the interest group COYOTE, mentioned earlier, was its challenge to the discriminatory nature of the testing regimes (Weitzer 1991: 3). A number of states in the USA had instituted compulsory gonorrhoea screening in the 1970s and 1980s. This system, by omitting customers, operated in a similar way to the Contagious Diseases Acts regime, clearly undermining any public health benefit. By highlighting the discriminatory nature, and given that sex workers did not demonstrate significantly higher levels of infection, COYOTE was able to fight this significant intrusion on this occasion.[8] This discursive challenge to representations of sex workers as 'vectors of disease' in public health regulation has proved to be particularly important in countering the stigma encountered by prostitutes and other groups; for example, gay men, who provide convenient scapegoats in public health panics.

Rights continue to be an important vehicle through which to challenge criminal regimes that threaten health. The international medical journal *The Lancet* (2014) recently devoted a whole issue to the topic of HIV and sex workers arguing that criminalisation exacerbated poor health outcomes and explicitly called on all governments to decriminalise sex work. Indeed, the World Health Organization (2013) and UNAIDS (2009) both recognise that criminalisation increases sex workers' vulnerability to HIV.

Feminists in exile: rights offer a counterpoint to homogenising victimisation discourse

Alongside challenging the negative cultural stigma associating prostitution with disease and deviancy, sex worker groups have also sought to challenge a dominant strand in feminism's depiction of prostitution as the epitome of female sexual slavery and the consequent portrayal of sex workers as hapless victims of male avarice. Rights have been an important element in this struggle. By stressing agency, they provide an alternative to abolitionist discourse, which dismisses sex workers as dupes of a global sex trade, human marionettes suspended forever in webs of control (as depicted in the previous image of the trafficked victim in Chapter 3) only recognised as subjects when they behave like 'good girls' and exit.

Inclusion into the feminist movement was central to the first movement of sex workers' rights in the West, which was formed directly in response to legal discrimination but also in response to feminist hesitations around viewing prostitution as work (Bell 1987; Delacoste and Alexander 1988). As Pheterson noted:

> Never have prostitutes been legitimized as spokespersons or self-determining agents, not by those who defend them against male abuse and not by those who depend on them for sexual services.
>
> (Pheterson 1989: 3)

8 Testing regimes, of course, often remain a feature of regulatory systems, as the later discussion of regulatory systems shows.

By reframing prostitution as work, groups such as COYOTE campaigned to challenge abolitionist rhetoric and raise awareness for the rights of women working in the sex industry; similarly, by emphasising human rights, contemporary movements attempt state recognition, a form of representation beyond victimhood.

Rights continue to be an important device to challenge abolitionist state control, which is in the ascendency in recent years. Sex workers' rights' organisations have tried to utilise a more inclusive vocabulary of human rights to try to 'force' entry into a political dialogue that has in recent years been dominated by the rhetoric of violence, as radical feminist concerns have been intertwined with state efforts to secure borders and prevent trafficking in women and children to create a new wave of abolitionism. For example, during the United Nations 'Fourth World Conference on Women', held in Beijing in 1995, the National Sex Work Projects (NSWP) issued the following statement:

> The dominant ideology about prostitution within the United Nations is a form of sexual exploitation that should be abolished. This view has been legitimized and passed into resolutions and laws at conferences such as Beijing with no input at all from sex workers themselves. Many sex workers feel that it is time to demand that we are heard . . . [and that] resolutions which reflect our demands for human rights . . . [be] passed rather than the resolutions which lead to repressive measures to abolish prostitution.
>
> (NSWP, quoted in Kuo 2002: 21)

Rights challenge criminalisation and highlight the structural role of law

Rights also provide a challenge to the widespread criminalisation of this group. Research and advocacy have shown that regimes of criminalisation are *as* damaging to individuals as the particular practice of prostitution. Such work exposes the forms of discrimination and state brutality that sex workers experience as a result of criminal justice interventions such as policing, fines, arrests and imprisonment – all of which have a disproportionate impact on poor, racially marked women. Criminal regimes simply represent a further 'trapping' factor (Sanders 2007) which as Jeffrey and Sullivan note, 'really ramps up the consequences for women engaged in sex work' and 'makes them more, *not less* vulnerable to coercion by third parties' (Jeffrey and Sullivan 2009: 64, emphasis added).

Criminalisation and quasi-criminalisation are also harmful as they stymie the potential that labour recognition and protections could bring to this group of precarious workers. As Rubin notes:

> [T]he underlying criminality of sex-oriented business keeps it marginal, underdeveloped, and distorted . . . It . . . renders sex workers . . . vulnerable to exploitation and bad working conditions. If sex commerce were legal, sex

> work would be more able to organize and agitate for higher pay, better conditions, greater control, and less stigma.
>
> (Rubin 1984: 289)

The International Labour Organisation (ILO) advocates for economic recognition of the sex sector, stating that a key benefit of recognising sex work as a form of labour is that it reduces the harms of criminalisation (Lim 1998). Jeffrey and Sullivan similarly note that in regimes where some forms of sex work are recognised as being legal:

> It is no small thing for workers to be less vulnerable to arrest, prosecution, fines and imprisonment, to not have to be concerned about the life long impact of a criminal record or the removal of their children in the wake of criminal proceedings.
>
> (Jeffrey and Sullivan 2009: 64)[9]

Claiming rights for sex workers provides a recognisable and potent language with which to challenge criminalisation and highlight law's role in structuring the marginal position of sex work. A pertinent example is the recent Canadian Supreme Court ruling in *Bedford* vs. *Canada*, discussed in more detail in Chapter 5. In this recent landmark decision, laws relating to prostitution (keeping or occupying a bawdy house, living on the avails of prostitution and communicating in a public place for the purposes of prostitution) were held to be unconstitutional because they infringed sections 2 and 7 of the Charter of Rights and Freedoms, which protected freedom of expression and the right not to be deprived of life, liberty or security of the person. In a unanimous decision, the court held that the combined effect of the provisions prevented sex workers from protecting themselves by hiring security, working indoors or in groups, or screening their clients and thus materially contributed to a growing incidence of physical and psychological violence.

This decision and similar violence-reduction initiatives in other parts of the world (such as efforts to recognise violence against sex workers as a form of hate crime (such as that in Merseyside; see Campbell 2014)), the rolling out of a national 'ugly mugs' scheme, which allows sex workers to report on dangerous and violent clients[10] and efforts to recognise rape in sex work (discussed in more detail in

9 The quotation goes on to say:

> As sex workers themselves have pointed out (SWOP undated), the criminalization of prostitution leads to a 'costly legal merry-go-round' for many sex workers; they are arrested and fined but are unable to pay these fines without returning to sex work. So criminalization really ramps up the consequences for women engaged in sex work and this makes them more vulnerable to coercion by third parties.
>
> (Jeffrey and Sullivan 2009: 64)

10 This scheme has been pioneered by the UK Sex Workers Projects (UKSWP). Individuals using this reporting mechanism do not have to record their details, as involvement in sex work is recognised to be a barrier to reporting crimes. See https://uknswp.org/um/.

Chapter 5) can help reduce the harms of the criminal frame by emphasising the safety needs of women *in* prostitution as citizens and members of the polity.

This criticism of the current operation of the criminal law does not necessarily imply that the practice should be legalised or that its state recognition does not come with its own consequences; nor is it to displace the important role of the criminal law in dealing with the violence that is experienced by sex workers. It does involve recognising where criminalisation helps to structure patterns of violence against sex workers and acknowledging the contradictions and limitations of criminal law when it performs dual roles, i.e., it designates certain groups as the instigators of offence, crime and nuisance, while also casting them as vulnerable. Moving beyond either/or may open up the possibility of law being used for more progressive means, such as in recent challenges in the Canadian courts.

Demands for rights *in* sex work are a powerful tool as they invoke laws' ethical duty to concrete subjects (Benhabib 1985) demanding more be done to protect women's rights in situ – not casting sex work as inherently dangerous and predicating state and ethical responsibility on exit.

The problem with rights

While noting the real potential that rights discourse has to challenge abolitionist hegemony and the harms of criminalisation, their ability to mobilise resistance and the promise of justice offered via inclusion to universal citizenship, it is important to expose the rights-bearing subject to the same governmental analysis as I did the victim discourse in the previous chapter. This chapter therefore also considers the more problematic aspects of seeking recognition as a 'rights-bearing subject'.

My analysis draws upon a more general critique of rights that, while vibrant in critical legal scholarship, has thus far not penetrated the sex work domain. That such work has not been widely recognised in the context of sex workers' rights should not be a surprise. The legacy of criminalisation, which remains a pressing and dominant issue for most, means that rights, which are in their infancy, have tended to be uncritically embraced by this marginalised constituency. While inclusion in the political realm remains restricted for so many, the recognition and positive gains that rights discourse delivers will inevitably overshadow any of the possible negative consequences, the implications of which are only just being worked through.

Nevertheless, it is important, even at a time when rights are in the ascendancy, to urge critical caution. In the sections that follow, I introduce the reader to key concepts in critical accounts of rights, and apply these insights to emerging empirical work in the contexts in which sex workers' rights have been asserted around the universals of 'sexual identity' and 'work', which highlight, perhaps not a darker side of rights, but certainly a greyer, more ambivalent experience.

Rights, like the concepts of autonomy and consent, occupy a central place in liberal political and legal discourses, and practices. They have inspired a rich and varied jurisprudence, with scholarship and perspectives ranging from naive and uncritical endorsement to cynicism and even outright rejection. Natural lawyers regard rights as an expression of core moral principles (Fuller 1964; Finnis 1980) and liberals, such as Ronald Dworkin herald them as 'trumps' in any moral, political or legal conflict (1977). Rights hold at bay the intrusions of state power. They are the embodiment of reason held by individuals by virtue of their personhood, by subjects (embodied in the autonomous (male) subject) who stands apart from (rather than, as I will argue, being constituted by) politics.

As a counter to this uncritical valorisation, theorists and activists on the left have been more sceptical of rights as a means to effectively challenge power. Rights confer membership of the polity but this is a polity that was formed and is maintained, in conditions of oppression and servitude. Rights are, of course, not capable of eradicating this inequality, although that is what their proponents would have us believe they are intended to do. Moreover, the individualising nature of rights acts as a foil for liberalism, operating to buttress power and concealing the root causes of inequality such as the impact of global capitalism (Kingdom 1991; Marks 2011; Douzinas 2013).

Scholarship that highlights rights' constitutive relationship to modern technologies of power (Sarat and Kearns 1995; Brown and Halley 2003; Golder 2010, 2011) is of more relevance to a critical analysis of the deployment of rights' claims by sex workers. This suggests a more ambivalent approach to rights, recognising that while they provide a strategic language for activism, they also rest on a false universalism and an abstract humanity, that acts to mask their complicity with, and constitutive relationship to, modern technologies of power (Brown 2000; Golder 2011: 284).

Rights can cut both ways

The fact that rights have no ontological essence, no intrinsic definition, means that they can be used by the powerful to maintain their position and stymie demands from those who demand recognition. Rights can, in essence, cut both ways. This has been the experience of feminists in struggles for access to safe abortion, where claims for reproductive rights have been met with counter-claims of rights for unborn children's or fathers' rights (Smart 1995). Demands for sex workers' rights have also been met with counter-claims: that sex work is degrading and an affront to sexual freedom; that sex work violates all women's human rights; and that women as a 'class' have the right to be free from its inherent victimisation. This is the language used in many radical feminist-inspired campaigns and those utilised by the moral right (see, for example, the 'Not for Sale' campaign – http://notforsalecampaign.org). Protecting the human rights of women as a group provides a justification for abolitionist laws, such as the criminalisation of clients in Sweden and anti-trafficking protocols and campaigns, which state that sex work must be abolished in order to protect fundamental human rights.

Rights as instrument effects

Moreover, in contrast to their apolitical, context-less portrayal in mainstream legal theory, critical accounts of rights, view them not as mere ideals, as universal or as 'trumps' (Dworkin 1977) but as regulatory regimes. Drawing on Foucault's insights, rights are not voluntarily taken up by individuals as liberalism implies, but rather, rights shape the political subjects that seek to claim them.

This is not simply to argue, as those on the left do, that rights individualise, which they may do, but rather to argue that the individual is unconsciously constituted and shaped by their invocation. The subject of rights does not stand outside regimes of rights but is constructed in and through them (Golder 2011: 292). As Foucault observed:

> The individual . . . is not the vis-à-vis of power; it is, I believe, one of its prime effects . . . and at the same time, or precisely to the extent to which it is that effect, it is the element of its articulation. The individual which power has constituted is at the same time its vehicle.
>
> (Foucault 1980: 98)

Golder, citing Ivanson's work, notes, that we use rights as tools to fight power but that they are in fact 'instrument effects' of politics, 'conduits of power' implicated in relations of power as much as criticising them, shaped by them as much as constrained by them (2010: 75–76):

> [Rights] do not simply represent a pre-given or already established identity but rather – through the various legal and political mechanisms of representation, lobbying, enactment and enforcement – go to constitute that very identity in the guise of its recognition.
>
> (Golder 2011: 293)

Rights do not simply oppose the state, they also confirm it. They tie subjects to 'governable forms' of being (Simons 1995: 98), integrating subjects into the apparatus of governmentality and, as such, function just as much as regulatory tools as they do vehicles of freedom (Golder 2011). Rights are complicit with power, they have a constitutive relationship to modern technologies of power, reinforcing 'the very sovereignty which they claim to limit, contest or displace' (Golder 2011: 284–285).

Rights as regulatory regimes

Finally, these constitutive insights alert us to the regulatory capacity of rights. A right is not simply a mechanism that converges with disciplinary power but is itself, from the onset, a potent disciplinary practice. The emancipatory function of rights cannot be separated from the bureaucratic judicial apparatus through which they are negotiated. As Brown explains:

> [This] popular and available currency . . . may subject us to intense forms of bureaucratic domination and regulatory power even at the moment that we assert them in our own defence.
>
> (Brown 1995: 121)

These critical insights are not simply academic musings but have resonance on the ground as I demonstrate using empirical examples whereby rights have been claimed around the identities of sex or work. This highlights a more ambivalent experience of rights. I draw attention to the political and constitutive nature of sex workers' rights in these examples, highlighting the regulatory consequences of such regimes, as they operate as 'regulative narratives' (Honig 1992: 79), generating some possibilities but in so doing, foreclose others.

The problem of sex workers' rights: claiming rights as a repressed, marginalised sexual minority

Sex worker rights emerged from political confrontation not only with the state but also with a dominant feminist discourse that has struggled to accommodate the voices and experiences of sex workers. Rights are asserted alongside other values such as agency and autonomy by those who claim a different 'experience' from the 'injured prostitute' as the 'ontological and epistemological basis of feminist truth' (Doezema 2001: 28; Scoular 2004b).

These campaigns sought to argue that the categories of sex worker and feminist were not antithetical. Jill Nagel describes feminist politics from the perspective of sex workers, holding accountable both traditional feminism for stigmatising sex workers, and also the sex industry for its sexist practices (Nagel 1997). Even before this, Pheterson subverts Wollstonecraft's early liberal feminist manifesto to include sex workers as part of an ongoing feminist campaign for the civil rights of women in the sex industry (Pheterson 1989). Seemingly flippant at times, for example, the demand for the right 'to charge for what other women give for free' (Delacoste and Alexander 1988: 273), this work raises important normative questions about the assumed distinctions made between sex work and other intimate relations such as marriage, dating, divorce and care work.

In these challenges sex workers' rights campaigners have frequently invoked sex-positivist or sex-radical arguments, citing the existence of rights, agency and pleasure as a means to resist both state control and victim models (Rubin 1984; Perkins 1991; Sprinkle 1991; McClintock 1993; Califia 1994; Nagel 1997; Queen 1997; Lopes 2001; Lopes 2002: 22; Ringdal and Daly 2005).[11] COYOTE and their allies utilised

11 Sex positivists oppose any control on women's sexuality whether governmental or feminist. They were involved in a fiercely polarised battle (dubbed the 'sex wars' or 'porn wars') with anti-porn

feminist consciousness-raising techniques and promoted cultural activities such as Hookers' Film Festivals, Hookers' Congresses (Weitzer 1991) and Hookers' Balls (see Pheterson 1989: 4) in order to raise self-esteem and fashion a more positive identity, resonating with a wider sexual liberation movement that was active at the time.[12] Indeed, across many political campaigns and writings, sex workers' rights are presented as an example of, or alongside, other sexual minority rights. Gayle Rubin draws parallels between prostitution and other supposed sexual 'deviations', in particular, homosexuality (Rubin 1984: 286). Whilst recognising their difference (sex work, she notes, is an occupation while sexual deviation is an erotic preference), she explains that both feature at the bottom of a hierarchical system of sexual value (an erotic pyramid) that structures modern Western society.[13] She explains:

> Like homosexuals, prostitutes are a criminalised sexual population stigmatised on the basis of sexual activity . . . The legal persecution of both populations is justified on an elaborate ideology that classifies them as dangerous and inferior undesirables who are not entitled to be left in peace.
>
> (Rubin 1984: 286)

By claiming rights as a sexual minority, sex workers seek to harness support from other maligned groups, in order to both challenge sexual hegemony and gain recognition. Making connections with other sexual minority struggles has been beneficial to sex workers in a number of ways. Given the failure to mount a common feminist position due to real ideological differences, support has been welcomed from those who similarly oppose dominant notions of appropriate sexual behaviour and campaign against the legal constraints on their apparent 'deviant' identities.

Too much sex?

While this alliance is understandable given the lack of unconditional support from large parts of the feminist movement and the shared experience of engaging in

feminists (radical feminists) disagreeing vehemently on issues regarding sexuality, pornography and other forms of sexual representation, prostitution, the role of trans women in the lesbian community, lesbian sexual practices and sadomasochism. The feminist movement was deeply divided as a result of these debates (see Duggan and Hunter 1995) and these positions still appear in contemporary debates on sex work and pornography.

12 This cultural work continues to be an important part of the sex worker movement – there is a biennial San Francisco Bay Area Sex Worker Film and Arts Festival. Sex worker film festivals have also been organised in Hamburg, Copenhagen and London with a number of films produced by sex workers themselves. Examples include the 'Red Umbrella Diaries' from New York-based Red Umbrella Project, 'The Honey Bringer: Stories from the Sex Worker Freedom Festival' by the UK's Sex Worker Open University and 'Last Rescue in Siam' by Thailand's Empower Foundation.

13 Rubin uses the imagery of an erotic pyramid, 'to depict the stratification of sexual populations and practices'. Married heterosexuals appear on top, stable gay relationships are next, the promiscuous below and sex workers appear at the bottom, 'among most despised sexual deviants' (1984: 286).

sexual activity outside the legitimated boundaries of married, heterosexual monogamy, comparing sex work with a sexual identity, is at times, problematic as this overlooks the wider material context, in particular, the structures of gender and the market that frames the institution of prostitution.

Viewing sex work as a sexual identity is empirically problematic. This discourse often just does not chime with the experience of many sex workers who view prostitution simply as a way to make money, a form of labour undertaken in what are often makeshift economies (see Chapter 2). Moreover, due to the highly gendered nature of the sex industry, many feminists are rightly sceptical of, if not hostile to, the idea of equating commercial sex to erotic diversity (Scoular 2004b). Shrage, for example argues that 'prostitution . . . is a cultural institution that is produced by, and reproduces, repressive norms of female sexuality' (Shrage 1994: 134, referencing McIntosh in Smart and Smart 1978).

Yet this wider context is often overlooked by certain prostitutes' rights campaigners, who at times, when seeking to counter objections to prostitution as inherently degrading to women, respond with an equally essentialist position that asserts its role in universally promoting sexual expression and economic freedom for those involved. The argument here is that by engaging in identity politics, sex workers appear to naturalise what are *politically* constituted differences. This criticism has been made in relation to the other struggles for sexual liberation. As diverse and nuanced as the work in the area of sexuality is,[14] there has been a tendency among the most rhetorical writers to cast sexual identity as normative, especially when striving for legal recognition, at the expense of more pluralistic struggles around sexuality (Bower 1994; Herman and Stychin 1995; Stychin and Herman 2000). Sex worker discourses can also, at times, fall into this mode of thinking when claims for sex workers' rights are made in terms of an inherent human right to sexual expression or a sublimated identity. For example, Pheterson maintains that law 'contributes to the stigmatisation and suppression of all active and autonomous expressions of female desire' (1989: 23, 194; Shrage 1994: 134).

While law clearly has negative effects, these cannot always be attributed to its functioning as a repressive force on apparently autonomous and intrinsic desire.[15] By equating the restrictions on women's sexual activity with the suppression of an

14 More nuanced work on sexuality (e.g., Rubin 1984; Valverde 1989a; Vance 1993) recognises the political aspects of sexuality. Rubin's radical pluralist approach offers, I think, a more realist perspective in that it calls for us to 'analyze and oppose the manifestations of gender inequality specific to the sex industry without attempting to wipe out the sex industry' (Rubin 1984: 302). This work also questions the apparent naturalisation and inevitability of male power and the apparent singularity of male sexuality, recognising that it too is constructed and that sites of injustice are multiple, and include not simply sexuality but also the 'family, religion, education, child-rearing practices, media, state, psychology, job discrimination and unequal pay' (Rubin 1984: 302). These are all sites that reproduce negative social norms.

15 I am critical of writers and indeed activists who either explicitly, but more often than not implicitly, presume that each individual actor has some sort of essential or instinctual sexuality that is prevented from being freely expressed or enjoyed by 'repressive social forces'. There is a tendency

apparent 'natural' sexual drive, Pheterson inadvertently reinforces dominant notions of sex as pre-social and confirms the centrality of sexuality to subjects' identity. Such an approach ignores the role of law and material structures in producing, as well as constraining, sexual preferences and acts (Foucault 1976). As Minow notes:

> Just as radical convention notions of objectivity have failed to recognise the authority of the voices of the relatively powerless, alternative notions of authority in subjective accounts are at times inattentive to material, historical experiences beyond individual subjectivity.
>
> (1993: 1437)

Thus what begins as a response to social exclusion, criminalisation and feminist disavowal may fall into the trap that has befallen other identity-based politics, in that by attempting to provide a coherent counter discourse they inadvertently take on the mantle of essentialism that they should instead seek to deconstruct.[16]

This is not to deny that pleasure, sexuality and agency are not important factors, but instead to caution against mobilising solely around such an uncritical and fixed identity and attempting to universalise one aspect of a more complex, intersectional experience. It is to highlight the role of other material factors (such as the economy), which, for many, render sex work less an issue of pleasure, or expression of a sexual identity, and more as a form of 'dull economic compulsion' (O'Connell Davidson 2002: 94; Kotiswaran 2011).

The problem of sex workers' rights: sex work: work like any other?

Emphasising the labour dimension of sex workers' rights has been a more fruitful avenue for campaigners – allowing them to build solidarity through collective organising and unionisation and to increase legal protection and recognition through work-based recognition. Yet, here again, I want to draw attention to the tendency when articulating rights from this perspective, for work to operate as a 'regulative narrative', a site of closure obscuring other perspectives, such as the gendered dimension of the work, which although perhaps overplayed by radical feminist and sex positivists, is constitutively important to the experience of sex work.

Early prostitutes' rights groups cited lack of legitimacy in the labour market as a determining factor in sex workers' marginal status (Pheterson 1989; Jenness

in some work to essentialise both sexuality and agency and to elide the two so that agency is almost defined by the free asocial expression of biological drives. A constitutive position would argue that sexuality is always and everywhere socially constructed (albeit out of instinctive or biological material). It may be legally regulated or subject to other forms of governance but these do not constrain some essence.

16 This point has been made in relation to gay rights essentialism (see Warner 2000).

1990). In *Making It Work*, Valerie Jenness (1990) describes the efforts of COYOTE to reframe prostitution as a service industry, staffed by professional sex workers. She shows their efforts to present sex workers as agents, choosing a form of service work that has an intrinsic social value and is deserving of respect and recognition as a form of legitimate labour.

This perspective continues to inform campaigns[17] and manifestos and has led to increased unionisation and spawned a small number of legal actions by workers seeking protection from unfair employment practices in the context of sex work and adult entertainment industries. In the 2006 case of *Everitt* vs. *Datapro Service*, the GMB union supported an adult chatline worker to take an unfair dismissal action to an employment tribunal, the first of its kind in the UK (Hencke 2006)

More recently, in the case of *Quashie* vs. *Stringfellows Restaurants Ltd*, the Court of Appeal in England held that, despite the common characterisation of lap dancing as a form of self-employment (a status that accrues little by way of employment protection), in principle, there was sufficient mutuality of obligation and sufficient control to constitute an employment contract and to ground a potential unfair dismissal action, although not in this particular instance.[18]

Worker's rights have also been formally recognised in some US states, such as Nevada, parts of Australia and Germany, which have instituted systems of positive regulation. Implementation is, however, often uneven.[19]

Failure of a movement or the perennial problem with rights?

Despite the apparent vibrancy of the sex worker movement and some of the gains discussed previously, progress has not been as hoped, and sex workers' rights in the

17 The IUSW state that sex workers should be able to 'access the full range of employment, contract and property laws' (http://www.iusw.org/).

18 The applicant was thought not to be an employee in this situation due to the fact that she had represented herself to Her Majesty's Revenue and Customs as self-employed. The court held this meant she had performed the contract illegally, which barred a successful claim. As one commentator noted: 'sex workers could not have cake and eat it' (Clarke 2012), although another way of viewing this is to recognise that sex work is a precarious form of work with minimal protections and that workers are invoking the identity of worker and the law strategically in the absence of clear formal protection.

19 In Germany, for example, local regions (*Länder*) never implemented the national system of legalisation (Pates 2012) rendering subsequent claims about the success or failure of regulation difficult to make, although many do anyway (Der Spiegel 2013). Pates notes: 'In reaction to the ProstG, many federal state governments run by a coalition involving the Christian Democratic Party stated either outright that they found the ProstG to violate moral law and thus to be unimplementable (Bavaria, Saxony) or, if run by a Social-Democrat coalition government, the Länder simply failed to ask its administration to come up with implementation guidelines (North Rhine-Westphalia,Hamburg, Thüringen, and others). The ProstG might in fact have the distinction of being the only federal law intentionally not implemented by Germany's public administration' (von Galen, personal communication) (Pates 2012: 213–214).

workplace remain in a rather embryonic state, leading some writers to declare the movement a failure (Weitzer 1991; Van der Poel 1995; Mathieu 2003).[20]

The reasons for this lack of progress can be attributed, in part, to feminist division – with the very idea of sex workers' rights being anathema to large sections of the women's movement and thus stymying important forms of solidarity and political capital.

Poor material resources are also an issue in terms of sustaining political representation. Profits in the sex industry, in part due to the assumed illicit nature, the impact of poverty and third-party involvement, rarely operate to fund long-term sustainable political organisation. State funding and support from international bodies increasingly tend to be contingent on adopting a prohibitionist approach and adhering to a victim status. Busza (2006), for example, describes the experience of many organisations working with those involved in prostitution, struggling to maintain their activities and very existence, in an increasingly politicised environment. In a context of a moral panic over trafficking, accessing funding for work focused on harm reduction is increasingly being limited and any initiatives not signing up to an abolitionist agenda or promising to exit victims, are simply not being supported by central and local governments.[21]

Moreover the competitive and individualised nature of the industry does not make it easy to develop effective union organisation (see West 2000). Gall notes that sex workers tend to operate as independent contractors and that individual rather than collective responsibility is emphasised in a market where colleagues are in direct financial competition with each other (2007: 81), creating 'significant

20 Weitzer made this assessment when reviewing the progress of prostitutes' rights' campaigns that began in the US in the 1980s under COYOTE. He notes that while COYOTE had some initial successes, in challenging local police harassment, in public health and were good at embedding organisation and goals within the leading social discourses of the day, around choice and civil rights, sex workers' rights failed to take off as a social movement. This he agrees was due to the effects of weak social capital and the difficulties of mobilising around a spoiled identity. Key goals, such as decriminalisation of prostitution, could not be achieved due to a chronic deficiency of material and human resources – both of which, he says, could compensate for lack of moral capital in struggles to achieve legal and institutional change and broader normalisation of the constituency's deviant status (Weitzer 1991: 25). While Weitzer's analysis focuses on the USA and the efforts of the vanguard organisation COYOTE and its struggle to make a lasting impact as a social movement, Mathieu (2003) and Van der Poel (1995) make similar points in relation to the legacy of sex workers' rights in Europe and these issues continue to plague the potential of contemporary movements, making Weitzer's insights pertinent beyond this period and location.

21 A prime example is the 'anti-prostitution pledge' that the US government requires developing countries to sign before they are eligible to receive state aid. While this has been declared unconstitutional by the Supreme Court (in the case of *Agency for International Development* vs. *Alliance for Open Society International* 133 S.Ct. 928), this ruling only applies to US-based organisations and the pledge continues to restrict the activities of overseas-based NGOs. Similarly, funding in many parts of the United Kingdom, and in other abolitionist systems, is increasingly conditional on services adopting 'exiting' as a primary objective of intervention (UK Home Office 2006; Scoular and Carline 2014).

obstacles to collectivism and solidarity in terms of both consciousness raising and organising' (Gall 2007: 81). This has meant that the potential for unionisation is limited, membership of unions is low, not necessarily representative and rarely captures the poorest sections of the industry. Gall's recent work, for example, found only 5,000 members across the seven countries in which unionisation existed (Gall 2007: 81).

The structure of the sex industry also places severe limitations on the potential of collective action in this field due to the power dynamics between prostitutes, those who buy sex and those who manage the industry. This tripartite relationship (which exhibits considerable power dynamics) sits uneasily within the standard employment relations usually reflected in union organisation and contract law (Lopes and Webber 2013). This, and the very precarious nature of the work, means that there are real difficulties in establishing successful employment tribunal cases, as previous cases attest. While the cases of *Everitt* and *Quashie* in the UK signals the possibility of a certain recognition for some sections of the industry, such gains are very individualised and remedial in nature and, without greater changes taking place in the industry and economy, are unlikely to be on offer to many.

Further, as Cruz notes, these employment-based rights are only ever likely to be claimed *post facto* by a small number of individuals as the degree of control required to meet the standard required to constitute employment relations, may be too onerous for many sex workers, who may prefer to remain 'unmanageable'.[22] While being unmanageable may be an asset in the context of a more radical politics – as will be discussed in Chapter 5 – it is problematic in a liberal system when seeking entry into the mainstream economy. In current terms, it would appear that the future potential for collective rights and unionisation, if based on incorporation to an existing work model, is 'quite tenuous' (Sanders et al. 2009: 108).

Yet, while these analyses of the sex movement would appear to question the viability of rights or signal their failure, as Weitzer and others suggest, I would resist any assessment of sex workers' rights that rests on a simple binary of success or failure. Rather, I would offer two main insights: first, that, rather than representing the failure of a movement as professed by some, the lack of progress in mainstreaming rights is evidence of the limitations of focusing solely on market-based solutions and casting identities in similarly narrow terms. Sex workers' demands often exceed the current political economic structure (see Cruz 2013: 5).

Second, viewing rights in the context of governmentality, which highlights their instrumental effects and regulatory nature, means that we should only ever be ambivalent about their utility (Golder 2011).

22 As Cruz observes, the individual result of an employment tribunal cannot be generalised and the cases thus far relate to a very particular section of industry. Unless, of course, it were accompanied by collective action to change conditions as was the case in Australia where the sex workers union have been active in drafting uniform terms and conditions. This is an interesting example of sex workers using law in more progressive ways – not simply to achieve individual gains but acting in solidarity to change the bargaining power of parties (see Chapter 5).

The limits of market mainstreaming

Claims that sex work is 'work like any other', made by sex work advocates and others who seek to normalise the activity, are often, although not always,[23] made along 'essentially liberal' lines, whereby selling sex is viewed as 'nothing but' a market transaction[24] (Zelizer 2005) and consent to this exchange is considered relatively straightforward. This is typified in this statement by Ericsson (1980), who considers prostitution as a straightforward contractual relationship in which the prostitute sells not her body, but sexual services (Ericsson 1980: 341–353). He argues that:

> If two adults voluntarily consent to an economic arrangement concerning sexual activity and this activity takes place in private, it seems plainly absurd to maintain that there is something intrinsically wrong with it.
>
> (1980: 338–339)[25]

Yet, while reframing the debate from being a social and criminal justice problem to questions of economic practice has had the benefit of shifting attention away from issues of stigma and has highlighted the importance of the labour dimension of prostitution, in so doing, scholars and activists have, at times, tended to 'represent the employment contract as a mode of equitable exchange and individual agency', ignoring the economic and gendered factors that also structure such relations (Weeks 2011: 67). As Hobson notes:

> [W]hile the progressive reform portrait of the prostitute women as enslavement was simplistic . . . the present-day representation of prostitution as women-entrepreneurs is equally naïve.
>
> (Hobson 1990: 235)

To see sex work as nothing but a failure of market recognition, misses the constitutive role of gender and the embodied nature of sexual services.[26] This point is made most forcefully by radical feminists, but can also be expressed in a less deterministic way, by a constitutive approach that recognises the embodied nature of the labour.

23 Not all prostitutes' rights' groups adopt this liberal position (Freeman 1990). Over the last decade sex worker advocates have also developed much more nuanced accounts of power and consent (see Bindman and Doezema 1997: 5; Doezema 1998: 34–50).

24 Ironically, this position is often met by similary myopic claims by radical feminists who view prostitution as 'nothing but' the operation of gendered power, i.e., patriarchy (see Zelizer 2005 for a critique of these 'nothing but' perspectives).

25 For Ericsson, 'satisfaction of sexual desires is . . . *intrinsically good*, love or no love' (1980: 341); 'coition resembles nourishment . . . if it cannot be obtained in any other way it can always be bought. And bought meals are not always the worst' (1980: 355).

26 It also ignores the intersection of other structures, such as race, which cannot, however hard some on the left try, be simply reduced to market dynamics. There is also the issue of market pluralism as capitalism is far from universal.

More than just work?

The liberal position on prostitution and consent has been thoroughly critiqued, most notably by feminist writers. Carole Pateman (1988) argues that the liberal language of contract has been used – both historically and in the present day – to mask the operation of sexual power. The representation of prostitution as a 'free contract' is, according to Pateman, simply another example of the way in which women's sexual submission is routinely confused with consent and free association. In societies marked by patriarchy (where 'the difference between masculinity and femininity is the political difference between freedom and subjection'), prostitution should not be viewed as a 'transaction' but instead as a form of slavery. For Pateman, when a man contracts to buy the sexual use of a woman in prostitution, 'his masculinity, and so his political freedom, is renewed and affirmed' (Pateman 1988: 206–207). Payment, she states, occurs in place of real consent and the prostitute does not simply contract out the use of her body but rather is 'selling *herself* in a very real sense' (1988: 207).

Similar arguments are made by Sheila Jeffreys who criticises *all* sex worker rights and third-wave feminist arguments, for operating effectively as 'cheerleaders for the sex industry' (Jeffreys 1997a: 15):

> [G]loss[ing] over the social and economic conditions that lead to prostitution . . . view[ing] a woman's decision to engage in prostitution as an economically-savvy way of maximizing her own assets . . . taking advantage of men's apparent need to sexualize and degrade women.
>
> (Crawford 2007: 57)

A parallel is made to traditional liberal theory, which radicals state is similarly 'committed to autonomy, individualism, and minimal state interference in private choice, more so than any sustained critique of relations between men and women [and] gender subordination and social structures . . . that reinforce that subordination' (Freeman 1989: 75).

While these perspectives raise important issues, I am not sure it is necessary to go so far as to equate sex work with slavery,[27] in order to recognise the gendered component of this labour, to acknowledge the commonplace inequality of the contracting parties or to question the ideas of unfettered autonomy that underlie many liberal approaches. A way round the rather tortured argument about what

27 I will return to the issue of consent in more detail in Chapter 5 but for now it is important to note that while it is vital that unfettered consent be questioned, there are dangers when a political analysis of structure overwhelms agency. As I argued in Chapter 3, it is politically and morally 'dangerous' to regard prostitution and rape as the same thing. While this may have some rhetorical effect, it is achieved at the expense of a recognition of the consensual capacity of this group to define meanings themselves. It renders sex workers dupes. Even more gravely, it condones the rape of this already highly stigmatised group, as O'Connell Davidson notes: 'If prostitution is rape, then it is logical to define prostitutes as women who are publicly available to be raped' (1998: 122).

is sold in sex is to take on board the insights from recent feminist work on embodiment. Such an approach can recognise that 'the body matters in prostitution' (O'Connell Davidson 2014), without falling on one side of a binary which either casts prostitution as a unique form of self-commodification (as portrayed by radical feminists or moralists) or generalises it as simply work like all others (as ironically both Marxists and liberals do).[28]

These two binaries rest on the liberal fiction that the economy and sex exist in hostile worlds, when, in fact, the existence of social practices such as sex work, surrogacy and alimony, for example, show that, no matter how much laws and morals try to keep them apart, they are connected (Zelizer 2005).

The notion of embodied labour is useful as it challenges the liberal fiction of disembodied labour power (O'Connell Davidson 2014), recognising that all waged labour is embodied (Horschild 1983) yet acknowledging that not all embodied labour is the same.

Despite attempts to de-exceptionalise sex by arguing that what is sold is not the body but rather sexual services, analogous to sale of labour (Scibelli 1987: 157; Overall 1992: 705 at 717), O'Connell Davidson (1998) argues that the gendered nature of this form of body work means that it is not work like any other. This is not the same argument that some radical feminists make that the prostitute is 'selling herself in a very real way' (Pateman 1988: 207) – this exceptionalises sex and fails to recognise that commodification is not distinctive to prostitution. While there are parallels to all forms of alienable labour – it is because of its link to sexuality that we may want to distinguish sex work from other forms of labour, because sexuality *is* a site of embodied personhood (O'Connell Davidson 2014).

This reading is evidenced by the fact that many sex workers' demands are often as much about bodily autonomy as they are about economic freedom, as the slogan 'My Body My Business' attests. The market alone is unlikely to help increase the sexual capacity of sex workers and sex workers as Cruz notes 'often advance a more antagonistic politics that stresses protections *from* the capitalist labour market as much as seeking protection within it' (Cruz 2013). As O'Connell Davidson notes:

> Prostitution is not currently socially organised in such a way that proletarianised workers sell their commodified sexual labour power to employers to direct and control in some kind of capitalist prostitution labour process, and those calling for sex worker rights do not wish to see it reconfigured in this manner.
>
> (O'Connell Davidson 2014: 527)

28 Marxists equate prostitution with all wage labour: 'Prostitution is only a particular expression of the universal prostitution of the worker' (Marx 1964). Yet, this begs the question of why is it overwhelmingly women's, and not men's, sexuality that is commodified and as Zatz notes, '[W]hy is it that prostitution has been so differentiated from other forms of waged work?' (Zatz 1997: 288).

Too much work? Limitations of the 'work' model

O'Connell Davidson and Cruz see the opportunity for formal economic and labour inclusion as limited given both the distinctive features of sex work and the limitations of wage labour itself in achieving equality. Moreover, they argue that sex work will only ever be partially incorporated within traditional employment relationships as much of it is ultimately unmanageable within the current strictures of labour law.

Failure to recognise these more complex political claims means that rights claims and reforms will continue to reduce sex workers' complex claims into narrow regulatory narratives, meaning that their accommodation within capitalist economy will only ever be incomplete and at the expense of other material aspects. This has been the experience where workers' rights have been mainstreamed.[29] Rights' talk, which relies exclusively on fixed notions of 'work' or 'sex' and agency, misses the complexity and challenge of sex workers' rights and subjects rights bearers to bureaucratic power and surveillance in regimes of legalisation. The requirement of adherence to one or other of these opposite approaches is self-defeating both intellectually and politically.

The regulatory dimension of sex workers' rights

The regulatory dimension of claiming 'workers' rights is highlighted by emerging, critically informed empirical work on legal regimes, such as Australia (Scott 2005; Sullivan 2010), the Netherlands (Hubbard et al. 2007; Scoular 2010), Nevada (Brents and Hausbeck 2007) and emerging critical work, New Zealand (Harrington 2012).

Each of these jurisdictions has attempted to institute positive forms of regulation and to create spaces in which sex work can be performed without violating the criminal law. Yet, as is clear from my analysis, the removal of criminal law does not

29 There are many limitations to labour inclusion under present conditions. Employment status is not an option for many illegal workers. And even for those who could meet conditions, as Cruz points out in relation to Quashie, sex workers have to accept high levels of control, required if they are to come under the ambit of employer/employee protections, for very partial returns. Given the precarious and intimate nature of the work, this level of control is not desirable for the majority in this area. These rights are unlikely to be used by many individuals and even then will be claimed retrospectively. As Cruz perceptively notes:

> It is one thing for a sex worker to offer a retrospective account of having been controlled for purposes of constructing her employment relationship as a contract of service for an unfair dismissal claim; it is quite another to argue that the level of control seen in the *Quashie* case is desirable and should be rolled out across the industry through individual contracts of employment.
> (Cruz 2013: 478)

Because sex work involves sex, there are limits to what the market can do. Think, for example, of the inapplicability of the general contract remedy of performance (whereby the courts compel performance of a contract) which would seriously undermine sexual autonomy (and amount to state-sanctioned rape). Again, we see that these claims are more complex than either sex or work.

signal the end of all forms of regulation and control. Just as the earlier chapter considered the regulatory effects of victim-focused interventions, in this chapter, I look beyond the rhetoric of legal models of work, which are often claimed to enhance sex worker capacity and rights, and examine instead what law is doing via licensing and public health regimes, offering insights into the forms of governance emerging in these complex and varied arenas.

This is an example of a constitutive approach. The operationalisation of rights through law makes the social world in a particular way which we find out about through the analyses of practices. It does not put into practice some idealised normative view of the world. I do this by offering an, admittedly selective, account of experiences of legalisation in the Netherlands and Australia and decriminalisation in New Zealand, all of which centre on an agential, rights-bearing model of citizenship.

Decriminalisation and self-governance: the Netherlands

In 1999 the Dutch parliament voted to lift a previously imposed 'brothel ban', a law which, although seldom enforced (due to the Dutch system of 'regulated tolerance' (Brants 1998)), officially outlawed the sale of sex in brothels. The ban's removal effectively legalised commercial sex in this setting. This reform took place the same year that the Swedish law criminalising purchasing came into force. Despite offering diametrically opposed responses, it is interesting to note that the motivations in both jurisdictions were similar, in that reforms sought to tackle gendered exploitation and curb trafficking. In the Dutch context, given its culture of pragmatism in public policy and the different political constituencies in debates (sex workers' voices were better represented in Dutch parliamentary debates and a greater diversity in feminism perspectives was displayed than in Sweden politics), it was thought this could be achieved by drawing a clear distinction between voluntary and forced prostitution, permitting those forms deemed to be voluntary, while enforcing the law in cases where there was coercion or force. As Outshoorn explains:

> Prostitution is no longer a controversial moral issue, but is now defined as sex work, provided the work is done voluntarily. Prostitutes are entitled to social insurance and can unionise if employed; they also have to pay taxes. Sex employers have to observe labour law, health and safety regulations, and pay social insurance and taxes. Brothels are permitted within certain areas and have to comply with local regulations; pimping is no longer a criminal offence. Forced prostitution, often tied to the trafficking of women, is to be eliminated.
> (Outshoorn 2004a: 165)

Outshoorn presents this new framework as a straightforward liberal pragmatic solution to the problem. However, a governmental analysis highlights the political nature of any problematisation, which, in this case, does not remove but reconfigures power and reconstitutes subjects and power in ways that align with liberal interests.

Despite claims that refiguring prostitution in this way makes it 'no longer a controversial moral issue', a certain form of morality remains, that of state non-interference, figured around simplistic notions of force and freedom. Indeed, a careful understanding of the reforms and their implementation shows that the grafting of essentially liberal notions of subjectivity, which deem prostitution as *either* forced *or* free, onto the more messy and complex world of sex work, results in what will inevitably be a selective and uneven approach to the issue.

While it is clear that, although they were rarely imposed, the removal of the threat of criminal sanctions brings significant benefits for those deemed to be voluntarily engaged in sex work in regulated brothels. For those who could meet these conditions of the regulatory system, conditions have improved (Vanwesenbeeck et al. 2002; Daalder 2007; Hubbard et al. 2007). Yet, these workers also experienced increased controls as the previous system of regulated tolerance was replaced with a system of licensing and regulation. Workers now had to comply with the bureaucratic structures of a new licensing regime. This system is more onerous and encourages sex workers, rather than clients, to self-regulate their behaviour in the interests of public health promotion. Social workers and public health workers took an increased policing role, encouraging prostitutes to conform to certain modes of working according to licensing conditions and business norms (Vanwesenbeeck et al. 2002; Hubbard et al. 2008). In order to meet the conditions of registration, workers were required to produce identification documents to verify their age, residential and immigration status.

Thus, the law operates alongside practices, such as public health, to create and maintain what Scott calls a 'responsible prostitution population' (Scott 2005: 252). Scott notes, in relation to similar legal moves in some states in Australia, that in such systems, inclusion is offered to those who 'can perform the rituals of middle class society' (Scott 2005), with all of the typical exclusions based on age, nationality, race, health and class that this entails. He illustrates his point by citing an advert which followed the decriminalisation of brothels in New South Wales, which gives a vivid description of the 'ideal' type, the rational subjects encouraged by these processes:

> [T]all, blonde and stylish, she recently completed her tertiary marketing course and is looking for employment in the field . . . She provides her own condoms . . . and comes complete with a medical certificate.
>
> (Harris and Haverkamp 1995, cited in Scott 2005: 264)

In the Netherlands, the costs of compliance and conditions imposed by this new system prioritised certain businesses and locations, especially the more corporatised forms of prostitution, constricting the legal market in sexual services (Hubbard et al. 2008). Research suggests that legalised systems create a two-tiered industry, as the costs and norms of compliance are too onerous for most individuals and small brothel owners to bear. Thus it overwhelmingly favours profitable sex businesses, who as Brents and Hausbeck note, can now hardly be described as 'other' to late capitalist industries (2007).

As the majority of sex workers lacked the financial resources to set up on their own, and preferred to retain an independent contractor status rather than subscribe to a formalised employer/employee relationship, many were not able to take up the new forms of legality. According to reports at the time, the number of legal brothels in Amsterdam halved when the new law was introduced ('Amsterdam to Cut Brothels in Half', BBC 6 December 2008). According to Lotte de Pol:

> The objective of the legalization, to recognize prostitution as a normal profession and so decriminalize it, has not been fulfilled . . .The majority of prostitutes work illegally and those with work permits have so far shunned to come into the open, proclaim themselves as prostitutes and pay taxes.
>
> (Lotte de Pol, cited in Hovet et al. 2005, referenced in Agustín 2008: 82)

The low take-up rate in the Netherlands indicates that very few can conform to this responsibilised model. This means that while licensing offers some increased improvement in the working conditions for a small section of workers, it also operates to identify and exclude those who cannot meet the increasingly conditional nature of citizenship, for example: migrants, drug users, who by virtue of age, nationality or health status, continue to be excluded from the formalised system and are thus outwith the framework of regulatory protection.

Also notably street sex work does not feature in the system of positive regulation. A number of Dutch authorities made a typical, yet erroneous assumption that by licensing some brothels they dispensed with any need to provide a safe space for outdoor workers.[30] This is based on the false premise that the industry is homogeneous and that the needs of different groups of sex workers are the same. This meant that *tippelzones*,[31] the areas in which sex work was previously tolerated, in Amsterdam, Rotterdam, The Hague and in Herleen, have faced closure since the repeal of the brothel ban,[32] leaving many more vulnerable and forced to work in less visible spaces. This is a prime example of how law constitutes the phenomenon that it is designed to regulate. Prostitution does not have an independent existence outside law, but rather it is shaped by it. Law plays a part in the construction of prostitution. The constitution of prostitution as a social fact in the Netherlands has changed as a result

30 This assumption is a common one, made, for example, in some states in Australia in which sex work was legalised (see Chapter 5) and in New Zealand where sex work was decriminalised but space was not made for street sex work.

31 These are areas where street prostitution is tolerated by the police and where certain services, for example, medical and social, may also be provided.

32 The *tippelzone* in Amsterdam closed in 2003 (City of Amsterdam 'Voortgangsrapportage sluiting tippelzone (de ontwikkelingen sinds de sluiting van de Theemsweg)' (2004); in Rotterdam in 2005 and The Hague in 2006 and then in Herleen on 1 January 2013.

of legal reform. Thus the net effect of the changes in the Netherlands has been a transformation from a large sex work sector operating under 'regulated tolerance' into a much smaller and constricted legal sector with better working conditions for a minority of workers who are now also subject to increased regulation. It has also led to the displacement of a large number to an unregulated illegal sector which as Daalder notes, is 'characterised by a lack of supervision and by poor accessibility for support workers, leaving [them] even more vulnerable to exploitation and making their position worse rather than better' (Daalder 2004: 50).

Decriminalisation: New Zealand

These themes are picked up by Harrington in the context of New Zealand's celebrated decriminalisation model. At the end of the 1990s, in the same period as the Swedes were busy outlawing buying sex and the Dutch were attempting to legalise it, the New Zealand parliament, after much debate, decriminalised prostitution. The Prostitution Reform Act (PRA) 2003 removed the laws governing prostitution, in order to make the sex industry 'subject to the same controls and regulations as those under which other businesses operate' (Abel, Fitzgerald, Healy and Taylor 2010b: 8).

While removing sex work from the criminal law brings with it undoubted benefits (Abel et al. 2010b; Abel 2014), there will also be other consequences. The removal of sovereign law does not extinguish power but rather reconstructs it. Harrington offers an important insight into the new configurations of knowledge and power that accompanied reform. She shows how the New Zealand Prostitutes Collective (NZPC) (a group of Wellington-based female prostitutes formed in 1987 who have had a prominent role in shaping public health knowledge of prostitution in New Zealand) and academics, helped to *produce* the decriminalisation approach (Abel and Fitzgerald 2010: 218; Abel, Fitzgerald and Brunton 2010a: 159).

Harrington notes that the NZPC claimed and were given authority to speak for women in the sex industry, due to their gatekeeping role. The focus on participatory models of knowledge production is productive of particular subject positions and the decriminalisation discourse was heavily influenced by subjects as rational agents who manage the risks associated with sex work.

Demands for a voice and participation, while *described* as inherently radical and synonymous with political resistance, when examined in practice, may also be understood within an advanced liberal framework which encourages individuals to make rational choices within a free market setting, self-governing, without disrupting existing hierarchies.

Public health policy regards sex workers as in need of empowerment, de-stigmatisation and reintegration into the wider society. The rational subject informs the New Zealand policy model, which is grounded in liberal notions of individual choice and responsibility in a market economy and confines state intervention in commercial sex markets to questions of health, safety and human rights. As Harrington notes:

> The New Zealand model may do away with the sexual double standard of past law, but replaces it with one that demonstrates a more consistently liberal policy of minimal intervention with the sexual conduct of apparently genderless free individuals in the marketplace.
>
> (Harrington 2012: 343)

The state concerns itself with clients only insofar as they refuse to wear condoms, solicit sex from someone under-aged or become violent. As Harrington argues, such an approach does not foster critical analyses of commercial sex markets and their contribution nor is it attentive to its effects on gendered social relationships.[33] This model treats social inequality and sexual exploitation as inevitable and focuses on 'harm reduction' for individuals. It places a great deal of faith in the free market resolving problems of violence and exploitation in the sex industry (Eden 1997: 152–153; Weatherall and Priestley 2001: 338).

Thus while we can recognise the undoubted benefits to this model (Abel 2014) that may render it a more pragmatic response, especially when compared with criminalised regimes (see Chapter 5), this is not because it is value free. Rather, the forms of governance it institutes may simply be less harmful and more compatible with other social justice interventions and politics.

A governmental analysis reveals a regulatory system that prioritises certain subjects and elevates state non-interference and market norms over other social values. By looking beyond the rhetoric and instead at what law is doing through empirical studies of regulatory systems, it becomes clear that promoting voluntary forms of sex work does not produce a system that neatly distinguishes good from bad, but rather one that actively constructs governable forms and subjects of sex work that become subject to increased bureaucratic control. While rights and space may accrue for some who are now 'legal', this does not extend to all, as many struggle to fit increasingly narrow models of citizenship and are thereby left (sometimes further) outside of the ambit of formal legal protection.

The irony is that these patterns of governance, although framed in different terms, display *some* of the same dynamics and patterns as abolitionist victim-oriented models, despite being cast as its polar opposite. Indeed, this was the conclusion of my own work with colleagues, which found that that the system of

33 Harrington cites Weatherall and Priestley's discourse analysis of how New Zealand prostitutes construct sex work. 'Sex worker voices construct masculinity as requiring uncomplicated sexual release and sex workers as providing a necessary social service' (Weatherall and Priestley 2001). She then argues: 'Sex markets are explained by an unchanging male sexual culture . . . sex workers view their clients' needs as unproblematic and the sex industry as responding to a pre-existing demand, rather than generating it, responding to a pre-existing need rather than constructing it' (Harrington 2012: 342) and 'to the extent that sex workers' livelihood depends on thriving sex markets, they have little interest in questioning the wider politics of commercial sex' (Harrington 2012: 341). I only partially accept this – as I think that some sex workers do display an interest in the wider politics of commercial sex, with a similar variation in political consciousness to other workers in many parts of the economy.

regulationism in the Netherlands, of abolitionism in Sweden and decriminalisation in New Zealand can all be seen to encourage similar forms of self-governance and produce analogous exclusions and which began my whole enquiry of how law matters in sex work (Scoular 2010).

Conclusion

In this chapter, I have sought to expose the rights-bearing sex worker to the same critical scrutiny as I have previous subject formations. In so doing, I have revealed the promises and paradoxes and politics of contemporary rights discourse.

Framing political demands in the idiom of rights can provide a powerful strategic language to build solidarity between diverse civil social actors both nationally and internationally (Steans 2007) and has led to a number of important gains by sex worker social movements. Yet any optimism must be measured against the experience of rights in action; as the abstract language of rights is often far removed from everyday struggles and is often silent on governmental effects. Drawing on wider critical literature on rights that resonates with empirical accounts of sex workers' rights in action, I consider the constitutive nature and regulatory capacity of sex workers' rights.

Just as my analysis did not seek to deny the important gendered insights by radical feminists, in this chapter, I do not suggest that we abandon rights but I do urge a critical caution. My intention is, as it was previously, to ensure critical enquiry in the face of approaches that seek to present themselves as *the* singular route to emancipation on behalf of fully constituted and stable subjects, whether they be victims or rights-bearing agents. In both cases, I argue, such naive, unicausal and universal approaches, which fail to reflect on the governmental features of identity claims, risk co-opting subjects in ever more complex webs of social control. The failures in the sex workers' movement in the past are, I argue, in a large part, to do with the difficulties of fitting sex work into a universal model of work or sexual identity. Just as rights-claims centred around sexual identity may miss materialist and economic elements, workers' rights, at their most rudimentary, can also ignore the embodied nature of the work involved. Such flattened subject positions, like their victim counterparts, easily aligns with systems of liberal and neoliberal governmentality (Scoular 2010) and rights may only be meaningful for a small section of self-governing individuals at the upper end of the market. This does not mean that rights are not useful as political 'tactics' but, rather, that when they are asserted as 'truth' and not tied to wider political change, they may simply operate to buttress the status quo; operating in the interests of profitable sex businesses, and a privatised, non-collective responsibilised prostitution population while leaving many outwith their grasp, yet subject to their differentiation. This explains the mixed success of a labour rights approach and the variable experience of legalised models.

Sex workers' rights, therefore, must be viewed in a critical light. This does not mean rejecting them altogether, but it does mean embracing them with a necessary ambivalence, and recognising that sex workers' rights, like rights in general, are as replete with paradoxes as they are fecund with promise. The radical potential of rights is not guaranteed by their mere invocation but rather requires a more critical engagement with the supposedly stable subject of rights and the apparently modern discourse of law than has been the case up until now.

The point that I am making is that rights do not, as many assume, provide a simple solution to the messy business of politics. They are not, as Dworkin claims, trumps that provide a right answer in hard cases – rather they are instrumental modes of power, not morals, not principles, but tools in political projects (Golder 2010: 75–76). They have no political or ontological priority but are part of the politics of the game. Campaigns are fundamentally flawed if they consider rights as an end game, as a solution, as a way of asserting an 'objective' legal norm that obviates the need for politics. What they are not is anti-politics, despite the fact that, as Wendy Brown notes, they often masquerade as 'something of an antipolitics – a pure defence of the innocent and the powerless against power' (Brown 2004: 453). Rights we must remember are not about democratising power or about protection from power – but are, in themselves, a mode of power, thus we must proceed strategically, empirically informed and with a certain ambivalence and concern when rights take over from broader justice projects.

Rights may be useful *tactics* in political movements but we must think how we can utilise them to resist power, rather than simply folding back into state and bio-political power. This is a theme that I will explore in the final chapter of the book.

Chapter 5

Reconstructing the subject of prostitution

> The most [human beings] can do is to manipulate the tensions within their own epoch in order to produce the beginning of the next epoch.
>
> (Rorty 1989: 51)

> Critique doesn't have to be the premise of a deduction which concludes: this then is what needs to be done. It should be an instrument for those you fight, those who resist and refuse what is . . . It doesn't have to lay down the law for the law. It isn't a stage in a programming. It is a challenge directed to what is.
>
> (Foucault 1991: 84)

Introduction

Having offered a critique of modernist approaches that attempt to fix subjects within frameworks of sovereign law, in this chapter I wrestle with the implications of a post-structural approach to the subject. I say 'wrestle', because a post-structural methodology raises certain dilemmas in terms of how to engage with legal reform in this arena. If having established that the prostitute subject is an effect of power, and that law – frequently appealed to as a neutral arbiter in contemporary political battles – is, as a result of its constitutive role, in fact a part of the social 'reality' that it seeks to reform – what are the implications for future legal engagement? How do we appeal to law and indeed can or should we, if it is itself part of the problem? Should we eschew law altogether or could legal reform initiatives perform some role in delivering justice for those in sex work. Can we reconcile post-structural insights with a progressive politics?

While I recognise that even the use of the term post-structural tends to induce anxiety, not least by those who want ready-made policy solutions, my project here is not simply an abstract exercise but one which fundamentally alters how we understand the field. The way in which we comprehend law transforms the kind of policy questions and assessments we can make. My contribution to the study of regulation is to show, by way of genealogy, the constitutive effect of law on the definition of sex work. Law does not stand outside politics and regulate 'prostitution', it, in part, makes prostitution what it is. Thus changes to law can change what prostitution is, which can have positive practical impacts on the lives of sex workers.

I recognise that an anti-foundational approach can appear unsettling. There is a danger that not taking up a position and 'urging caution' and 'reassessment' (Scott 2005) in the face of grave injustices, may look suspiciously like fence sitting (Veitch et al. 2007). Marshall, for example, notes: '[T]he de-centred subject, lacking in autonomy or any kind of identity, is unlikely to be an effective agent of social transformation' (2006: 20). Others argue that post-structural approaches are nihilistic,[1] lacking in any basic guidelines or collective aims that can compel mutual solidarity (McNay 1992). This point has particular resonance in systems such as law and politics, which require constituencies to align with liberal legal concepts (of citizenship and rights) to be recognised. By critically engaging with norms, then, it is possible to both address these concerns without endorsing liberal law and to move away from these foundations without becoming disorientated, immoral, and blind to injustice.[2]

A main concern in writing this book has been to give a more empirically accurate and critical account of how law matters in the field of sex work. This challenges both formalist accounts that over-determine the significance of law but also analysis that appear to suggest that a post-structural approach rendered law irrelevant (see Scoular 2010, re Agustín 2009). The governmental approach developed in this book helps not only to elucidate the significance of law, it may also offer *some* hope for law's potential, albeit limited, to challenge injustices. Understanding how law operates constitutively opens up ways to imagine how law *could* matter better, suggesting ways in which it could deliver a different and better form of justice.

1 The charge of nihilism, I argue, leads us back to absolutes and creates an impasse with regards strategy. We are seemingly forced to either do nothing or take sides. I reject this binary and suggest that using norms as tactics, to perform a strategic intervention, provides a middle ground between eschewing law and its uncritical adoption (see Golder 2011: 295).

2 I think it is entirely possible to make ethical and pragmatic decisions without necessarily adhering to a system of universal ethics (Levinas 1991; Bauman 1993; Butler 2004b) or least recognising their contingency. Post-structuralism does not suggest some laissez-faire apolitical engagement, but rather suggests a different kind of solidarity. Foucault's rejection of normative criteria aims to 'expose the compulsion that binds each political intervention to a proof of justification, to a norm of identity or, as what he called, a "test of legitimacy"' (Lemke 2003: 175). This does not mean that, for Foucault, all exercises of power are ethically and politically equal, of course; what it means is simply that one has to empirically investigate how power relations work in a particular setting. Power exists everywhere, but its workings cannot be predicted from a scientific model (O'Malley and Valverde 2014: 333). Thus, in this context, urging 'caution and reassessment', an approach urged by Scott, whose work I found particularly inspiring for this book, is, as he notes 'not to denounce public health practices as repressive, dismiss liberal-humanist agendas, or obscure the possibilities that may arise under programmes of decriminalization' (Scott 2005: 272). It simply means that we cannot accept their claims at face value and need to test them via careful empiricism. We need to consider what law does not what it says, as any intervention produces complex, unpredictable social effects as law operates alongside other discourses in complex social fields (see Smart 1989).

A further benefit of Foucault's work is his insight into resistance. As power is immanent in our social practice, then, so too is resistance, albeit circumscribed by the context within which it operates. This is not to suggest that power is a 'bad' thing that comes from on high and has to be resisted. But that, in order to deliver change, power has also to be exercised. Strategies have to be developed, tactics deployed, debates conducted and compromises made. These engagements with politics take place within *existing* social arrangements. There is no 'essential freedom' to be achieved, as imagined by Marxist, liberal, anarchist or feminist utopias, but rather freedom is to be understood as a practice conducted in resistance to power, the process of legal change necessarily involves a process of 'agonism' or 'reciprocal incitation and struggle' (Foucault 1982b: 221–222). As Valverde notes:

> Foucault was extremely careful to avoid developing a new model, a grand social theory that might replace the Marxism that was dominant then. Instead, he cultivated more empirically grounded, historically specific habits of thought [where] the basic terms are themselves tactical weapons, and hence do not have fixed meanings. That is, the terms are not concepts. This has gone largely unnoticed in the literature.
>
> (Valverde 2010: 45)

These insights can be usefully applied to the dilemma of legal reform. Given there is no 'outside' of law, due to its constitutive relationship to society, we must work within its structures. As the structures of modern law expand beyond sovereign law and extend to its bio-political manifestations, so too must resistance. We cannot eschew law (or legal processes, actors, norms), although we may want to decentre it and think differently about its engagement. Law does not operate ideologically (as there is always resistance) or directly via consciousness (as it is more than simply what people think and do) but through its increased governmentality as it increasingly forms part of wider normalising processes that constitute and shape the subjects and spaces of modern life. It is thus within these spaces that we must apply some leverage.

Engaging critically *within* the institutional spaces of liberalism constitutes a potent strategic intervention. As Christodoulidis explains:

> [T]he 'strategic' imports a specific reflexivity that does not necessarily fall within, but may situate itself incongruently to the spaces, interstices and speaking positions that the system makes available.
>
> (Christodoulidis 2009: 22)

I therefore outline the strategic and pragmatic[3] importance of engaging with liberal language, concepts such as rights, consent, autonomy that already structure

3 If readers are not convinced by post-structuralism then there is also pragmatic argument to be made for engaging with law in this critical manner. A pragmatic approach recognises that it is not possible

a range of literatures (theoretical, legal, policy) and debates about prostitution. In the sections that follow I consider:

- struggles to legally establish sex workers' sexual non-consent
- attempts to establish workplace rights and protections for those engaged in sex work.
- challenges that seek recognition of sex workers' constitutional rights in the case of *Bedford* vs. *Canada*
- the novel use of rights in claims for 'entertainment rights'

My aim is not to offer some 'improved sociology of modernity' (Valverde 2010).[4] I show that these concepts do not have a 'predetermined content'; nor do they represent 'some enduring metaphysics of humanity', assuming they do simply results in circular normative discussions that centre around force vs. free, freedom vs. slavery and victims vs. agents. Rather their meaning 'rests on much more contested ground', as Golder explains:

> For Foucault, norms themselves are part of the historical field under investigation and not outside it. Norms are not something laid out in advance of political struggles that guide and govern them; rather they are constituted in struggle. Recognising the political nature of rights does not mean abandoning them but using them as tactics.
>
> (Golder 2011: 288)

I use examples where sex workers *have* been critically engaging with law, to show that legal norms can be used as tactics, in the service of radical ends, to encourage struggle, resistance and imagine new ways of being, beyond tired aporias and their 'enlightenment present'. By pragmatically engaging with liberal legal language (concepts such as rights, consent and autonomy), we can 'manipulate the tensions within their own epoch in order to produce the beginning of the next epoch' (Rorty 1989: 51).

to engage in debates about prostitution without also engaging with liberal language of consent and rights, but sees these norms not as truths, end points but as cultural concepts (Valverde 1989b: 157) which are amenable to cultural change and 'reflect not [some] objective truth but the grammar of what it means to be us' (Williams 2000: 63). Engaging with norms also helps to offer a 'reassuring tone' (Williams 1991: 175) in the face of what some consider to the nihilism of writers such as Foucault, Derrida, Nietzsche and what some consider to be their 'alienating of style aesthetics' (Williams 1991: 175).

4 It is important to carefully elucidate such an agenda to ensure that it offers something more than what Valverde (2010) refers to as 'an improved sociology of modernity', a term she uses alongside 'post-structuralism-lite' to describe ways of engaging that simply serve to 'prop up' or make minor renovations to existing academic edifices (Valverde 2010: 46). She urges us instead to 'question our own desire to call ourselves modern and challenge our yearning for static models' (Valverde 2010: 45).

Critical engagements with the subject: consent

Consent is a defining feature of the voluntary liberal subject and as such is a foundational concept in liberal legal system. Alongside autonomy, it has been a controversial concept for feminists who are critical of the asocial and gendered nature of the concept that masquerades under the myth of legal neutrality as consent in law has tended to be constructed and interpreted in ways that reflect an unencumbered and masculine subject (Cowan and Hunter 2007). Debates regarding the extent to which material factors and gender inequalities structure, or indeed undermine, consensual capacity have been particularly heated in the areas of sexual offences, pornography, reproductive rights and sex work.

The very possibility of consent in prostitution has been questioned by a significant section of the feminist movement, most notably radical feminists Jeffreys (1997a), Barry (1979, 1995) and MacKinnon (1987, 1989). Given the universal conditions of male supremacy and endemic male violence which mean that women are 'forced' into many abusive situations – including prostitution – in order to survive, 'consent is not a good divining-rod to the existence of freedom [as] . . . consent to violation is a fact of oppression' (Barry 1995: 65). Barry talks about 'the ideology of consent' which is used to 'obscure the real effects of women's multi-layered oppression on their ability to exercise individual free will' (Barry, cited by Jeffreys 1997a: 137) and 'falsely' separates prostitution from rape. For radical feminists, prostitution is always a coercive sexual practice. Even if women express their 'consent' to prostitution sex, it is not *real* consent, as this quotation from a recent campaign to criminalise the purchase of sex in Scotland illustrates:

> Although women in prostitution are agreeing to sexual activity, this is unwanted sex. In order to repeatedly endure this unwanted sex women have to dissociate, and many use alcohol or drugs to do so. This is the case irrespective of whether the prostitution happens on the street, in a brothel, or in a fancy hotel.
>
> (Scottish Coalition Against Sexual Exploitation 2010: 1)

This radical feminist approach to prostitution and consent has, in turn, been subject to critique. As discussed in Chapter 3, the omnipotence of gender domination in this schema eclipses all other structures. Crucial factors such as race and colonialism and the economic coercion that sex workers experience due to pervasive poverty, rather than informing a more contextual, intersectional framework are rendered secondary (see Scoular 2004b).[5]

Patriarchy so overwhelms the subject that it renders agency irrelevant, creating practical issues for feminist justice efforts. Concrete forms of resistance (what I like

5 An intersectional framework recognises the multiple ways in which different forms or systems of oppression, for example, race, gender and class, intersect.

to call 'in situ' rights) are irrelevant, to the quest for an ideologically perfect solution that fits with the radical world view.

Critics highlight the political and moral problems associated with disregarding consent. While equating prostitution with rape makes a strong rhetorical statement, it is dangerous as it appears to condone the violence that this group experiences, casting it as in some way inevitable, an occupational hazard. This renders harms by clients, employers, pimps or others less visible and sex workers less able than other women to pursue complaints of rape in the criminal justice systems. As O'Connell Davidson argues:

> If prostitution is rape, then it is logical to define prostitutes as women who are publicly available to be raped, and this is precisely the position taken by many police officers, judges and jurists around the world who refuse to accept that a woman who works as a prostitute can ever be raped.
>
> (1998: 122)

Moreover, to say that sex work involves only 'a veneer of consent' (O'Connell Davidson 1998: 121) or is a manifestation of false consciousness is at odds with the subjective, lived experience of sex workers. As Sullivan notes, while sex workers negotiate consent within a particular set of power relations, they *do* make a distinction between their 'consensual' work as prostitutes and non-consensual acts of rape. This, she argues:

> [S]uggests . . . not that sex workers are the deluded victims of false consciousness . . . but that the nature of their consent – and their specific non-consent – needs to be taken more seriously by feminist and other theorists of prostitution.
>
> (Sullivan 2000: 3)

This insight does not seek to fall back onto liberal orthodoxy – whereby free-floating autonomous individuals consent to exactly the type of sex they want in some sexy, hedonistic social vacuum.

Indeed, the problem with *both* liberals and some dominant feminist ideas of consent is that they view it in such stark terms, not as a process or construction but as a state to be achieved only in the absence of power relations – when individuals are completely free and autonomous. Consent becomes a marker of the distinction between legitimate and illegitimate exercises of power, the absence of consent equals coercion and that its presence equals freedom.[6]

6 Over the last decade, sex worker advocates have also developed much more nuanced accounts of consent beyond the binaries of 'forced and free', particularly in the wake of new international debates about 'trafficking' for the purposes of prostitution (see Bindman and Doezema 1997: 5; Doezema 1998: 34–50).

Critical theorists have questioned this stark binary of free/unfree and consent/non-consent. Freeman (1990: 98), for example, argues:

> The fixed nature of liberal consent fails to appreciate the importance of social context and human mediation . . . we must look at the factors that minimize, undermine or extinguish it in order to work toward authentic consent.

These insights rely on Foucault's insights as regards power (1982b) – that power is immanent in all relations and that it operates to construct the possibilities of human action, including 'free' action. For Freeman (1990: 96), consent is always 'relative and socially contingent' and we participate in processes that construct the meaning of consent in any given context. Except in conditions of domination, human subjects – produced as an effect of power – will be able to practice some freedom and some resistance (see Hindess 1996: 98–104).

This approach moves us beyond an abstract binary of forced/free in feminism and calls attention to the importance of context and power relations in the construction of consensual capacity. It is not to deny power dynamics or to ignore material insights of radical feminism, but it does allow them to overtake. It calls into question the conceptualisation of prostitution as 'always involving rape', but does so not by invoking some naive, liberal notion of freedom but by recognising that capacity to consent or indeed register non-consent is an effect of power relations, one that is socially, politically and legally constructed.

This brings to mind the progress that has been made as regards consent. As Sullivan notes, consent has been a site of considerable feminist struggle as women have sought to work within and to extend its normative strictures to recognise their lived experience in legal reforms on rape, abortion and many other issues *including* sex work. Indeed, feminist critical engagements have helped to create the very possibility of sex workers' non-consent and in so doing have served not only to enlarge consent but to redefine sex workers as citizens capable of exercising non-consent.

Engaging with law strategically – being remade in law

Sullivan points to feminist efforts in reforming the law of rape in order to create the very possibility of sex workers' non-consent. For centuries, sex workers, like married women, have found it incredibly difficult, if not impossible, to pursue complaints of rape. Legal discourse, informed by social mores, presumed that both married women and sex workers always consented to sex. By virtue of marriage and by prostitutes being 'commonly' available to men, these women effectively gave up their right to refuse sex forever[7] (Edwards 1981: 62). In a number of common law jurisdictions (United Kingdom, Australia, Canada and New Zealand)

and in many other systems, evidence of involvement in prostitution was deemed relevant in determining whether the complainant's non-consent could be believed by a jury.[8] This was reinforced by the practice of cross-examination, which focuses on complainants' sexual reputation.[9] These legal constructions meant that, in practice, those engaged in sex work were considered as being incapable of withholding consent and therefore were effectively incapable of being raped. This is a significant issue given the high rates of sexual assault women experience generally and in this context (analogous again to marriage and other intimate heterosexual relations).

However, as Sullivan notes, as a direct result of feminist activism that campaigned for significant reforms in rape law and improvements in social attitudes towards women working in prostitution, things have begun to change. In a number of countries in the 1980s and 1990s, men for the first time were prosecuted for raping those involved in sex work[10] and convictions for rape and associated crimes began to slowly increase. Building on these reforms, evidence of prior history as a sex worker was deemed to be no longer admissible (Sullivan 2000), neither can it now be used to justify a lesser sentence for rape, as J Kirby of the New South Wales Supreme Court explained when overturning the previous position:[11]

> [P]rostitutes, male or female, were entitled to the same protection of the law as any other citizen. They have their human dignity and their privacy and ought not unconsensually to have that invaded by fellow citizens.
>
> (J Kirby in *R* vs. *Leary*)

Thus, as Sullivan notes, sex workers have recently been 'remade' in law as women vulnerable to rape, as individuals able to give and withhold sexual consent.

7 This was also the case for married women who had to struggle to gain legal recognition for rape. Change was incremental; the first case of legal recognition for non-consent related to a separated couple then extended to those in relationships (see *Stallard vs. HM Advocate* 1989 SCCR 248 and *R* vs. *R* [1991] UKHL 12).

8 See *R* vs. *Krausz* (1973) 57 Cr App R 466.

9 See *R* vs. *Bashir* [1969] 1 WLR 1303; *R* vs. *Barker* (1829) 172 ER 558; these cases parallel the problematic use of sexual evidence history of women more generally.

10 In Australia, see *R* vs. *Leary* BC 9302383 Supreme Court of NSW Court of Criminal Appeal CCA 060254 of 1992; *R* vs. *Myers and Ward* BC 9300725 Supreme Court of Victoria Court of Criminal Appeal 40 and 83 of 1993; *R* vs. *Heros Hakopian* BC 9100584 Supreme Court of Victoria Court of Criminal Appeal 168 and 871 of 1991; in the United Kingdom, see *R* vs. *Charles Grenville Shaw* [1997] EWCA 165, *R* vs. *Arjumand Hussein* [1996] EWCA 606, *R* vs. *Kevin Davis* [1997] EWCA 3655; in New Zealand, see *R* vs. *Clark* [1987] 1 NZLR 380.

11 Kirby overturned an increasingly controversial line of authorities that maintained it was permissible to reduce the sentence of those who were convicted of rape where the victim was a sex worker, see, e.g., the *Hakopian* case where the judge imposed a lighter sentence on the accused because 'the likely impact of the rape on the victim was "much less a factor in this case and lessens the gravity of the offences"' (B. Sullivan 2007: 134). Public outrage at this decision helped to pressure for change.

Through legal struggle sex workers have made their non-consent visible and legally relevant and in doing so have been *(re)constructed* as citizens with new rights and as subjects with new capacities:

> [T]hese capacities are not unreal or ideological. They are an effect of changing power relations and, in particular, of those feminist challenges to gendered power relations which led to new social attitudes to prostitutes and statutory reform.
>
> (Sullivan 2000: 5)

Feminist and sex workers' efforts to gain recognition for rape, look to law, less to define some abstract notion of consent, but rather to recognise legal subjectivity regarding rape, and to help create conditions for consent to be utilised for more progressive ends.

Reforms have allowed *some* sex workers to successfully pursue complaints of rape. Barriers continue to exist: attrition rates are high; successful cases tend to be limited to where an assault has been accompanied by violence; low sentences are common in sex work cases, and sexual history evidence is, despite legislation being in place, still presented to undermine the credibility of *all* rape complainants.

The fact that these problems apply in cases of rape more generally and that many victims of sexual violence struggle to be heard in legal processes[12] underlines the importance of working together in solidarity rather than setting up sex workers as antithetical subjects. Establishing legal subjectivity and enlarging consensual capacity increases the space for women to challenge the boundaries of consent and are of benefit to all women and survivors of sexual abuse.

Thinking beyond consent: moving beyond the Hamlet question

This focus on the conditions of consent is pertinent to the subject of prostitution where the search for a universal ethic has resulted in binary arguments and political stalemate. Feminist scholarship and activism that orientates feminist concerns to the *structure* rather than the existence of commercial sex is particularly useful (Fraser 1993). It urges us to abandon what Williams calls the Hamlet question – 'to commodify or not' and consider instead how we would want to structure such social relationships that involve elements of both economy and identity (Williams and Zelizer 2005). As Radin notes:

> If neither commodification nor non-commodification can put to rest our disquiet about harm to personhood in conjunction with certain specific kinds

12 Despite legislation being in place, sexual history evidence is still routinely presented to undermine the credibility of all rape complainants (see Henning and Bronitt 1998; Burman 2009).

> of transactions . . . [or] can satisfy our aspirations for a society exhibiting equal respect for persons – then we must rethink the larger social context within which this dilemma is embedded. We must think about wealth and power redistribution.
>
> (Radin 1996: 125)

We also need to think of the role that law and legal process may have in this. Given the constitutive role that law plays in modern societies, there is a need to move beyond approaching law in binary form, as either a repressive or a facilitative power, as envisaged in legal/illegal models and see law rather as a dynamic that can effect both positive and negative changes in the distribution of power between parties.

Moreover, the difficulties of easily distinguishing between forced and free (Doezema 1998) means that there is much potential in what a number of writers call for a 'contextual and plural ethics of commercial sexual transactions' (Bernstein 2007). This ethical framework moves beyond legal/illegal universal categorisation (sex work is all good or all bad) and is able to accommodate feminist concerns regarding gendered power alongside an appreciation of prostitution as a complex commodity form.

Moving beyond hypothetical, binary on/off questions about whether to commodify sex or not, recognises the fact that such services *are* currently marketised and highlights more pressing concrete issues, such as who controls the process and proceeds, to what extent can law, market reform, trade union rights, criminal justice interventions and different forms of social solidarity help to bring about more egalitarian effects to the sex market? This more nuanced approach looks beyond banning or legalizing, to addressing in situ needs. This does not mean being blind to injustices neither does it signify a laissez-faire approach, as there remains a deep concern about the effects of commodification at a material level that create the conditions for 'desperate exchanges' (Satz 1995: 65–66) and render the issue of choice problematic. Satz (1995) uses this term when she considers what is wrong – and, potentially, right – with different commercial sexual modalities (see Bernstein 1999). She argues that it is possible to distinguish between markets in sexual labour, and contrasts the activities of, for example, a Park Avenue call girl, a man selling sex to another man and the desperate exchanges of a 14-year-old heroin addict (Satz 1995: 65–66). This offers a context for a more grounded and plural ethics of consent.

Yet the fact that these desperate exchanges come about, often sadly as the result of women's disproportionate poverty,[13] means that for many, the 'concern over women's lives becoming entirely commodified seems by comparison an abstract worry' (Silbaugh 1997: 84). Funnelling these concerns into a binary of legal/illegal

13 Indeed, one of my concerns with regards the uncritical promotion of individualised exiting programmes is their utility in the face of economic recession (see Scoular and O'Neill 2007).

or choice/no choice unfortunately comes up against empirical findings that for many, living on or below the poverty line, 'there is "just enough" choice in such exchanges' (Rosen and Venkatesh 2008). Preventing desperate exchanges necessitates a wider politics than that of prostitution control or identity politics that are currently prevailing. The focus then should be to struggle to improve the context in which such exchanges are made, to create the conditions for a non-alienated sexuality (Valverde 1989a: 254), or the possibilities for 'sexual communism' (Van der Veen 2002: 208),[14] which, in turn, may make for a more meaningful legal subjectivity.

Law and social policy can be more creative than simply condemnation and criminalisation but have a role in creating and strengthening what Satz (1995) calls 'barriers to degradation'. Barriers to degradation can be established by working to create conditions in which sex workers have an ability to refuse to perform and to exercise informed consent, have the freedom to work without male brokerage and have other viable options in life.

Critical engagements with the subject: reconfiguring rights

In the previous chapter, I considered some of the key paradoxes of sex workers' rights and spent some time highlighting the perils of emancipatory discourses that continued in the modernist tradition. I was critical of the current operation of sex worker rights that overly relies on fixed notions of 'work' or 'sex' and agency. Such 'rights' talk' I argued, may only foster the inclusion of a small elite, who are mainstreamed into an existing sexual or economic order, reifying, rather than challenging, bureaucratic structures of control.

Yet, there was also a hint at the end of the chapter that we may not want to abandon rights altogether. Given their current political and legal currency, rights may still have potential to provide some leverage in certain situations, provided they are reconstructed in the light of post-structural insights. This requires viewing rights with a certain ambivalence and utilizing them strategically (rather than ontologically) and as tactics in the context of, not in place of, a wider feminist materialist politics (Scoular and O'Neill 2007; Cruz 2013; O'Connell Davidson 2014).

A critical, ambivalent affirmation of rights

> The allure of human rights persists because they can, and do, mean many things at once. Human rights can be sources of empowerment and protection for persons against the societies on which they live, or they can constrain the

14 In a similar vein, Cruz calls for sex workers to join campaigns for a basic income (Cruz 2013). While these may appear idealistic goals, imaginaries are important in feminist justice projects (Cornell 1995). Yet they must, I argue, be balanced with pragmatic legal engagements with concrete, rather than idealised, others.

> same persons. Additionally, they can liberate or limit the imagination of the possible; they can revolutionize or conserve . . . [they can] authorize action and yet undermine authority's claims. They are, by definition, mandatory claims, yet they are fecund with interpretative possibilities. They both constitute us as subjects and provide a language through which we can resist that construction and forge new identities.
>
> (Sarat and Kearns 2002: 6–7)[15]

I am inspired by critical work that seeks to occupy a middle ground between the avowal of rights and naive engagement. Working in this space requires a certain ambivalence; taking advantage of the present currency of rights yet not being seduced by their rhetoric. Thus I advocate the tactical use of rights to mitigate harms suffered by prostitutes (i.e., a pragmatic approach) which transcends approaches that either embrace rights as *the* answer or those which argue that rights are liberal smokescreens and can *never be* the answer.

Recognising the political character of rights does not have to be fatal to feminism or sex worker activists if we take a more expansive notion of politics and law and move beyond viewing such claims as if they are made by a readymade, 'natural' constituency in a fixed polity.[16] By approaching rights critically we can tap into their political currency and benefit from what Sarat calls their 'interpretive possibilities' (Sarat and Kearns 2002). Yet this requires that we begin from a different starting point; that we 'depart from the standard legal and political idiom of rights' (Golder 2011: 286), which rests on an orthodox liberal humanism. Rather than affirming some pre-existing subject that is beyond power, critical rights do not profess a predetermined content – 'some enduring metaphysics of humanity' but are framed on much more contested ground (Golder 2011: 288). If we see rights as illimitable and based on less solid ground, this opens up, rather than stifles, politics.

This is particularly pertinent to the case of sex workers' rights, where the very act of rights' claiming by this constituency, challenges the established boundaries of what it means to be 'human', extending the previously tightly drawn polity[17] and has the *potential* to perform an important political rupture, as Figure 4.2 playfully suggested.

15 Golder makes a similar point:

> [A] critique of the limits of humanism, as both a form of thought and a technology of power which works to circumscribe the limits of human possibility, is indeed compatible with an affirmation of human rights.
>
> (Golder 2011: 288)

16 See Minow 1988, 1989, 1995, 2002, who argues for more expansive notion of rights.

17 Sex workers' rights also highlight the problematic relationship between rights and citizenship. Rights-based activism in this area reveals 'some exclusionary practices of citizenship' as access to rights is often mediated through a statism that many migrants cannot access and on a separation between public and private that excludes many undertaking caring and affective forms of labour (see Merry 2006; Elias 2007).

Liminal subjects: sex workers' rights to have rights

There is a liminal nature to sex workers' rights. Foucault's archeological method shows that what has passed as human is, in fact, an a-temporal construction, one that nevertheless has been universalized as the basis for a human essence and serves as a basis for liberal rights claims. His genealogy of 'knowledge' shows that Western reason is founded on a series of constitutive silences and exclusions, he gives the examples of madness (Foucault 1996: viii) and homosexuality (Foucault 1976) to which we could add women (Lloyd 2005) and sex worker as subjects excluded from the polity in order to establish the boundaries of citizenship.

Yet, when those previously excluded from the polity speak and seek rights as 'human rights', they perform 'a rhetorical, ironical, strategy of pointing out law's antinomies, and of challenging law's contingencies' (O'Donovan 1997: 63). By claiming 'the right to have rights', this group (may) begin to challenge the tight strictures within which subjects are recognised and moves us beyond the modernism that has flourished through the exclusion and management of 'others'. The very possibility of such rights, their articulation and potential recognition, simultaneously serves to widen meanings of what it is to be 'human' or a 'rights-bearing subject' (Lloyd 2007) and in so doing creates new relations of power. Golder talks of 'anti-humanist human rights', which are used not as an attempt to insert a new ontology, but critically and strategically to extend the political community (2010). Sex workers' rights, I argue, are an example of anti-humanist human rights.

Sex workers' rights as anti-humanist rights

While I have been critical of sex workers' rights framed solely around the axis of sexuality or work, it is important to recognise that such claims can be more complex. Sex worker narratives offer important counter-hegemonic insights that contest the artificial split between sexuality and intimacy, on the one hand, and productive work and commercial exchange, on the other (Zatz 1997: 306). Their claims for rights in the context of embodied labour *can* fuse sexual autonomy and economic control in a way that goes beyond the current sexual economy and the capitalist market. By mobilising rights in this way, I argue, sex workers are not simply affirming the essence of what it is to be a sex worker (there is no such thing) but constituting a strategic challenge to ideals of humanity based on fictions that separate work and affect.

In the sections that follow, I give examples of a more critical deployment of rights in the context of:

- the creation of new workers' protections and rights in labour reforms that combine safety, sexual and economic autonomy
- a recent Supreme Court judgment whereby sex workers for the first time have been able to access fundamental constitutional rights

- the novel use of rights in the campaigning activities of the DMSC sex workers' union in India which calls for 'entertainment rights'.

'Rights' are deployed in these examples in ways that help to reconstitute the legal definition of what it means to be a sex worker while simultaneously mitigating some of the negative consequences. Sex workers are still operating in a liberal democracy, the new utopia is still not with us, but the pragmatic deployment of rights claims, I show, have helped to generate some change and prostitution is a little different from what it was before.

Getting rights to work

> The test of a first rate intelligence is the ability to hold two opposed ideas in the mind at the same time, and still retain the ability to function.
>
> (Scott Fitzgerald 1936)

I want to return to consider sex workers' workplace-based rights in the context of a more critical appreciation of rights doctrine. The previous chapter warned of the necessary limitations of claims that were premised on simply being mainstreamed into the formal economy. By taking themselves off to market and naming their price, O'Connell Davidson (2013) warned that sex workers were more petty bourgeois entrepreneurs than radical subjects (Bell 1994: 122). These concerns have been realised in some of the empirical examples I cited where there have been attempts to regulate prostitution as work in legalised or decriminalised systems (Chapter 4). However rather than abandon work-based rights, it is important to recognise that there are cases where such rights claiming represents more than simply 'petty bourgeois demands' for recognition, where they go beyond the limits of the market and begin to challenge its bare protections.[18] While recognising the need to connect up to larger material and political struggles, I nevertheless argue that it is possible to engage with workplace rights while recognising the gendered and exploitative elements that typify many struggles in late capitalist economies.

One of my concerns about the way that rights are currently configured is that sex workers' rights are often assumed to present some uncritical endorsement of legal regimes. Sex workers' rights are often pitted against radical feminist abolitionist ideas, as if a feminist cannot accommodate both ideas – i.e., that some workers' protection may help those in the sector and that a gendered and materialist analysis is important. This influences the treatment of law, which is also often presented in binary form – legal vs. illegal.

18 The concern, as O'Connell Davidson (2013) notes, is not commodification per se but what this means under the conditions of capitalism, the effects of which may be felt more intensely by some groups than others (Weeks 2011).

The constitutive role that law plays in modern societies dictates that we move beyond approaching law in binary form, as either a repressive or a facilitative power, and see law rather as a dynamic that can effect both positive and negative changes in the distribution of power between parties.

This refers back to my earlier point that notes the value in considering the *structure* rather than the existence of commercial sex (Fraser 1993). The empirically grounded work of Barbara Sullivan and Prabha Kotiswaran highlights the positive role that workplace struggles can have in terms of enlarging worker capacity and redistributing power between the different constituents. Both authors offer rich ethnographically informed analysis of the impact of law (in its widest sense)[19] on the organization of sex work in very different contexts, in states in Australia where: 'some sex work is legal' (Jeffrey and Sullivan 2009; Sullivan 2010) and in the diverse sex markets of two Indian cities.

Both studies recognise that 'consensual adult prostitution can be work and exploitation' (Sullivan 2004). As Kotiswaran notes, the heterogeneity of sex markets makes it impossible to have a uniform 'theory of exploitation' (Kotiswaran 2011) as sex workers are differently situated, and various laws will have different impacts upon them. By carefully drawing on empirical work they each examine how law matters as they consider the distributional effect of different policies on concrete and heterogeneous sex and markets.

Even in such different contexts, both conclude that criminalisation is rarely a good policy option. Kotiswaran argues that criminal models, by treating sex work as an exceptional economic activity, *always* place women in inferior bargaining positions to those who seek to exploit power differentials (and she includes property owners, the state and men in this category). Sullivan similarly notes, 'criminalization really "ramps up" the consequences for women engaged in sex work and this makes them more vulnerable to coercion by third parties' (Jeffrey and Sullivan 2009: 64). Additionally, Sullivan notes:

> [S]ex workers who operate in a legal environment – that is, who are not subject to arrest, imprisonment and deportation for working in prostitution

19 Realists describe law in the context of a plural rule network that provides background rules for the ordering of social life:

> We do not assume that the legal system as a whole deliberately decrees one thing or another . . . Rather, we conceptualize the network as providing background rules that constitute the actors, by granting them all kinds of powers under all kinds of limitations, and then regulating interaction between actors by banning and permitting, encouraging and discouraging particular tactics of particular actors in particular circumstances.
>
> (Kennedy 2002: 80)

Kotiswaran points to the importance of tenancy, property law and criminal law – all of which constitute a complex rule network pertinent to sex work. Using insights from legal pluralism, socio-legal studies and anthropology (Santos 2002), she shows formal law to be in a constant state of interaction with several other legal orders, social norms, custom, community-based dispute resolutions mechanisms, social practice and market structures. She shows that these background

> – are more able to resist power and practice their freedom. They are, for example, more able to call on the same official channels as other citizens if they are sick, robbed, assaulted or mistreated by employers. Sex workers whose employment is regulated by occupational health and safety codes and/or by employment agreements will also benefit from the construction of new rights as workers . . . which . . . specify the rights and duties of both employers and employees. These agreements indicate how much a worker will be paid, the extent of agency fees and, importantly, the right of workers to both refuse clients and pursue complaints against clients through the justice system.
>
> (Sullivan 2000: 7)[20]

Beyond this, both recognise that law and policies can have a significant, yet differing impact on the safety of sex workers, their working environments, their civil and labour rights and capacities (Sullivan 2010).

Sullivan's study considers the variations between the 'legal regimes' of Queensland and New South Wales (NSW) (Sullivan 2010), testing the distributive effects of what are, in fact, very different policy interventions.[21] Queensland introduced a licensing scheme for brothel owners and operators, overseen by an independent statutory authority (the Prostitution Licensing Authority (PLA)), with their location approved by local councils. As a result new possibilities for legal sex work have opened up for workers that have to some extent enlarged the safety, rights and capacities of some sex workers, who can receive some of the benefits of mainstream work environments and are more able to call on state bodies (such as police, anti-discrimination and employment rights authorities) to help them protect their rights.

Sullivan notes, however, that while these offer some legal recognition they give limited control. Recognising changing modes of governance, she shows that in this new bureaucratic system, significant power over workers has been handed over to third parties such as the PLA, brothel operators and local authorities (Jeffrey and Sullivan 2009: 65). Sex workers are not represented in licensing boards, meaning

rules both govern the conduct of parties during prostitution bargaining and structure possible alternatives (Kennedy 1993: 87) as she considers the likely impact of reform.

20 This criticism of the current operation of the criminal law does not necessary imply that the practice should be legalised or that its state recognition does not come with its own consequences; neither is it to displace the important role of the criminal law in dealing with the violence that is experienced by sex workers. It does involve recognising where criminalisation helps to structure patterns of violence against sex workers and acknowledging the contradictions and limitations of criminal law when it performs dual roles, for example, where it both designates certain groups as the instigators of offence, crime and nuisance, while also casting them as vulnerable. Moving beyond either/or may open up possibility of law being used for more progressive means, such as in recent challenges in the Canadian courts.

21 This is in contrast to reductive descriptions of legalization by authors such as Mary Sullivan (2005) who claims, with no solid evidence base, that legalisation per se has led to a rise in trafficking and worsening conditions (and see Sullivan and Jeffreys 2001, 2002).

that they have no direct voice in the regulatory regime and as a result there is no focus on establishing good working conditions and no complaints mechanism. Self-governance, which would redress this balance, is precluded by the high costs and onerous procedures involved in becoming a licensee.

Furthermore, those now working 'legally' in licensed brothels do not enjoy 'good' working conditions. Sexual Service Providers Advocacy Network (SSPAN) describes legal brothels as 'oppressive work environments' (SSPAN 2006: 2). Conditions are often poor and workers are subject to oppressive and discriminatory health screenings. Workers are paid as independent sub-contractors rather than as 'employees', which means that they are not entitled to normal employment rights such as sick leave, holiday pay, employer contributions, or pensions and they have to pay their own taxes. As SSPAN notes:

> Brothel work is simply not an attractive option for the silent majority of sex workers . . . Given the inordinate amount of control brothels have over workers and the lack of worker unionization, brothel workers are often referred to as 'employees without benefits'.
>
> (SSPAN 2006: 2)

Thus for those outwith licenced brothels, working privately (which is inherently more dangerous) remains the only other legal option under the new regime, as street sex work and escort agencies remain illegal.

In NSW, by contrast, a licence is not required to work legally in a brothel setting,[22] and more importantly, some street-based sex work has been decriminalised. This allows workers greater freedom to choose between different types of employment. As Sullivan notes, this moderates the power between workers and sex businesses and operators, reduces the need for third-party protection (see Harcourt et al. 2001: 18–19), improves safety and allows workers to organise in protection of their safety and rights (Jeffrey and Sullivan 2009: 64, citing evidence from Perkins 1991; PLA 2004). Thus the reforms in NSW, while not ideal,offer some real advantages to sex workers particularly in terms of their safety, rights and capacities.

By utilising a granular, empirical approach, Sullivan shows that it mattered, for example, whether brothels are licensed or not. It also mattered if street sex work is decriminalised. Representation of sex workers in regulatory regimes and the balance between the various sectors – all effect quite different results for sex

22 Although brothels in NSW are not subject to onerous licensing conditions, they do require local council planning consent. In administering planning consent councils have zoning powers to designate certain areas in which brothels are prohibited. Councils have differing attitudes to sex work businesses and use their zoning powers to varying degrees. For example, some local councils permit brothels only in industrial zones, 'which effectively outlaws home-based businesses (including private workers) and many existing small brothels' (Sullivan 2010: 97).

workers (see Sullivan 2010). She shows that these distributive effects are a matter of empirical testing rather than ideological faith.

Kotiswaran's study, although distinct, makes complementary points. Her work *Dangerous Sex, Invisible Labor* offers a rich ethnography of brothel work in Sonagachi (Calcutta), contrasting it with the more dispersed practices of prostitution in the temple city of Tirupati in Andhra Pradesh. She also undertakes a hypothetical exercise in which she assesses the likely distributional consequences of four reforms measures (partial decriminalisation, complete decriminalisation, two forms of legalisation) using Sonagachi as case study. While this perhaps stretches realist methodology, looking at the possible outcomes of laws on concrete and complex sex markets is probably the best we can do, and takes us beyond much of the rhetoric of law reform in this area.

Kotiswaran assesses various regulatory proposals, taking into account the interaction of different forms of laws (including criminal law, property law and customary law), the different modes in which sex work is organised (recognising that markets are complex and varied) and the different relationships that exist between different stakeholders. From this, she concludes that decriminalisation is likely to achieve the most beneficial effects for women, as it allows more space for them to self-organise and creates opportunities to restructure labour relations and tenancy agreements. In contrast, she notes that prohibitionist or abolitionist models operate to solidify existing power relations.

Both writers' work show that while there are many avenues to resist power and enhance the freedom of sex workers, the mode of regulation is an important factor in determining the safety, rights and capacities of workers in the sex industry, with some reforms delivering better outcomes than others. Decriminalisation would seem to offer sex workers and advocates some space in which to begin to articulate and assert rights. There is evidence from Australia that legal sex workers are more likely to take actions to protect their rights, to report assaults to the police (PLA 2004: 68–69), to challenge police discrimination, unfair arrests and failure to act and may be able to challenge other aspects of discriminatory treatment, for example, in advertising, banking and accommodation. There is also increased dialogue and cooperation regarding safe areas to work (Wotton 2005). In other words, sex workers increasingly consider themselves as being entitled to the same rights as other citizens and the space for political engagement increases rather than decreases.

A recent case from New Zealand supports this contention. New Zealand, as noted, has recently decriminalised sex work meaning that the labour rights of sex workers are to some extent recognised and workers are able to pursue complaints of abuse and exploitation. In an action before the New Zealand Human Rights Tribunal in March 2014, a sex worker won a compensation award of $25,000 after being sexually harassed by a brothel operator. The judgment underlined the importance of sex workers' human rights:

> Sex workers are as much entitled to protection from sexual harassment as those working in other occupations. The fact that a person is a sex worker is

> not a licence for sexual harassment, especially by the manager or employer at the brothel. Sex workers' have the same human rights as other workers.[23]

This moves us well beyond binaries of legal/illegal. Legal norms and workers' rights are used as tactics that can, in certain circumstances, help to establish conditions that can support and enable consensual capacity. Only by paying attention to what law achieves in practice can we make judgements about law's effects, recognising that law operates in complex regulatory networks and that influential contextual factors may result in different outcomes for different constituencies.

Constituting subjects: *Canada (Attorney General)* vs. *Bedford*

The potential of rights discourse can also be seen in a recent series of constitutional challenges taking place in the Canadian courts[24] – culminating in the recent Supreme Court decision of *Canada (Attorney General)* vs. *Bedford* 2013 SCC 72 in which sex workers have sought inclusion in the constitution protections of the Canadian Charter of Rights.

The background to the case involves a legislative context similar to that in the UK, and other analogous prohibitionist jurisdictions, in which the act of prostitution while legal, is rendered, *de facto* criminal by the operation of several laws that penalise central activities, such as keeping a 'bawdy house' (the equivalent of brothel keeping in the UK), living off the avails of prostitution and communicating in public places for the purposes of prostitution.[25]

This disconnect creates an ambiguous and dangerous legal space for those working in sex work and gave rise to a legal challenge by three Canadian current and former female sex workers, Terri-Jean Bedford, Valerie Scott and Amy Lebovitch. They argued that the laws materially contributed to a growing incidence

23 *DML* vs. *Montgomery and MT Enterprises Ltd* [2014] NZHRRT 6, see para. 146. http://www.nbr.co.nz/sites/default/files/images/2014-NZHRRT-6-DML-v-Montgomery-and-M-T%20Enterprises%20Ltd.pdf. These types of action are, of course, limited in scope. Julia O'Connell Davidson (2014) notes that sex discrimination actions are unlikely to be taken given that that the industry plays on these and other power dynamics (race, age etc.). Yet, even if small in number, actions recognising the personhood and legal subjectivity of sex workers are important in challenging some of the myths that persist with regards femininity and powerlessness and in challenging the heterogeneity of the industry.

24 *Bedford* was the most prominent case in the context of increased legal activism by sex workers and organisations in Canada. Others include *Canada (Attorney General)* vs. *Downtown Eastside Sex Workers United Against Violence Society* [2012] 2 SCR 524 (and see Van der Meulen et al. 2013).

25 The Canadian Criminal Code criminalises the 'keeping or occupying a bawdy house' (*Criminal Code*, RSC 1985, c C-46, s 210), 'living on the avails of prostitution of another person' (*Criminal Code*, RSC 1985, c C-46, s. 212(1)(*j*)) and 'communicating in a public place for the purposes of engaging in prostitution' (*Criminal Code*, RSC 1985, c C-46, s. 213(1)(*c*)).

of physical and psychological violence against this group as they prevented sex workers from protecting themselves by hiring security, working indoors or in groups or screening their clients through initial questioning for fear of arrest. As such the laws infringed sections 2 and 7 of the Charter of Rights and Freedoms, which protected freedom of expression and the right not to be deprived of life, liberty or security of the person.

In response, the government of Ontario argued that the criminal law had a legitimate role to play in preventing sex work from becoming normalised, which should outweigh minimal human rights violations. They also claimed that bawdy houses and other prostitution-related activities commodified women and so violated sex workers' dignity and equality. Further arguments were presented to the court by interveners in the case, REAL Women Canada, the Christian Legal Fellowship and the Catholic Civil Rights League, who argued that sex work was not a 'Canadian value', that it was an act that offends the conscience of ordinary Canadian citizens, was harmful to the women involved and that the state was permitted to protect against its 'moral corruption' through its criminal laws (see paras 23 and 24 Himel J).

After a series of appeals, the case was heard in the Supreme Court of Canada on 28 September 2010. In *Bedford* vs. *Canada*, the court found that while the Criminal Code provisions had a legitimate role in protecting state interests around nuisance, the operation of the laws increased the risk of violence experienced by sex workers and therefore violated the right to free expression and personal security of those involved in street sex work. As a result, the bench of nine justices unanimously declared all three provisions as unconstitutional – effectively striking down Canada's prostitution laws.

Analysis: not binary but multivocality

Inevitably, this landmark case has been discussed in polarised terms, as a battle between sex workers rights' and victimhood perspectives. Much was made of this in media, where the clash was even played out at the level of celebrity biography[26]

26 *Souled Out* by Tania Fiolleau, is a first-hand victim narrative that aims to expose the horrors facing women caught up in the sex trade. The sex industry is described as 'a sick world, full of broken dreams and empty promises, battered, shattered, sexually abused women, men and children', (22 December 2010 (LifeSiteNews.com)). The author, who previously worked in prostitution, has now dedicated her life to fighting the sex trade, launching a website called SavetheWomen.ca, aimed at raising awareness and helping women exit the industry. She has been a prominent voice in the media debates on Canada's prostitution laws.

Terri-Jean Bedford's *Dominatrix on Trial: Bedford vs. Canada* is the memoir of Canada's most famous dominatrix. In the book, she describes her journey from abject poverty and abuse into the elite world of the professional dominatrix and her experience as a plaintiff in a major constitutional challenge that resulted in Canada's prostitution laws being struck down in 2010.

Of course, neither experience has to override the other but this is just the sort of binary drama that the media and public adore. In a late modern culture obsessed with celebrity personal narrative, these biographies may be as powerful as legal discourse in the public imagination.

(*Souled Out* and *Dominatrix on Trial* were biographies that appeared at the same time as the legal proceedings).

Yet these efforts to force back binaries and the government's subsequent effort to restrict the impact of the decision[27] (via the Protection of Communities and Exploited Persons Act 2014) detracts from what is a much more nuanced legal judgment. The case is not about a constitutional right to prostitution but rather about a group, previously denied access to the public discourse of law, being able to claim rights as citizens – 'the right to have rights', discussed previously. The court does not make an authoritative pronouncement on prostitution as being good or bad, but recognises that this is 'a complex and delicate matter'. In contrast to the previous legal position, which cast much of the activity on a binary of legal/illegal and excluded many different voices, by viewing the activity through the lens of constitutional rights, the court allows varied claims for justice to thrive. The case, and the judge at first instance Justice Susan Himel's reasoning (in the Ontario Superior Court (*Bedford* vs. *Canada* (2010) ONSC 4264) in particular, demonstrates the utility of rights discourse and the benefits of engaging politically with norms in legal forums. She interprets law in context, treating the rights of freedom of expression and security of person not as static norms but as cultural artefacts that are open to reinterpretation and political contestation.

Freedom of expression

In determining whether the communicating offence infringed on freedom of expression, the Court of First Instance had to contend with established precedent of the highest order. In the *Prostitution Reference* case,[28] the Supreme Court had previously held the 'communicating' offence to be a reasonable limit on freedom of expression, with CJ Dickson stating: '[I]t can hardly be said that communications regarding an economic transaction of sex for money lie at, or even near, the core of the guarantee of freedom of expression.'[29]

In her judgment, Justice Himel acknowledged the role of precedent in ensuring consistency, certainty and predictability but she also noted its hegemonic potential;

27 The Protection of Communities and Exploited Persons Act 2014 amended the Canadian prostitution law as narrowly as possible to comply with the decision in *Bedford*. However, rather than repealing the laws that were considered to be harmful by the Court in *Bedford*, the government amended the provisions only marginally. For example, rather than repealing the communicating in public for the purposes of prostitution provisions they were amended to make it a criminal offence to communicate 'in a public place, or in any place open to public view, that is or is next to a school ground, playground or daycare centre' (s. 15 2014 Act). The Act also introduced a raft of new prostitution-related offences including criminalising the purchase of sex and other offences that can be used against sex workers such as a prohibition on advertising for the purpose of offering sexual services. The Act frames prostitution exclusively as a violent, exploitative practice and source of social harm.

28 [1990] 1 SCR 1123.

29 Page 1136 of Prostitution Reference [1990] 1 SCR 1123 per Chief Justice Dickson.

that strict adherence to previous decisions can lead to 'injustices in individual cases [via the] continued application of legal principles long since outdated as society has changed'.[30] Given the changes in the social and political environment that have occurred over the 20 years since the *Prostitution Reference* has been decided and the amount of research that had been produced on the subject in the intervening period (especially around the issues of criminalisation and violence – in fact, 88 volumes of evidence were provided to the court),[31] she considered that she was within her authority to reconsider whether the communicating offence minimally impaired freedom of expression. In her view, the negative effects of the provision were not outweighed by its positive effects.

Central to her assessment was the previous ruling's interpretation of communicating for prostitution as a trivial act which did not 'lie at, or even near, the core of the guarantee of freedom of expression', Justice Himel was able to offer a different interpretation by distinguishing the case before her as one in which, she noted, communication was 'ultimately directed at *safely* exchanging sexual services for payment',[32] which was she concluded *was* 'near the core of expression'[33] that the Charter seeks to protect. The Supreme Court agreed with this assessment, CJ McLachlin finding that face-to-face communication was an 'essential tool' in enhancing street prostitutes' safety.[34]

This is a good example of a judge creatively engaging with norms. Free speech (which in many analyses has been said to preserve 'masculine' values (MacKinnon 1993b)) becomes amenable to gender considerations and has to accommodate safety – a value inserted by Himel – by listening to the experiences and rights claims of in situ sex workers.

The case shows the importance of contextual and ethical decision making that considers embodied interests rather than relying on abstract individualism. It is also an example of the transformative possibilities when those excluded from public discourse speak. Sex worker narratives presented to the court talk not in terms of binaries, or of simple 'economic transactions' but of a particular form of embodied labour, a bifurcation between work and affect, where safety is central to sexual and bodily autonomy. A recognition of this perspective makes for a contextual ethics, in which the judge decides that the increased danger for prostitutes due to the restrictions on communicating was 'simply too high a price to pay for the alleviation

30 Para. 121 of *David Polowin Real Estate Ltd.* vs. *Dominion of Canada General Insurance Co.* (2006), 76 OR (3d) 161, [2005] OJ No. 2436 (C.A.) per Justice Larkin cited by Justice Himel at para. 68 of *Bedford* vs. *Canada* (2010) ONSC 4264.

31 Eighty-eight volumes of contradictory expert evidence, and examples from international jurisdictions were presented to the court. Prostitution is being reconstituted legally by the judgment of the court but this reconstitution has been generated by the work of many other agencies and individuals including, researchers, sex workers and activists. So, while the legal decision is vitally important, it is only one piece of a much larger jigsaw of constitutive material.

32 Para. 461 *Bedford* vs. *Canada* (2010) ONSC 4264.

33 Para. 462 *Bedford* vs. *Canada* (2010) ONSC 4264.

34 Para. 69 *Canada* vs. *Bedford* (2013) SCC 72.

of social nuisance', especially as *safely* exchange became a value to protect, to temper the market and move beyond liberalism's bare protections.

Security of person

A second normative issue that the court had to consider was the claim made by sex workers that the Criminal Code provisions infringed their Article 7 rights which protects their 'security of person'. The applicants, while acknowledging that the direct cause of violence against prostitutes was usually their clients, argued that the law also 'materially contributed' to the harms faced by prostitutes and that this was sufficient to engage the 'security of the person' protections. The government's response was to claim that there was *no* causal connection between the provisions and the harm, that prostitution was inherently dangerous, regardless of the way in which it is practised and as such any deprivation in security cannot be attributed to the laws in question.

Justice Himel's reasoning did not rest on a liberal assessment that sex work was either inherently dangerous or work like any other, but was much more nuanced. She focused on whether the provisions 'sufficiently contributed' (Himel J para. 362) to the violence experienced by sex workers, thus giving space to recognise the role of men, commercial sex, misogyny and wider sexual inequality, alongside the law in fostering their precarious position.[35]

Himel's reasoning is an excellent example of the virtues of interpreting law in context. She noted that while each of the laws pursued a legitimate state purpose, the way in which they were *experienced cumulatively by sex workers*,[36] as concrete subjects, was arbitrary in that they 'materially contributed' to the

35 The Attorney General argued that the causal connection between the provisions and the infringement of the right was broken by (a) the actions of third-party johns and pimps, *or* by (b) prostitutes' 'choice' to engage in prostitution. The court rejected these arguments noting that:

> [I]t makes no difference source of the harms suffered by prostitutes. The impugned laws deprive people engaging in a risky, but legal activity of the means to protect themselves against those risks. The violence of a john does not diminish the role of the state in making a prostitute more vulnerable to that violence.
>
> [Para 89]

36 Rather than a universal generalised self, the judgment recognises sex workers' perspectives as 'the concrete "other"'. This refers to an ethical approach where we see the other person as an individual with a 'concrete history identity, and affective-emotional constitution' (Benhabib 1985). This can be seen in the way that the judge recognises the reduced choices available to sex workers operating in an environment, where prostitution is legal but its practice heavily circumscribed. 'In-call' work – where the clients come to an established place of business – was prevented by the provisions on bawdy houses. While prostitutes can legally work 'out-call', where they go to a hotel or other location that varies from client to client, this type of work is more dangerous. Moreover, Justice Himel considered these risks are increased because the 'living on the avails' offence prevents prostitutes from entering into business relationships that could enhance their safety. The final

harms of prostitution and thus deprived prostitutes of their right to security of the person.

This was not a state centric view but based on the perspectives of those involved actors who experienced violence and fear for their personal security. The prohibitions were found to heighten the risks the applicants face in the legal activity of prostitution. The judge noted that prostitutes, especially those working on the street, are at high risk of physical violence, yet the three offences made it illegal for sex workers to engage key methods of harm reduction in order to reduce those risks. Preventative measures, such as working indoors and in close proximity to others, using drivers or bodyguards or having a regular clientele were prevented by the laws.

The court found that the laws did not merely impose conditions on how prostitutes operate, but went a critical step further by 'imposing *dangerous* conditions on prostitution; they prevent[ed] people engaged in a risky – but legal – activity from taking steps to protect themselves from the risks'.[37] An analogy was made to the case of *Canada (Attorney General)* vs. *PHS Community Services Society*, 2011 SCC 44, [2011] 3 SCR 134 where the Supreme Court held that drug possession laws could not be applied in order to prevent a safe injection site operating, as this had the effect of denying health services to this group and the risk of death was grossly disproportionate to the objectives of public health and safety.[38]

The Court of First Instance rejected the claim that prostitution was inherently dangerous and that there was nothing the law could do to alleviate these risks or protect women in situ. This was echoed by the Supreme Court which stated that 'the violence of a john does not diminish the role of the state in making a prostitute more vulnerable to that violence'.[39] They also rejected the claim that women's safety in sex work should be compromised, for the greater good of a generic women's safety (similar arguments are, of course, made in abolitionist systems such as Sweden). The court noted:

> The analysis is qualitative, not quantitative. The question under s. 7 is whether *anyone's* life, liberty or security of the person has been denied by a law that is inherently bad; a grossly disproportionate, overbroad, or arbitrary effect on one person is sufficient to establish a breach of s. 7.[40]

This is vitally important. The Supreme Court recognises that the law cannot sacrifice the rights of some (in situ workers) for the comfort of the majority.

option available to prostitutes is working on the street. This, however, as Justice Himel noted, puts them at risk of violating the 'communicating' offence and is the most dangerous way to engage in prostitution. (See para. 361 *Bedford* vs *Canada* (2010) ONSC 4264 as per Justice Himel.)

37 Para. 60 *Canada* vs. *Bedford* (2013) SCC 72 per Chief Justice McLachlin.

38 Para. 104 *Canada* vs. *Bedford* (2013) SCC 72 per Chief Justice McLachlin.

39 Para. 89 *Canada* vs. *Bedford* (2013) SCC 72 per Chief Justice McLachlin.

40 Para. 123 *Canada* vs. *Bedford* (2013) SCC 72 per Chief Justice McLachlin.

Moreover, the court noted that these restrictions (on working together, communicating in a public place, and on bawdy houses) operated in the context of high levels of violence including the specific threat, posed by the serial killer, Robert Pickton, who preyed on vulnerable women, including sex trade workers from Vancouver's poor Downtown Eastside.[41] The court made specific mention of this: 'If screening could have prevented one woman from jumping into Robert Pickton's car, the severity of the harmful effects is established.'[42]

The court also condemned the closing of local safe houses, such as Grandma's House, established in Vancouver to support street sex workers in Downtown Eastside.[43] Recognising the vital function they perform as places of safety for those with nowhere else to go, the court noted: 'For these people, the ability to work in brothels or hire security, even if these activities were lawful (which at time they were not) may be illusory.'[44] That such safe havens were rendered illegal (under s. 210: keeping bawdy house provision), at same time as a large number of women were disappearing, presumed murdered, the court had sanguine sobering thoughts:

> Parliament has the power to regulate against nuisances, but not at the cost of the health, safety and lives of prostitutes. A law that prevents street prostitutes from resorting to a safe haven such as Grandma's House, while a suspected serial killer prowls the streets, is a law that has lost sight of its purpose.
>
> (CJ Lachlin [para. 136])[45]

41 In the years leading up to the constitutional challenge, more than 60 women – mostly sex trade workers from Vancouver's troubled Downtown Eastside – had disappeared. Investigations culminated in the arrest of pig farmer, Robert Pickton, who was charged with 26 counts of first-degree murder and was convicted, in 2007, of six of those counts – making him the most prolific serial killer in Canadian history. A 2006 Statistics Canada report found that 171 female prostitutes were murdered between 1991 and 2004, and that 45 per cent of those cases went unsolved.

42 Para. 158 *Canada* vs. *Bedford* (2013) SCC 72 per Chief Justice McLachlin.

43 'For some prostitutes, particularly those who are destitute, safe houses such as Grandma's House may be critical. For these people, the ability to work in brothels or hire security, even if these activities were lawful (which, at the time, they weren't) may be illusory [CJ Lachlin, para. 64].

44 Para 64. *Canada* vs. *Bedford* (2013) SCC 72 per Chief Justice McLachlin.

45 Para. 136 *Canada* vs. *Bedford* (2013) SCC 72 per Chief Justice McLachlin. The court has to balance state interests against those of sex workers – in doing so, attention was paid to context and balance power. The Court, for example, notes that while bawdy house provisions may legitimately protect against nuisance, that such complaints are rare and the harmful effects of the bawdy house provision prevented women working in proximity to others, in familiar surroundings, with security and CCTV and were thus disproportionate. The Court of Appeal noted that moving indoors was a 'basic safety precaution for prostitutes', which the bawdy house provision made illegal and the Supreme Court agreed.

One commentator (Abdul 2010) has suggested that, although the reasoning is grounded in 'multiple Supreme Court cases, this standard was set in cases that involved alleged terrorism and repatriation from a foreign military prison. He argued that 'security of persons' was inappropriate in a prostitution case, as it would set the bar too low for the security interest to be engaged'. Given the background to this action, the very high levels of violence directed towards a group of persons, and the disappearance and homicide of sex workers, this point is worthy of debate.

Rights and multivocality

This case is illustrative of the interpretive possibilities of rights and law's potential as a site for agonism. The Canadian constitution, in this instance, shows potential to accommodate a 'multivocality of views' as the meaning of legal norms are openly contested (Valverde 1999a).[46] The right to freedom of expression and to personal security, and indeed other open-textured norms, can be viewed not as a site of epistemic closure as many formalists would claim, but rather as 'a site upon which to reflect on the ways in which courts continuously open up new avenues for political challenges even as they attempt to reinstitute sovereignty and limit epistemological "pluralism"' (Valverde 1999a: 181). Seeing norms as open textured, as cultural artefacts that can be contested and can change over time, allows the 'Canadian Charter' to do the work it should – to operate as an open and evolving, living instrument of the community – not simply protect an already formed political community, created in exclusion.[47] Rights function, not as a bright line that determines the content of law or the boundaries of criminal law, despite attempts at various points in the case to restrict meaning in such a way, but they instead emerge as a vehicle through which multiple, at times agonistic voices can demand inclusion within a more pluralistic community and, through doing so, can secure a platform from which to contest and ultimately reconfigure the boundaries of that community. The case demonstrates that rights may prove fecund for justice in this area, creating a space for agonism and for an enlivened engagement between protagonists.[48]

The theme of being 'remade' in law is again pertinent here as the decision increases sex worker legal subjectivity which has a positive impact on sex workers' perceptions – their legal consciousness, a point that has not gone unnoticed in the sex work community. Indeed, one of the applicants in the *Bedford* case, Valerie Scott, thanked the justices in the earlier Appeal Court decision for: '[P]retty much declaring sex workers persons today. I didn't think I would see it in my lifetime, but here we are' (Humphreys 2012).

46 Valverde uses this phrase in the context of 'the risk of harm test', which has become the legal test in Canadian courts with regards the regulation of pornography. Valverde recognises that the reliance on the language of risk evokes neoliberal connotations and could, and indeed has, perpetuated existing forms of 'patriarchal and heterosexist moral regulation', citing a number of cases where its use supports a conservative reading of the test, e.g. restricting breasts on display or lesbian porn. Nevertheless, it also has, she argues, the innate potential to facilitate more progressive outcomes, since it 'allows a multivocality of views' from different communities, as they speak to law about their divergent perceptions of harm (Valverde 1999a: 181).

47 The foundation of many liberal democracies rests on a number of exclusions: of women, non-whites, property owners and non-nationals.

48 Commenting on the reforms, Nikki Thomas, executive director of Sex Professionals of Canada, said all levels of government now needed to discuss with sex workers the regulatory framework for opening and running brothels and other aspects of the sex trade. And, she said, the sex industry needs to convince the public there is no need for them to fear the new regime (Humphreys 2012). I like this idea of mutual responsibility and dialogue, although, sadly, the new legislation in Canada closes this down.

Rights, redistribution and recognition: DMSC and precarious workers' rights

A final point I wish to make is while there may be an important strategic role in seeking rights for those excluded from the polity (which as ever, must be empirically tested), rather than simply proliferating rights, there is also a need to explore what Brown calls 'the historically and culturally specific ground for their demand' (Brown 1995: 12). This requires that we take 'proper notice of the material, disciplinary conditions of rights regimes – conditions which structure rights claims in advance' (Golder 2011: 291).

Yet this wider materialist account should not necessarily preclude rights – provided they are viewed in context and considered critically. In earlier work with Maggie O'Neill, inspired by Laclau and Mouffe (1985; see also Smith 1998) and Nancy Fraser's work (1997, 2000), we advanced a politics of 'rights, recognition and redistribution', as a means to develop a radical democratic politics that resists rather than supports modes of governance that have such poor outcomes for so many, especially the most vulnerable female sex workers. Politics, including rights claiming, we argued, needed to move away from regulatory categories of identity. However, there remains a role for the strategic deployment of rights in the context of a more radical form of politics that is disruptive of binaries and instead facilitates forms of solidarity, however temporary, in order to challenge the injustices that accompany global capitalism and its stark material inequalities.

A good example of such radical rights claiming, which can complement a materialist approach, comes from the campaigning activities of the Durbar Mahila Samanwaya Committee (DMSC) of Kolkata, West Bengal, in India. This group of 65,000 organized sex workers campaign against what they see as the oppressive features of work in the twenty-first century, poor labour conditions and long hours, which lead to exploitation and little time for leisure and entertainment. To counter this widespread alienation the group demand 'the Right to Leisure/Pleasure/Play/Entertainment [. . .] to safeguard and enhance the social, legal, labour and human rights of all the entertainment workers across the world' (Durbar Mahila Samanwaya Committee 2007: 19, from Agustín 2008).

While, on the one hand, these claims seem fairly utopian,[49] they have, on the other, the potential to be transformative as they are not based on narrow identity rights, nor do they envisage being mainstreamed in the existing economy, which, as discussed earlier, may simply serve to reinforce capitalism. Rather, these rights claims are non-foundational – they do not form around a single closed identity, neither do they isolate identity from wider structural inequalities as they seek wider forms of redistribution. Instead, sex workers are seeking to ally themselves with

49 It could be said that such rights cannot be actualised without attending to a host of interlocking social and economic arrangements. Yet this does not mean rights without specific realisable obligations are merely aspirational, as the value of human rights does not depend strictly on whether they are immediately justiciable – they have important constitutive functions – helping in the development of legal consciousness – the effects of which we cannot know immediately.

other low paid and under-regulated workers (such domestic, reproductive and agricultural labourers), forming alliances and broader strategic coalitions with those marginalised in late capitalist/global economies to form a wider movement against precarious work.

This suggests a different kind of human rights, which move away from the enshrined statism and possessive individualism of liberalism, towards a radically different ontology, what Foucault called 'mutual solidarity based on the "shared difficulties" of international citizens', a 'community of the governed' (Foucault 2000b: 474)[50] or what Illan Wall more recently terms 'being-together' (Butler 2004b; Pratt 2005) in constituent struggle (Wall 2011).[51]

A more radical politics is envisaged in this rights claiming. Rights can be seen as displaying an 'open' constituent power within which campaigners reimagine ideas of community. The political tactical deployment of rights operates as a ruptural force – rather than as a site of closure of a constituted order (Wall 2011). The issue is not inclusion for an upper elite or accommodation in a neoliberal market as is, but wider forms of redistribution, recognition and restructuring.

In looking beyond mere identity politics, DMSC's wider claims resist attempts to fit women's diverse experience into a binary rights claims – as workers or as sexual subjects – both of which obscure the context in which sexuality or work is performed. This goes well beyond a discussion of the legal system's treatment of sex work but connects to other forms of entertainment and precarious work and attempts to address the contemporary alienating situation in late capitalism for a wide range of workers. It addresses Valverde's call to feminism more generally to reconceptualise the terms of the debate, to turn away from narrow, essentialist definitions of women's bodies and instead to *contextualise* sexual behaviour in order to bring about the conditions for a non-alienated sexuality:

> The task before us is perhaps best envisaged as the effort to discern and bring about the conditions for a non-alienated sexuality, rather than as an attempt to maximize the sexual rights of individuals or groups.
>
> (Valverde 1989a: 254)

Conclusion

In arguing for the continued relevance of law, I do not intend to reinstate an imperialist, uncritical positivist position. I recognise the need to decentre law as a

50 Foucault used the term 'community of the governed' in 1984 in the context of stranded stateless migrants (a topical issue) to describe the basis of 'responsibility' for their rescue. In doing so, he questions the exclusive nature of safe citizenship when he asks 'Who appointed us, then? No-one. And that is precisely what constitutes our right' (Foucault 2000b: 474).

51 He talks of a more radical form of human rights that is more than 'just a moralistic cover for biopolitical subordination, but as a constituent potential; the coming to presence of a radical sense of being-with, and a very different human right-ing' (Wall 2011).

singular signifier and recognise that it may be marginal in some, although not all political struggles.

Its constitutive role, however, means that it cannot be ignored and therefore I propose that we engage with law strategically, in order to 'pursue a deconstructivist agenda *within* legal arenas and discourses' (Sandland 1995: 14). This is different from embarking on an institutional project (as suggested by projects that seek to establish '*a* feminist theory of the state' (MacKinnon 1989) or provide *a* blueprint for prostitution reform. Rather than create a new orthodoxy or take a position in an already fixed political system, I critically engage with law to 'generate new schemas of politicisation' (Lemke 2003: 175).

In each of these examples, of consent, and in cases of constitutional and workplace rights, I highlight the possibilities of a critical engagement with law, showing what reconstituting legal norms and the subject of prostitution can offer.

I consider the struggles that have taken place to enlarge sex workers' consensual capacity in the context of rape, efforts that have effectively remade sex workers as subjects in law, as subjects capable of exercising non-consent. I suggest a less normative approach to prostitutes' rights, not as 'another configuration of sexual desire and pleasure' but as a strategic intervention that inhabits and disrupts present political idioms. The case of *Bedford* is a prime example of the value in those previously excluded from the polity, accessing the public discourse of law and seeking inclusion into its constitutional protections. By asking for *their* experience of safety to be recognised, sex workers reconstruct norms in ways that allow the constitution and its courts to do the work it should – to operate as an open and evolving instrument of the community. *Bedford* offers an opportunity to critically reflect on the role of criminal law as a creator of exclusions, risks, and precariousness, as well as a source of protection and redress. It breathes life into the law by envisaging a more positive role for it in ensuring that constitutional protections and norms operate to protect all of the community. Finally, the campaigning activities of the DMSC and its use of novel rights claims provides an institutional space to connect up to wider political and material struggles.

A final point on empiricism

> Struggle is indeed everything, but there is no privileged position from which to say that one struggle is always more significant than others or that one kind of power is always the most important one.
>
> (O'Malley and Valverde 2014: 333)

A final point to make by way of clarification is that these examples do not constitute a programme for law reform. They are simply examples of ways in which law has been utilised constructively to advance the interests of sex workers and to reconfigure the subject of prostitution. They demonstrate that law can be utilised in ways that create some space for struggle and may produce better outcomes for some.

While it is impossible to accurately predict the outcome of political engagement, those involved have a responsibility to try to weigh up the likely consequences before deciding on a particular strategy. The task of an academic observer, *post facto*, is to trace the processes of political reform, mapping the consequences, intended and unintended. These examples highlight the value of engaging empirically with law in context rather than at a purely abstract level, and of looking critically at what law does rather than what it says.

Indeed, the main lesson of a post-structural perspective is that one cannot determine the outcome of any particular approach. We cannot anticipate the effect of such engagements. There are always intended and unintended consequences as governmental projects are implemented and indeed produced in varying social contexts and through social interactions between actors and spaces, which are always ad hoc and complex. Thus an eye must always be kept on the empirical effects of any interventions. We cannot assume these attempts to refashion norms will be more inclusive or that they will serve all equally – their effects will inevitably be varied for different constituencies.

This not does not mean that engaging with legal rights is redundant – it simply means that they are political and have to be examined as such, with careful attention paid to their varied and complex empirical effects. Rights have the *potential* to be transformative – but this cannot be guaranteed by mere invocation as effects will always be varied. This task – of how law matters in concrete situations – is the one that I would strongly urge socio-legal and feminist scholars to focus on, rather than the endless normative question or 'Hamlet question' (Williams and Zelizer 2005) whether to legalise or criminalise selling sex, that ends up in circular arguments and overbroad rhetorical legal reforms that are far removed from the constituencies they are supposed to, or at least should be, serving.

Chapter 6

Conclusion: moving beyond the subject of prostitution

> Without absolutes, anything is possible, but everything remains difficult.
>
> (Williams 1991: 154)

> Definitions belonged to the definers – not the defined.
>
> (Morrison 1987: 190)

A principal aim of this work has been to advance an understanding of the subject of prostitution, not according to a set ideology; as a vector of disease, as the embodiment of patriarchal power, as the expression of an innate yet repressed sexuality or even as an unrecognised form of work, but rather by developing a more expansive framework and critical understanding of the many discourses and practices that constitute the subject in different ways at different times.

I begin from the premise that the 'prostitute' subject, a body exchanging sexual services in return for payment, has no inherent, fixed meaning but rather is, 'signified differently in different discourses' (Bell 1994: 1). I offer a selective genealogy that uncovers the discursive processes and regulatory practices that construct the problem of prostitution in different ways. Paying particular attention to the role of law in these complex processes of signification, my purpose has also been to provide a fuller and more critical account of modern legal power in the context of prostitution regulation.

This is not to suggest some dark, ideological ulterior motive at play but rather to stress that 'law' (legal processes, norms and actors) is itself not beyond power and to highlight its constitutive role. The fact that the law is already playing a part in constructing social spaces and norms of contemporary sex work makes appeals to it as a neutral arbiter all the more problematic. It changes the questions we ask of law, moving away from formalist accounts of what law says to consider what law does, as it acts, alongside other discourses and practices, to constitute, regulate and authorise the spaces, norms and subjects of sex work.

Moving beyond the modern subject of prostitution

In Chapter 2, I trace the origins of the 'modern prostitute' subject – describing its formation in the late Victorian era as resulting from the interaction of 'new' forms of knowledge – social science, public health and legal discourses and the operation of their associated regulatory techniques (e.g., lock hospitals, statistics, policing). Described as a 'metaphor of modernity' (Gilfoyle 1999), the 'prostitute subject' is closely associated with the ascendance of modern epistemes, the formation of the modern state and with changing forms of social organisation, which also instantiate distinctive normative standards. This includes legal power which, following changing in governmental style, moves from repressive forms of control to assuming an increasingly facilitative and normative role in society. This has far-reaching implications for feminist reform efforts as this and later chapters consider.

In Chapter 3, I offer a critical account of the prostitute subject as a 'victimised subject', an image that is gaining increased salience due to the influence of radical feminist and abolitionist approaches that seek to outlaw commercial sex and stymie demand. In Chapter 4, I consider the prostitute subject as a 'rights-bearing subject', a characterisation commonly utilised in sex worker social movements and in policies that seek to 'positively' regulate the activity.

Much of the book then focuses on the regulatory dimension of victim-centric interventions and on campaigns and legal initiatives that centre on sex workers' rights. Guided by Foucault's wonderful insight that '[p]eople know what they do; frequently they know why they do what they do; but what they don't know is what what they do does' (Foucault 1982b), I offer a critique of the regulatory dimension of identity politics that has so ensnared the politics of prostitution and feminism (and emancipatory politics more generally) in the last century.

I examine recent reforms in Sweden, New Zealand, Australia and the Netherlands, which in different ways sought to develop a more 'modern' and 'enlightened' model based on gender equality, democracy and human rights. Each arrived at distinctive definition of the issue: prostitution was constituted as a problem of pathology and inequality or a problem of recognition of workers and human rights. However, when viewed through a governmental lens, these processes, despite their different problematisations, also share much in common.

In both regulationist and abolitionist systems, campaigners and legislators looked to social science 'to transform knowledge about prostitution and to develop more critical methodologies, beyond the sexual double standard of past prostitution policy, where intervention and knowledge focussed on women as objects' (Harrington 2012: 347). Yet the forms of knowledge produced, whether they claimed to give a 'voice to the marginalized' or sought to turn the spotlight 'upon the powerful' (Harrington 2012: 347; see Axel Månsson's work discussed in Chapter 3), display *some* of the same dynamics and patterns, despite being cast as polar opposites.

Rather ironically, the patterns of governance facilitated by either advanced liberal technologies of agency (which utilise regimes of licencing and rights) or advanced liberal authoritarian techniques (which combines criminal sanction and welfare-inspired exit models) (see Bernstein 1999; Hubbard et al. 2007; Harrington 2012; Scoular 2010), are not as distinctive as they appear. Both can be seen to operate in the interests of profitable sex businesses, by consolidating a privatised, non-collective responsibilised prostitution population, while leaving those who cannot join this group further marginalised.

Thus I argue, as well meaning as reformers and campaigners on both sides may be, by defining the apparent 'problem' of prostitution in particular ways and aligning these within various sites of government that are pressured to respond, the complex justice issues that mark sex work are absorbed into the institutional procedures of the state in ways that support rather than challenge power. What is more, feminist concerns, whether based on a recognition of sex workers' inherent agency or victimhood, have been translated into techniques of governance, as social exclusion is being used as leverage for increased control rather than for increased social justice.

Beyond binaries – reviving the feminist subject

There is a pressing need to break out of the current aporia that stifles prostitution politics. Viewing accounts of sex workers' rights and exploitation as antithetical, I argue, not only serves to paralyse feminism, but also denies the lived reality of those involved in sex work who, in their everyday lives, have to integrate both perspectives. As I have previously argued with O'Neill:

> [F]eminism risks losing much of its transformative power when reduced to the binaries of identity politics. Both subject positions and politics are considered or forced as 'settled' and do not include the realities of contradiction and struggle in the lives of those involved in selling and buying sex or the ambiguities of activity which both challenges and reinforces many of the norms of heterosexuality and femininity and thus requires a more nuanced approach.
>
> (Scoular and O'Neill 2008: 27)

There is a need to reframe feminism in a way that recognises the governmentalisation of feminist critique, and tries to mitigate the co-opting and slowing of political resistance.[1] Feminism needs to accept that it is part of the governmentalisation process and to try to steer this in a direction that feminists consider to be progressive.

1 As Cornell notes:

> Feminism must not focus *solely* on what men have done to women. [It] must continuously seek ways in which women can unleash their own imaginary from the constraints that have been imposed upon them through rigid definitions of femininity.
>
> (Cornell 1995: 104)

As Segal notes:

> [The challenge for feminism is] to find a way to deliver both sexual freedom and freedom from sexism, both entitlement to pleasure and resistance to exploitation, abuse and market commodification of women's (and nowadays men's) sexual passions.
>
> (Segal 2006)

In order to creatively deploy and extend feminism, we need to see these positions as not necessarily mutually exclusive. Feminists needs to embrace this ambivalence and agonism rather than insisting on silencing one or other side of the dualism.

Post-structural feminist scholarship seeks to overcome this impasse, where it seems the only answer is to 'take sides'. It recognises that prostitution can be both a form of work and also a form of exploitation. Both approaches, if stripped of their essentialist underpinnings have the potential to inform a more inclusive and dynamic politics of prostitution, one that can combine sex workers' rights with challenges to male violence and power. This means that feminism must move beyond the binaries of identity politics and be guided instead by concrete, in situ claims, taking a pragmatic approach to both political and legal engagements.

My contribution to this debate is to show that that this approach can be extended to law, which can also benefit from post-structural insights. As noted, legal analysis has been stymied by a formalist analytical framework which revolves around legal/illegal binaries. A more nuanced approach emerges if we think of the subject as a political effect and engage critically with law, taking a pragmatic approach to its terms. Feminist politics also needs to understand how law can be used creatively, alongside other tactics, in ways that serve feminist agendas. As Brake explains:

> No one approach to legal theory can solve the thorny problems of gender oppression . . . pragmatism is a promising approach for feminist scholars, with its reminder to be vigilant in tailoring strategies to the full context of oppression and to treat legal theory as a work in progress, while relentlessly attending to changes in the social context. Rather than picking a theoretical approach for its consistency and abstract purity, feminist scholars should treat legal theory as contingent and context-specific, while continually evaluating it for how it serves our feminist agendas.
>
> (Brake 2007: 545–546)

We need to use law, legal norms, mechanisms and categories, not simply to confirm pre-established identities but to open up space for ambivalence and politics, for recognition *and* redistribution, if we are to imagine a more inclusive and potentially transformative politics of prostitution reform.

Moving beyond the subject

To facilitate such a politics, in Chapter 5, I suggest a way to pragmatically engage with legal norms as a means of pursuing a deconstructive agenda in legal arenas. By critically engaging and expanding the parameters of sexual consent, work place and human rights, I show the possibilities for increased justice that moves beyond universal and either or binaries. My critical engagements with the norms of sexual consent in the context of rape cases, sex workers' constitutional protections (*Bedford* vs. *Canada*) and workplace rights, seek to, as Rorty urges 'manipulate the tensions within our own epoch in order to produce the beginning of the next epoch' (Rorty 1989: 51).

I offer these examples, not as 'programmes' for reform, or as some improved sociology of modernity. They are not appeals to the existing system, in and on its own terms, but rather represent efforts to critically engage with law to open it up to political contestation – an agonism so essential to justice. It moves us beyond circular normative discussion and gets involved in the messy empiricism of what law does rather than what it says.

These are complex political projects. They require a move away from much that is safe and secure, in both the humanist legal project and from a politics that is authorised by fixed identities and binary subjects. By radically rethinking the relationship between the subject of prostitution and law, a post-structuralist approach signals a perhaps more unsettled yet invigorating place for law, which rather than being used in the service of identity politics can help to create space for multiple identities and to help create the material conditions that foster their proliferation.

To conclude then, this book on the subject of prostitution and law is not an end point but the beginning of a more critical approach that, it is hoped, inspires more work which looks beyond the binary of illegal/legal to the complexities of commercial sex and its regulation. The aim is not to dictate a reform agenda but to enliven a new politics of prostitution which features a less central, but perhaps more dynamic role for law and justice, one that avoids binaries and better responds to the issues raised by late modern sex work in its various manifestations.

Epilogue

I end this work with a final quote and an image, as reminders of the main themes of this work. The text is from Foucault, to whose ideas the book is indebted:

> Through these different practices – psychological, medical, penitential, educational – the certain idea or model of humanity was developed, and now this idea of man has become normative, self-evident, and is supposed to be universal. Humanism may not be universal but may be quite relative to a certain situation . . .This does not mean that we have to get rid of what we call human rights or freedom, but that we can't say that freedom or human rights has to be limited at certain frontiers. For instance, if you asked eighty years

> ago if feminine virtue was part of universal humanism, everyone would have answered yes. What I am afraid of about humanism is that it presents a certain form of our ethics as a universal model for any kind of freedom. I think that there are more secrets, more possible freedoms, and more inventions in our future than we can imagine in humanism as it is dogmatically represented on every side of the political rainbow: the Left, the Center, the Right.
>
> (Foucault 1982c: 15)

This passage from Foucault's later work, warns of the limitations of human rights if restricted to a humanist political imaginary. He talks of the political processes that have constituted citizenship in particular, exclusive ways and how rights have tended to follow a similar trajectory. Yet paradoxically, the political nature of human rights, reveals their potential – as those excluded from citizenship fight for inclusion, the social nature and the possibilities of rights are revealed. By highlighting the political processes involved in constructing universal citizenship, Foucault shows that the very nature of what it is to be human is subject to social change. This offers some hope that rights can be reworked, reconstituted in ways that can accommodate new possibilities which are not limited at 'certain frontiers'.

These insights are incredibly pertinent to sex work politics. Feminine virtue, once a marker of women's very partial political inclusion – was, in part, responsible for sex workers' exclusion from the polity. The fact that this value is no longer a sole marker of inclusion, and the fact that sex workers themselves demand 'the right to have rights' illustrates changing ideas of what it is to be human and the potential of law, in its constitutive capacity, to act both as a constraint but also as a vehicle for the constructions of new communities and rights.

A vacant chair for an inessential subject

Finally, in conclusion, I leave the readers with the image of an empty chair, which serves as a useful metaphor for the subject prostitution and law (see Figure 6.1). It features the Eames Chair, made famous in the iconic 1960s' photograph of Christine Keeler, the call girl whose brief affair with a government minister sparked the scandal[2] of the 'Profumo Affair'. Typical representations that show a naked Keeler, sitting provocatively astride the chair have a strong cultural resonance as it evokes the changing sexual mores, vice and transgression and perhaps more accurately sexual hypocrisy of the time.[3]

While others have used this image to invoke similar meanings of shame, scandal and vice, I use the vacant chair to evoke the main themes of the book. The chair

2 *Scandal* is indeed the title of the film based on the Profumo Affair and the 1989 Pet Shop Boys' song, featuring Dusty Springfield.

3 Interestingly, others have used this image to invoke similar meanings of shame, scandal and vice or even to play around with meanings by substituting Keeler for a different subject, such as Homer Simpson or a rotund male comedian, naked, straddling the chair, for comedic effect.

Figure 6.1 Iconic Eames Chair, made famous by Christine Keeler during the 'Profumo Affair'

is used to represent the edifice of law and previous attempts to fix the modern prostitute subject as sinful, diseased, abused or as rights bearing. Presenting a vacant chair seems to encourage us to put a new subject into the space. The absence of the subject, however, suggests the possibilities of a post-structural methodology; an approach to the politics of prostitution and law that is no longer essentially grounded by a foundational subject and which can generate new possibilities, 'more inventions', beyond the enlightenment present and beyond the current liberal humanist imaginary.

The chair's structure represents the continuing constitutive role of law and the continued need to engage with legal mechanisms, in all their complexity, working within and beyond their terms, to produce new futures that transcend current conventions. It reminds us of Derrida's (apparently paradoxical) call to use legal mechanisms, which are in themselves instruments of power, 'to get a little closer to the unachievable goal of justice' (Valverde 2010: 56). It is to that never ending end that this book aspires.

Bibliography

ABC News (2014) 'Prostitute wins Damages for Sexual Harassment in "World First" Case', ABC News, 1 March. http://www.abc.net.au/news/2014-03-01/an-nz-prostitute-harassment-case/5292738

Abdul, U. (2010) '*Bedford* vs. *Canada*: renewed debate on the "World's Oldest Profession"', *The Court*, 12 October. http://www.thecourt.ca/2010/ 10/12/bedford-v-canada-renewed-debate-on-the-worlds-oldest-profession/

Abel, G. (2014) 'A Decade of Decriminalization: Sex Work "Down Under" but not Underground', *Criminology and Criminal Justice*, 14(5): 580–592

Abel, G. and Fitzgerald, L. (2010) Risk and Risk Management in Sex Work Post-Prostitution Reform Act: a Public Health Perspective, in Abel, G. et al. (eds.) *Taking the Crime out of Sex Work: New Zealand Sex Workers' Fight for Decriminalization*, Bristol: Policy Press

Abel, G., Fitzgerald, L. and Brunton, C. (2010a) Christchurch School of Medicine Study: Methodology and Methods, in Abel, G. et al. (eds.) *Taking the Crime out of Sex Work: New Zealand Sex Workers' Fight for Decriminalization*, Bristol: Policy Press

Abel, G., Fitzgerald, L., Healy, C. and Taylor, A. (eds.) (2010b) *Taking the Crime out of Sex Work: New Zealand Sex Workers' Fight for Decriminalization*, Bristol: Policy Press

Abel, G., Healy, C., Bennachie, C. and Reed, A. (2010c) The Prostitution Reform Act, in Abel, G. et al. (eds.) *Taking the Crime out of Sex Work: New Zealand Sex Workers' Fight for Decriminalization*, Bristol: Policy Press

Acton, W. (1870) *Prostitution Considered in its Moral, Social and Sanitary Aspects*, London: Frank Cass (reprinted 1972)

Addams, J. (1912) *A New Conscience and an Ancient Evil*, Champaign: University of Illinois Press (reprinted 2002)

Agamben, G. (2005) *States of Exception*, Chicago: University of Chicago Press

Agustín, L. (2002) 'The (Crying) Need for Different Kinds of Research', *Research for Sex Work*, 5(June): 30–32

— (2005) 'New Research Directions: The Cultural Study of Commercial Sex', *Sexualities*, 7: 618–631

— (2007) *Sex at the Margins: Migration, Labour Markets and the Rescue Industry*, London: Zed Books

— (2008) 'Sex and the Limits of Enlightenment: The Irrationality of Legal Regimes to Control Prostitution', *Sexuality Research & Social Policy*, 5: 73–86

— (2009) 'Bad Reporting: Prostitution Law, Nationalism and the BBC', *The Naked Anthropologist: Dr Laura Agustín on Migration, Trafficking and Sex*, 20 March. http://www.lauraagustin.com/bad-reporting-prostitution-law-and-the-bbc

All-Party Parliamentary Group on Prostitution and the Global Sex Trade (APPG) (2014), *Shifting the Burden: Inquiry to assess the operation of the current legal settlement on prostitution in England and Wales*, APPG

Anderson, S.A. (2002) 'Prostitution and Sexual Autonomy: Making Sense of the Prohibition of Prostitution', *Ethics*, 112(4): 748–780

Andersson, L. and Östergren, P. (1998a) 'Ny Lag Förvärrar för Sexarbetare', *Aftonbladet*, 11 May

— (1998b) 'Med Lögner blev Sexarbetarnas kunder Kriminella', *Aftonbladet*, 15 June

Andrijasevic, R. (2007) 'Beautiful Dead Bodies: Gender, Migration and Representation in Anti-Trafficking Campaigns', *Feminist Review*, 86: 24–44

— (2009) 'Sex on the Move: Gender, Subjectivity and Differential Inclusion', *Subjectivity*, 29: 389–406

Aradau, C. (2008) *Rethinking Trafficking in Women: Politics out of Security*, Basingstoke: Palgrave Macmillan

Aronowitz, A.A. (2009) *Human Trafficking, Human Misery: the Global Trade in Human Beings*, Westport, CT: Praeger Publishers

Baksi, P. (2006) 'Why the so-called Immoral Traffic (Prevention) Act of India should be Repealed', self-published

Banach, L. and Metzenrath, S. (2000) 'Principles for Model Sex Industry Legislation'. http://www.scarletalliance.org.au/pub/

Barnard, M., Hart, G. and Church, S. (2002) 'Client Violence against Prostitute Women working from Street and Off-street Locations: a Three City Comparison', Swindon: Economic and Social Research Council

Barnard, M.A., McKeganey, N.P. and Leyland, A.H. (1993) 'Risk Behaviours among Male Clients of Female Prostitutes', *British Medical Journal*, 307: 361–362

Barry, K. (1979) *Female Sexual Slavery*, New York: Avon Books

— (1995) *The Prostitution of Sexuality*, New York: New York University Press

Bartley, P. (2000) *Prostitution: Prevention and Reform in England 1860–1914*, London: Routledge

Bassermann, L. (1993) *The Oldest Profession: A History of Prostitution*, New York: Dorsett Press

Bauman, Z. (1993) *Postmodern Ethics*, Oxford: Blackwell

— (1998) 'On Postmodern Use of Sex', *Theory Culture and Society*, 15: 19–33

— (2003) *Liquid Love: On the Frailty of Human Bonds*, Oxford: Polity Press

BBC News (2008) 'Amsterdam to Cut Brothels in Half', BBC News, 6 December. http://news.bbc.co.uk/1/hi/7769199.stm

Becker, H.S. (1963) *Outsiders: Studies in Social Deviance*, New York: Free Press

Bedford, T.J. (2011) *Dominatrix on Trial: Bedford vs. Canada*, Toronto: iUniverse Publishing

Bell, L. (1987) *Good Girls/Bad Girls: Feminists and Sex Trade Workers Face to Face*, Seattle, WA: Seal Press

Bell, S. (1994) *Reading, Writing and Rewriting the Prostitute Body*, Indiana: Indiana University Press

Benhabib, S. (1985) 'The Generalized and the Concrete Other: The Kohlberg-Gilligan Controversy and Feminist Theory', *Praxis International*, (4): 402–424

Bernstein, E. (1999) 'What's Wrong with Prostitution – What's Right with Sex Work – Comparing Markets in Female Sexual Labor' *Hastings Women's Law Journal*, 10: 91–117

— (2001) 'The Meaning of Purchase: Desire, Demand and the Commerce of Sex', *Ethnography*, 2(3): 389–420

— (2007a) *Temporarily Yours: Intimacy, Authenticity, and the Commerce of Sex*, Chicago: University of Chicago Press

— (2007b) 'The Sexual Politics of the "New Abolitionism"', *Differences: Journal of Feminist Cultural Studies*, 18(3): 128–151

— (2010) 'Militarized Humanitarianism Meets Carceral Feminism: The Politics of Sex, Rights, and Freedom in Contemporary Anti-Trafficking Campaigns', *Signs: Journal of Women in Culture and Society*, 36(1): 45–71

Bindel, J. (1998) 'Flushing the Johns', *Trouble and Strife*, 38: 35–36

— (1999) 'Streets Apart on Approach to Kerb Crawling' (letter), *The Guardian*, 18 August

Bindel, J. and Atkins, H. (2008) 'Big Brothel: a Survey of the Off-street Sex Industry in London', London: The Poppy Project

Bindman, J. and Doezema, J. (1997) *Redefining Prostitution as Sex Work on the International Agenda*, Anti-Slavery International/Network of Sex Work Projects. http://www.walnet.org/csis/papers/redefining.html

Bingham, J. (1996) *The Constitution of Interests: Beyond the Politics of Rights*, New York: New York University Press

Bloch, R. (1987) 'The Gendered Meanings of Virtue in Revolutionary America', *Signs*, 13: 37–58

Bordo, S. (1988) 'Feminist Skepticism and the "Maleness" of Philosophy', *Journal of Philosophy*, 85: 619–629

Borg, A., Elwien, F., Fruhling, M., Grönwall, L., Liljeström, R., and Månsson, S.A. (1981) *Prostitution: Beskrivning, Analys, Förslag till Åtgärder*, Stockholm: Liber

Bower, L. (1994) 'Queer Acts and the Politics of "Direct Address": Rethinking Law, Culture and Community', *Law and Society Review*, 28(5): 1009–1034

BRÅ: Brottsförebyggande Rådet (2000) *Förbud mot Köp av Sexuella Tjänster*, Stockholm, BRÅ

Brace, L. and O'Connell Davidson, J. (2000) 'Minding the Gap: General and Substantive Theorizing on Power and Exploitation', *Signs*, 25(4): 1045–1051

Brake, D. (2007) 'Title IX as Pragmatic Feminism', *Cleveland State Law Review*, 55: 513–546

Brants, C. (1998) 'The Fine Art of Regulated Tolerance: Prostitution in Amsterdam', *Journal of Law and Society*, 25: 621–635

Brents, B.G. and Hausbeck, K. (2007) 'Marketing Sex: US Legal Brothels and Late Capitalist Consumption', *Sexualities*, 10: 425–439

Brents, B.G., Jackson, C.A. and Hausbeck, K. (2010) *The State of Sex: Tourism, Sex and Sin in the New American Heartland*, New York: Routledge

Brewis, J. and Linstead, S. (2000) *Sex, Work and Sex Work: Eroticizing Organization*, London: Routledge

Brooks-Gordon, B. (2006) *The Price of Sex: Prostitution, Policy and Society*, Cullompton: Willan Publishing

— (2010) 'Bellwether Citizens: The Regulation of Male Clients of Sex Workers', *Journal of Law and Society* 31(1): 145–170

Brooks-Gordon, B.M. and Gelsthorpe, L.R. (2003) 'Prostitutes' Clients, Ken Livingstone, and a New Trojan horse', *Howard Journal of Criminal Justice*, 42(5): 437–451

Brown, W. (1995) *States of Injury, Power and Freedom in Late Modernity*, Princeton, NJ: Princeton University Press

— (2000) 'Suffering Rights as Paradoxes', *Constellations*, 7(2): 208–229

— (2004) '"The Most we can Hope for. . ." – Human Rights and the Politics of Fatalism', *South Atlantic Quarterly*, 103: 451–463

Brown, W. and Halley, J. (2003) *Left Legalism/Left Critique*, London: Duke University Press

Bullough, V. and Bullough, B. (1987) *Women and Prostitution: A Social History*, Buffalo, NY: Prometheus Books

Burman, M. (2009) 'Evidencing Sexual Assault: Women in the Witness Box', *Probation Journal*, 56(4): 379–398

Burman, M., Jamieson, L., Nicholson, J. and Brooks, O. (2007) *Impact of Aspects of the Law of Evidence in Sexual Offences Trials: An Evaluation Study*, Social Research: Crime and Justice, No. 2

Burton, A. (1994) *Burdens of History: British Feminists, Indian Women and Imperial Culture 1865–1915*, Chapel Hill: University of North Carolina Press

Busza, J. (2006) 'Having the Rug Pulled from under Your Feet: One's Project Experience of the US Policy Reversal on Sex Work', *Health, Policy and Planning*, 21(4): 329–332

Butler, J. (1990) *Gender Trouble: Feminism and the Subdivision of Identity*, London: Routledge

— (1993) *Bodies that Matter: On the Discursive Limits of 'Sex'*, New York: Routledge

— (2004a) *Undoing Gender*, London: Routledge

— (2004b) *Precarious Life: The Powers of Mourning and Violence,* London: Verso

Califia, P. (1994) *Public Sex: The Culture of Radical Sex*, Berkeley, CA: Cleis Press

Campbell, R. (2014) Not Getting Away With It: Linking Sex Work and Hate Crime in Merseyside, in Chakraborti, N. and Garland, J. (eds.) *Responding to Hate Crime: The Case for Connecting Policy and Research*, Bristol: Policy Press

Campbell, R. and Storr, M. (2001) 'Challenging the Kerb-crawler Rehabilitation Programme', *Feminist Review*, 67: 94–108

Castel, R. (1994) 'Problematization' as a Mode of Reading History, in Goldstein, J. (ed.) *Foucault and the Writing of History*, Oxford: Blackwell

Chapkis, W. (1997) *Live Sex Acts: Women Performing Erotic Labour*, London: Routledge

—(2003) 'Trafficking, Migration and the Law: Protecting Innocents, Punishing Immigrants', *Gender and Society*, 17: 923–937

Cheng, S. (2010) *On the Move for Love: Migrant Entertainers and the U.S. Military in South Korea*, Philadelphia: University of Pennsylvania Press

Chodorow, N. (1994) *Femininities, Masculinities, Sexualities: Freud and Beyond*, Kentucky: University Press of Kentucky

Chomsky, N. and Foucault, M. (1997) Human Nature: Justice Versus Power, in Davidson, A. (ed.) *Foucault and his Interlocutors*, Chicago: University of Chicago Press

Christodoulidis, E. (2009) 'Strategies of Rapture', *Law and Critique*, 20(1): 3–26

Church, S., Henderson, M., Barnard, M. and Hart, G. (2001) 'Violence by Clients towards Female Prostitutes in Different Work Settings: Questionnaire Survey', *British Medical Journal*, 322: 524–525

Clarke, M. (2012) 'Case of the Week: *Quashie* vs. *Stringfellows Restaurants Ltd*'. http://www.personneltoday.com/hr/case-of-the-week-quashie-v-stringfellows-restaurants-ltd/

Clark, P., Bellis, M., Cook, P. and Tocque, K. (2004) *Consultation on a Managed Zone for Sex Trade Workers in Liverpool*, Liverpool: Centre for Public Health, Liverpool John Moores University

Claude, K. (2010) *Targeting the Sex Buyer – The Swedish Example: Stopping Prostitution and Trafficking Where All Begins*, Stockholm: The Swedish Institute

Cohen, S. (1972) *Folk Devils and Moral Panics: The Creation of the Mods and Rockers*, London: Routledge
— (1985) *Visions of Social Control: Crime, Punishment and Classification*, Cambridge: Polity Press
Cohen, S. and Young, J. (1973) *The Manufacture of News: Social Problems, Deviance and the Mass Media*, London: Sage
Collins, A. and Judge, G. (2008a) 'Client Participation in Paid Sex Markets under Alternative Regulatory Regimes', *International Review of Economics*, 28: 294–301
— (2008b) Client Demand and the Regulatory Environment, in Munro, V. and Della Giusta, M. (eds.) *Demanding Sex: Critical Reflections on the Regulation of Prostitution*, London: Ashgate
Committee on Homosexual Offences and Prostitution (1957) *The Report of the Departmental Committee on Homosexual Offences and Prostitution*, (also known as the *Wolfenden Committee Report*), 4 September, London: HMSO
Connell, R.W. (1995) *Masculinities*, Cambridge: Polity Press
Cook, I.R. (2015) 'Making Links between Sex Work, Gender and Victimisation: the Politics and Pedagogies of John Schools', *Gender, Place and Culture*, 22 (6): 817–832
Corbin, A. (1990) *Women for Hire*, Cambridge, MA: Harvard University Press
Cornell, D. (1991) *Beyond Accommodation: Ethical Feminism, Deconstruction, and the Law*, New York: Routledge
— (1995) *The Imaginary Domain: Abortion, Pornography and Sexual Harassment*, London: Routledge
Council of Europe (2007) Resolution 1579 'Prostitution – Which stance to take?'. http://assembly.coe.int/Main.asp?link=/Documents/AdoptedText/ta07/ERES1579.htm
Cowan, S. and Hunter, R. (2007) *Choice and Consent: Feminist Engagements with Law and Subjectivity*, Bungay: Routledge Cavendish
Cox, P. (2007) 'Compulsion, Voluntarism, and Venereal Disease: Governing Sexual Health in England after the Contagious Diseases Acts', *Journal of British Studies*, 46(1): 91–115.
Coy, M. (2009) 'This Body which is not Mine: the notion of the Habit Body, Prostitution and Dis(embodiment)', *Feminist Theory*, 10: 61–75
Coy, M., Horvath, M. and Kelly, L. (2007) '"It's just like Going to the Supermarket": Men Buying Sex in East London', Report for Safe Exit Tower Hamlets, Child and Women Abuse Studies Unit
Crawford, B.J. (2007) 'Toward a Third-Wave Feminist Legal Theory: Young Women, Pornography and the Praxis of Pleasure', *Michigan Journal of Gender and Law*, 14: 99. http://digitalcommons.pace.edu/ lawfaculty/243/
Crenshaw, K. (1989) 'Demarginalizing the Intersection of Race and Sex: a Black Feminist Critique of Antidiscrimination Doctrine, Feminist Theory and Antiracist Politics', *University of Chicago Legal Forum*: 139–167
Cruikshank, B. (2004) *The Will to Empower: Democratic Citizens and Other Subjects*, New York: Cornell University Press
Cruz, K. (2013) 'Unmanageable Work, (Un)liveable Lives: the UK Sex Industry, Labour Rights and the Welfare State', *Social & Legal Studies*, 22(4): 465–488
Daalder, A.L. (2004) *Lifting the Ban on Brothels: Prostitution in 2000–2001*, Wetenschappelijk Onderzoek-en Documentatiecentrum. https://www.ncjrs.gov/App/abstractdb/AbstractDBDetails.aspx?id=207401
— (2007) *Prostitution in the Netherlands since the Lifting of the Brothel Ban*, WODC Research Study. http://english.wodc.nl/ onderzoeksdatabase/1204e-engelse-vertaling-rapport-evaluatie-opheffing-bordeelverbod.aspx

Dabhoiwala, F. (2012) *The Origins of Sex: a History of the First Sexual Revolution*, Oxford: Oxford University Press

Danna, D. (2012) 'Client-only Criminalization in the City of Stockholm: a Local Research on the Application of the "Swedish Model" of Prostitution Policy', *Sexuality Research and Social Policy*, 9: 80–93

Davidson, R. and Hall, L.J. (2001) *Sex, Sin and Suffering: Venereal Disease and European Society since 1870*, London: Routledge

Davies, N. (2009) 'Prostitution and Trafficking – the Anatomy of a Moral Panic', *The Guardian*, 20 October

Davies, P. and Feldman, R. (1997) Prostitute Men Now, in Scrambler, G. and Scrambler, A. (eds.) *Rethinking Prostitution: Purchasing Sex in the 1990s*, London: Routledge

Davis, N.J. (ed.) (1993) *Prostitution: an International Handbook on Trends, Problems, and Policies*, London: Greenwood Press

De Beauvoir, S. (1949) *The Second Sex*, trans. and ed. H.M. Parshley, London: Vintage (reprinted 1997)

De Lauretis, T. (1987) *Technologies of Gender: Essays on Theory, Film and Fiction*, Indiana: Indiana University Press

De Marneffe, P. (2009) *Liberalism and Prostitution*, Oxford: Oxford University Press

Dean, M. (1999) *Governmentality: Power and Rule in Modern Society*, London: Sage

— (2002) 'Liberal Government and Authoritarianism', *Economy and Society*, 31(1): 37–61

Delacoste, F. and Alexander, P. (1988) *Sex Work: Writings by Women in the Sex Industry*, London: Virago

Deleuze, G. (1995) *Negotiations 1972–1990*, ed. Martin Joughin, New York: Columbia University Press

Della Giusta, M., Di Tomasso, D.L. and Strøm, S. (2008) *Sex Markets: A Denied Industry*, London: Routledge

Department of Health (2000) *Safeguarding Children Involved in Prostitution*. http://www.dh.gov.uk/en/Publicationsandstatistics/Publications/PublicationsPolicyAndGuidance/DH_4006037

Der Spiegel (2013) 'Unprotected: How Legalizing Prostitution Has Failed', *Der Spiegel*, 26 May. http://www.spiegel.de/international/germany/human-trafficking-persists-despite-legality-of-prostitution-in-germany-a-902533.html

Dewey, S. (2011) *Neon Wasteland: On Love, Motherhood, and Sex Work in a Rust Belt Town*, Berkeley, CA: University of California Press

Diduck, A. and Wilson, W. (1997) 'Prostitutes and Persons', *Journal of Law and Society*, 24(4): 504–525

Di Stefano, C. (1990) Dilemmas of Difference: Feminism, Modernity and Postmodernism, in Nicholson, L. (ed.) *Feminism/Postmodernism*, New York: Routledge

Diu, N.L. (2014) 'Welcome to Paradise: Inside the World of Legalized Prostitution', *The Telegraph*. http://s.telegraph.co.uk/graphics/ projects/ welcome-to-paradise/

Doezema, J. (1998) Forced to Choose: Beyond the Voluntary v Forced Prostitution Dichotomy, in Kempadoo, K. and Doezema, J. (eds.) *Global Sex Workers. Rights, Resistance, and Redefinition*, New York: Routledge

— (1999) 'Loose Women or Lost Women? The Re-emergence of the Myth of White Slavery in Contemporary Discourses of Trafficking in Women', *Gender Issues*, 18(1): 23–50

— (2001) 'Ouch! Western Feminists' "Wounded Attachment" to the "Third World Prostitute"', *Feminist Review*, 67: 16–38

— (2010) *Sex Slaves and Discourse Masters: the Construction of Trafficking*, London: Zed Books

Douglas, M. (1970) *Natural Symbols: Explorations in Cosmology*, London: Barrie & Rockliff
Douzinas, C. (2002) *The End of Human Rights: Critical Legal Thought at the Fin-de-Siecle*, Oxford: Hart Publishing
— (2013) 'The Paradoxes of Human Rights', *Constellations*, 20(1): 51–67
Duggan, L. and Hunter, N. (1995) *Sex Wars: Sexual Dissent and Political Culture*, New York: Routledge
Durbar Mahila Samanwaya Committee, India (1998) 'We Demand Workers' Rights', self-published
Dworkin, A. (1981) *Pornography – Men Possessing Women*, London: Women's Press
— (1987) *Intercourse*, New York: Basic Books
— (1993) 'Prostitution and Male Supremacy', *Michigan Journal of Gender & Law*, 1: 1.
Dworkin, R. (1977) *Taking Rights Seriously*, Cambridge, MA: Harvard University Press
Eden, P. (1997) 'Sex industry worlds: massage parlours, escort agencies, and the social organization of sex work in Christchurch', a thesis submitted in partial fulfillment of the requirements for the Degree of Master Arts in Sociology, University of Christchurch
Edwards, J. (2005) '25,000 Sex Slaves on the Streets of Britain', *The Daily Mirror*, 19 October
Edwards, S.M. (1981) *Female Sexuality and the Law: A Study of Constructs of Female Sexuality as they inform Statute and Legal Procedure*, Oxford: Martin Robertson
— (1993) Policing and the Under-representation of Women's Interests, in Jackson, S. (ed.) *Women's Studies: A Reader*, Hemel Hempstead: Harvester
Eespere, K. (2007) 'The Hidden Side of Prostitution: Sex Buyers Speak', Social Policy Information and Analysis Department, Ministry of Social Affairs of the Republic of Estonia
Egger, S. and Harcourt, C. (2004) 'A Comment on John Scott, "Prostitution and Public Health in New South Wales"', *Culture, Health & Sexuality*, 6: 439–466
Ekberg, G. (2004) 'The Swedish Law that Prohibits the Purchase of Sexual Services: Best Practices for the Prevention of Prostitution and Trafficking in Human Beings', *Violence Against Women*, 10: 1187–1218
— (2008) 'Abolishing Prostitution: The Swedish Solution, an Interview with Gunilla Ekberg by the Rain and Thunder Collective', *Rain and Thunder: A Radical Feminist Journal of Discussion and Activism*, (41, Winter). http://www.catwinternational.org/Content/Images/Article/169/attachment.pdf
Elder, D. (ed.) (2000) 'A Guide to Best Practice: Occupation Health and Safety in the Australian Legal Industry'. http://www.scarletalliance.org.au/library/bestpractice
Elias, J. (2007) 'Women Workers and Labour Standards: the Problem of "Human Rights"', *Review of International Studies*, 33(1): 45–57
Ellis, H. (1897) *Sexual Inversions*, Oxford: Oxford University Press
— (1903) *Analysis of the Sexual Impulse, Love and Pain, The Sexual Impulse in Women*, Oxford: Oxford University Press
— (1910) *Sex in Relation to Society*, Oxford: Oxford University Press
Engle, K. (2008) 'Judging Sex in War', *Michigan Law Review*, 106: 941–962
Equality Now (2012) 'Global Sex Trafficking Fact Sheet'. http://www.equalitynow.org/node/1010
Ericsson, L.O. (1980) 'Charges against Prostitution: an Attempt at a Philosophical Assessment', *Ethics*, 90: 335–366
European Parliament (2014) 'European Parliament resolution of 26 February 2014 on Sexual Exploitation and Prostitution and its Impact on Gender Equality', 26 February.

http://www.europarl.europa.eu/sides/getDoc.do? pubRef=-//EP//TEXT+TA+P7-TA-2014-0162+0+DOC+XML+V0//EN

European Women's Lobby (2010) 'Towards, a Europe Free from All Forms of Male Violence Against Women', Position Paper, EWL Centre on Violence Against Women. http://www.womenlobby.org/spip.php?article934

Ewald. F. (1991) Norms, Discipline and Law, in Post, R. (ed.) *Law and the Order of Culture*, Berkeley: University of California Press

Ewick, P. and Silbey, S. (1998) *The Common Place of Law: Stories from Everyday Life*, Chicago: University of Chicago Press

Farley, M. and Barkan, H. (1998) 'Prostitution, Violence, and Post-traumatic Stress Disorder', *Women and Health*, 27(3): 37–49

Farley, M., Cotton, A., Lynne, J., Zumbeck, S., Spiwak, F., Reyes, M.E. et al. (2003) 'Prostitution and Trafficking in Nine Countries: Update on Violence and Posttraumatic Stress Disorder', *Journal of Trauma Practice*, 2: 33–74

Farley, M. and Patsalides, B.M. (2001) 'Physical Symptoms, Posttraumatic Stress Disorder, and Healthcare Utilization of Women with and without Childhood Physical and Sexual Abuse', *Psychological Reports*, 89(3): 595–606

Faugier, J., Hayes, C. and Butterworth, C. (1992) 'Drug Using Prostitutes, Their Health Care Needs and Their Clients', University of Manchester, Research Paper produced by the University of Manchester

Fine, S. (2013) 'Supreme Court strikes down Canada's Prostitution Laws', *The Globe and Mail*, 20 December

Finnis, J. (1980) *Natural Law and Natural Rights*, New York: Oxford University Press

Fiolleau, T. (2010) *Souled Out: an Insider Account of the Sex Trade from a Former Prostitute and Madam*, London: Off the Bookshelf

Fischer, B., Wortley, S., Webster, C. and Kirst, M. (2002) 'The Socio-legal Dynamics and Implications of "Diversion": the Case Study of the Toronto John School Diversion Programme for Prostitution Offenders', *Criminal Justice*, 2(4): 385–410

Fitch, C. (1996) 'Review of Reading, Writing and Re-Writing the Prostitute Body', *Sociological Review*, 44: 128–131

Florin, O. (2012) 'A Particular Kind of Violence: Swedish Social Policy Puzzles of a Multipurpose Criminal Law', *Sexuality Research and Social Policy*, published online 31 May

Foucault, M. (1975) *Discipline and Punish: The Birth of the Prison*, Paris: Gallimard

— (1976) *The History of Sexuality Volume 1: The Will to Knowledge*, London: Penguin

— (1978) 'About the Concept of the "Dangerous Individual" in 19th Century Legal Psychiatry', *International Journal of Law and Psychiatry* 1: 1–18

— (1980) *Power/Knowledge: Selected Interviews and Other Writings, 1972–1977*, New York: Pantheon

— (1982a) Madness and Civilization: A History of Insanity in the Age of Reason, in Dreyfus, H.L. and Rabinow, P. (eds.) *Michel Foucault: Beyond Structuralism and Hermeneutics*, Chicago: University of Chicago Press

— (1982b) The Subject and Power, in Dreyfus, H.L. and Rabinow, P. (eds.) *Michel Foucault: Beyond Structuralism and Hermeneutics*, Chicago: University of Chicago Press

— (1982c) Truth, Power, Self, in Martin, L.H., Gutman, H. and Hutton, P.H. (eds.) *Technologies of the Self: A Seminar with Michel Foucault*, London: Tavistock

— (1990) *The History of Sexuality: An Introduction*, New York: Vintage Books

— (1991) Questions of Method, in Burchell, G., Gordon, C. and Miller, P. (eds.) *The Foucault Effect: Studies in Governmentality*, Hemel Hempstead: Harvester Wheatsheaf

— (1994) *The Order of Things: An Archaeology of the Human Sciences*, New York: Vintage Books
— (1996) *The Birth of the Clinic An Archaeology of Medical Perception*, New York: Vintage
— (1997) *Ethics: Subjectivity and Truth (Essential Works, Volume 1)*, ed. Paul Rabinow, New York: New York Press
— (2000a) 'The Moral and Social Experience of the Poles Can No Longer Be Tolerated', ed. James Faubion, *Power (Essential Works, Volume 3)*, London: Penguin
— (2000b) Confronting Governments: Human Rights, in Foucault, M., Faubion, J.D. and Hurley, R. (eds.) *Essential Works of Foucault 1954–1984, Vol. 3: Power*, New York: The New Press
— (2001) *Fearless Speech*, ed. J. Pearson, Los Angeles: Semiotext(e)
— (2003) *Society Must Be Defended*, Collège de France Course Lectures
Frank, K. (2002) *G-Strings and Sympathy: Strip Club Regulars and Male Desire*, Durham, NC: Duke University Press
Frank, K., Egan, R.D. and Johnston, M.L. (eds.) (2006) *Flesh for Fantasy: Producing and Consuming Exotic Dance*, Seattle: Seal Press
Fraser, N. (1981) 'Foucault on Modern Power: Empirical Insights and Normative Confusions', *Praxis International*, 1: 272–287
— (1993) 'Beyond the Master/Subject Model: Reflections on Carole Pateman's Sexual Contract', *Social Text*, 37, A Special Section Edited by Anne McClintock Explores the Sex Trade: 173–181
— (1997) *Justice Interruptus: Critical Reflections on the Postsocialist Condition*, London: Routledge
— (2000) 'Rethinking Recognition', *New Left Review*, 3(May/June): 107–120
Freeman, J. (1990) 'The Feminist Debate over Prostitution Reform: Prostitutes' Rights Groups, Radical Feminists and the (Im)possibility of Consent', *Berkeley Women's Law Journal*, 5: 75–109
Freud, S. (1912) 'The Most Prevalent Form of Degradation in Erotic Life', *Collected Papers*, 4: 203–216
Frommel, M. (2014) 'Prostitution: Beyond an Infantilising Feminism', *NovoArgumente*, November. English language translation available at https://researchprojectgermany.wordpress.com/author/satellithias/
Fuller, L. (1964) *The Morality of Law*, Fredericksburg, VA: Yale University Press
Gaffney, J. (2002) Guidelines for the Development of Outreach Work with Men who Sell Sex, in Schiffer, K. (ed.) *Manual: Tips, Tricks and Models of Good Practice for Service Providers Considering, Planning or Implementing Services for Male Sex Workers*, Amsterdam: European Network Male Prostitution
— (2007) 'A Coordinated Prostitution Strategy and Response to Paying the Price – But what about the Men?', *Community Safety Journal*, 6(1): 27–33
Gaffney, J. and Beverly, K. (2001) 'Contextualizing the Construction and Social Organization of the Commercial Male Sex Industry in London at the Beginning of the Twenty-First Century', *Feminist Studies*, 67: 133–141
Gall, G. (2007) *Sex Worker Union Organising: An International Study*, London: Palgrave
Geertz, C. (1984) 'Anti Anti-Relativism', *American Anthropologist*, 86: 263–277
Giddens, A. (1992) *The Transformation of Intimacy: Sexuality, Love and Eroticism in Modern Societies*, Palo Alto, CA: Stanford University Press
Gilchrist, G., Cameron, J. and Scoular, J. (2005) 'Crack and Cocaine Use among Female Prostitutes in Glasgow: Risky Business', *Drugs Education and Prevention*, 12(5): 381–391
Gilfoyle, T.J. (1999) 'Prostitutes in History: From Parables of Pornography to Metaphors of Modernity', *American Historical Review*, 104(1): 117–141

Gilman, S. (1985) *Difference and Pathology: Stereotypes of Sexuality, Race and Madness*, Ithaca, NY: Cornell University Press

Giobbe, E. (1990) Confronting the Liberal Lies about Prostitution, in Leidholdt, D. and Raymond, J. (eds.) *The Sexual Liberty and the Attack on Feminism*, New York: Pergamon

Global Alliance Against Traffic in Women (GAATW) (2007), *Collateral Damage: The Impact of Anti-Trafficking Measures on Human Rights around the World*, GAATW

Golder, B. (2010) 'What is an Anti-humanist Human Right?', *Social Identities*, 16(5): 651–668

— (2011) 'Foucault's Critical (yet Ambivalent) Affirmation: Three Figures of Rights', *Social & Legal Studies*, 20: 283–312

Goode, E. and Ben-Yehuda, N. (1994) *Moral Panics: The Social Construction of Deviance*, London: Blackwell

Gordon, C. (1991) Afterword, in Gordon, C. (ed.) *M. Foucault: Power/Knowledge*, Hemel Hempstead: Harvester

Gould, A. (1994) 'Sweden's Syringe Exchange Debate: Moral Panic in a Rational Society', *Journal of Social Policy*, 23: 2

— (1999) 'A Drug-free Europe: Sweden on the Offensive', *Druglink*, 14: 2

Gould, A. (2001) 'The Criminalisation of Buying Sex: the Politics of Prostitution in Sweden', *Journal of Social Policy*, 30: 437–456

Gray, J. (1995) *Enlightenment's Wake: Politics and Culture at the Close of the Modern Age*, London: Routledge

— (2002) *Straw Dogs: Thoughts on Humans and Other Animals*, London: Granta Books

Grewal, I. (1994) Autobiographical Subjects and Diasporic Locations: Meatless Days and Borderlands, in Kaplan, C. and Grewal, I. (eds.) *Scattered Hegemonies: Postmodernity and Transnational Feminist Practices*, Minneapolis: University of Minnesota Press

— (1998) On the New Global Feminism and the Family of Nations: Dilemmas of Transnational Feminist Practice, in Shohat, E. (ed.) *Talking Visions: Multicultural Feminism in a Transnational Age*, New York: New Museum of Contemporary Art

Griffiths, P. (2008) *Lost Londons: Change, Crime, and Control in the Capital City, 1550–1660*, New York: Cambridge University Press

Groom, T. and Nandwini, R. (2006) 'Characteristics of Men who Pay for Sex: a UK Sexual Health Clinic Survey', *Sexually Transmitted Infections*, 82(5): 364–367

Guy, D.J. (1995) *Sex and Danger in Buenos Aires: Prostitution, Family and Nation in Argentina (Engendering Latin America)*, Lincoln, NE: University of Nebraska Press

Hall, S. (1978) *Policing the Crisis: Mugging, the State, and Law, and Order*, New York: Holmes & Meier

Haraway, D. (1985) 'Manifesto for Cyborgs: Science, Technology, and Socialist Feminism in the 1980s', *Socialist Review*, 80: 65–108.

— (1991) Cyborg Manifesto: Science, Technology, and Socialist-Feminism in the Late Twentieth Century, in Haraway, D., *Simians, Cyborgs and Women: The Reinvention of Nature*, New York: Routledge

Harcourt, C., Beek, I., Heslop, J., McMahon, M., and Donovan, B. (2001) 'The Health and Welfare Needs of Female and Transgender Street Sex Workers in New South Wales', *Australian and New Zealand Journal of Public Health*, 25(1): 84–89

Harcourt, C. and Donovan, B. (2005) 'The Many Faces of Sex Work', *Sexually Transmitted Infection*, 81(3): 201–206

Hardy, K. (2010) '(Sex) Working Class Subjects: Integrating Sex Workers in the Argentine Labour Movement', *International Labour and Working Class History*, 77(1): 89–108

Harrington, C. (2012) 'Prostitution Policy Models and Feminist Knowledge: Politics in New Zealand and Sweden', *Sexuality Research and Social Policy*, 9(4): 32–54

Harris, S. and Haverkamp, R. (1995) 'Happy Hooker's Rich Pickings: It's a Bed of Roses for $200 an Hour Beauty', *Sunday Telegraph*, 6 August

Harsin, J. (1985) *Policing Prostitution in Nineteenth-Century Paris*, Princeton, NJ: Princeton University Press

Hencke, D. (2006) 'Sex Chatline Worker Wins Dismissal Case', *The Guardian*, 17 January. www.theguardian.com/ money/2006/jan/17/ workandcareers.uknews.

Henderson, T. (1999) *Disorderly Women in Eighteenth-Century London: Prostitution and Control in the Metropolis, 1730–1830*, London: Routledge

Henning, T. and Bronitt, S. (1998) Rape Victims on Trial: Regulating the Use and Abuse of Sexual History Evidence, in Easteal, P. (ed.) *Balancing the Scales: Rape, Law Reform and Australian Culture*, Sydney: Federation Press

Herman, D. and Stychin, C. (1995) *Legal Inversions: Lesbians, Gay Men, and the Politics of Law*, Philadelphia, PA: Temple University Press

Hester, M. and Westmarland, N. (2004) *Tackling Street Prostitution: Towards a Holistic Approach*, Home Office Research, Development and Statistics Directorate

Hill Collins, P. (1990) *Black Feminist Thought: Knowledge, Consciousness and the Politics of Knowledge*, London: Routledge

Hindess, B. (1996) *Discourses of Power: From Hobbes to Foucault*, London: Wiley

— (2002) 'Neo-liberal Citizenship', *Citizenship Studies*, 6: 127–143

Hobson, B.M. (1990) *Uneasy Virtue: the Politics of Prostitution and the American Reform Tradition*, Chicago: University of Chicago Press

Hochschild, A.R. (1983) *The Managed Heart: Commercialization of Human Feeling*, Berkeley: University of California Press

Hoigrad, C. and Finstad, L. (1992) *Backstreets: Prostitution, Money and Love*, Philadelphia: Pennsylvanian University State Press

Holzman, H.R. and Pines, S. (1982) 'Buying Sex: the Phenomenology of Being a John', *Deviant Behavior*, 4: 89–116

Honeyball, M. (2014) 'Yesterday's Outcome on Prostitution Was a Victory for Genuine Choice', *Huffington Post*, 27 February. http://www.huffingtonpost.co.uk/mary-honeyball/european-parliament-prostitution-law_b_4864025.html

Honig, B. (1992) Towards an Agnostic Feminism: Hannah Arendt and the Politics of Identity, in Butler, J. and Scott, J. (eds.) *Feminists Theorise the Political*, London: Routledge

hooks, b. (1982) *Ain't I a Woman?: Black Women and Feminism*, London: Pluto Press

Horschild, A. (1983) *The Managed Heart: Commercialization of Human Feeling*, California: University of California Press

Hovet, J., Duda, M. and Smolovà, K. (2005) 'A Peek inside the Sex Industry', *The Prague Tribune*, 10 July

Howe, C., Zaraysky, S. and Lorentzen, L. (2008) 'Transgender Sex Workers and Sexual Transmigration between Guadalajara and San Francisco', *Latin American Perspectives*, 35(1): 31–50

Howell, P. (2009) *Geographies of Regulation: Policing Prostitution in Nineteenth-Century Britain and the Empire*, Cambridge: Cambridge University Press

Howell, P., Beckingham, D. and Moore, F. (2008) 'Managed Zones for Sex Workers in Liverpool: Contemporary Proposals, Victorian Parallels', *Transactions of the Institute of British Geographers*, 33(2): 233–250

Hubbard, P. (2015) 'Law, Sex and the City: Regulating Sexual Entertainment Venues in England and Wales', *International Journal of Law in the Built Environment*, 7(1): 5–20

Hubbard, P. and Scoular, J. (2009) 'Making the dangerous more dangerous?: The contradictions of British street prostitution policy' in Canter, D. (ed.) *Safer Sex In the City*, Aldershot: Ashgate

Hubbard, P.J., Matthews, R. and Scoular, J. (2007) *Regulating the Spaces of Sex Work: Assessing the Impact of Prostitution Law: Full Research Report*, ESRC End of Award Report, RES-000-22-1001

— (2008) 'Regulating Sex Work in the EU: Prostitute Women and the New Spaces of Exclusion', *Gender, Place and Culture*, 15(2): 137–152

Hughes, D. (2000) 'Scientific, Feminist and Personal Epistemologies: Conflicts and Opportunities', *Women's Studies Quarterly*, 28: 305–312

Humphreys, A. (1972) Biographical Note, in Acton, W. (1870) *Prostitution Considered in its Moral, Social, and Sanitary Aspects*, London: Frank Cass (reprinted 1972)

— (2012) 'Ontario Court of Appeal Greenlights Brothels, Sweeps Aside many of Canada's Anti-prostitution Laws', *National Post*, 26 March. http://news.nationalpost.com/2012/03/26/ontario-court-of-appeal-greenlights-brothels-sweeps-aside-many-of-canadas-anti-prostitution-laws/

Hunt, A. (1992) 'Foucault's Expulsion of Law: Toward a Retrieval', *Law and Social Inquiry*, 17(1): 1–38

— (1993) *Explorations in Law and Society*, New York: Routledge

— (1999a) 'Anxiety and Social Explanation: Some Anxieties about Anxiety', *Journal of Social History*, 32(3): 509–528

— (1999b) *Governing Morals: A Social History of Moral Regulation*, Cambridge: Cambridge University Press

Hunt, A. and Wickham, G. (1994) *Foucault and Law: Towards a Sociology of Law as Governance*, London: Pluto Press

Hunt, N. and Stevens, A. (2004) 'Whose Harm? Harm Reduction and the Shift to Coercion in UK Drug Policy', *Social Policy and Society*, 3(4): 333–342

Hunter, G. and May, T. (2004) *Solutions and Strategies: Drug Problems and Street Sex Markets: Guidance for Partnerships and Providers*, London: Home Office, Drug Strategy Directorate

Ilcan, S. and Phillips, L. (2008) 'Governing through Global Networks: Knowledge Mobilities and Participatory Development', *Current Sociology*, 56(5): 711–734

International Labour Organisation (2012) *ILO Global Estimate of Forced Labour: Results and Methodology*, 1 June. http://www.ilo.org/washington/areas/ elimination-of-forced-labor/WCMS_182004/lang—en/index.htm

Ivison, D. (1998) The Disciplinary Moment: Foucault, Law and the Reinscription of Right, in Moss J. (ed.) *The Later Foucault: Politics and Philosophy*, London: Sage

— (2008) *Rights*, Stocksfield: Acumen

Jackson, S. (1992) 'The Amazing Deconstructing Woman', *Trouble and Strife*, 25: 25–35

Jacobson, M. (2002) 'Why do Men Buy Sex? The Interview: Professor Sven Axel Månsson', *NIKK magasin*, (1): 22–25

Jarvinen, M. (1993) *Of Vice and Women: Shades of Prostitution*, Oslo: Scandinavian University Press

Jeffrey, L.A. and Sullivan, B. (2009) 'Canadian Sex Work Policy for the 21st Century: Enhancing Rights and Safety, Lessons from Australia', *Canadian Political Science Review*, 3: 57–78

Jeffreys, S. (1997a) *The Idea of Prostitution*, North Melbourne: Spinifex Press

— (1997b) *The Spinster and her Enemies: Feminism and Sexuality, 1880–1930*, North Melbourne: Spinifex Press

Jenness, V. (1990) *Making it Work: The Prostitutes' Rights Movement in Perspective*, Washington, DC: Society for the Study of Social Problems

Johansson, L. and Persson, K. (2004) *Perspektiv på Prostitution*, Lund: Lunds Universitet Statsvetenskapliga Institutionen

Joint United Nations Programme on HIV/AIDS (UNAIDS) (2009), Annual Report. http://www.unaids.org/sites/default/files/media_aset/2009_annual_report_en_0.pdf

Jouve, N. (1986) *The Streetcleaner: The Yorkshire Ripper Case on Trial*, London: Marion Boyars

Kapur, R. (2001) 'Post-colonial Economies of Desire: Legal Representations of the Sexual Subaltern', *Denver University Law Review*, 78(4): 855–885

Karras, R. (1996) *Common Women: Prostitution and Sexuality in Medieval England*, Oxford: Oxford University Press

Kelly, L., Coy, M. and Davenport, R. (2009) 'Shifting Sands: a Comparison of Prostitution Regimes across Nine Countries', Child and Woman's Abuse Study Unit, London Metropolitan University

Kempadoo, K. (1999) *Sun, Sex and Gold: Tourism and Sex Work in the Caribbean*, Lanham, MD: Rowman & Littlefield

Kempadoo, K. and Doezema, J. (eds.) (1998) *Global Sex Workers. Rights, Resistance, and Redefinition*, New York: Routledge

Kennedy, D. (1993) *Sexy Dressing Etc.* Cambridge, MA: Harvard University Press

— (2002) 'Legal Economics of US Low Income Housing Markets in Light of "Informality" Analysis', *Journal of Law in Society*, 4: 71–98

Kesler, K. (2002) 'Is a Feminist Stance in Support of Prostitution Possible? An Exploration of Current Trends', *Sexualities*, 2: 219–235

Kilvington, J., Day, S. and Ward, H. (2001) 'Prostitution Policy in Europe: a Time of Change?', *Feminist Review*, 46: 78–93

Kim, H.J. (2011) 'S. Korean Sex Workers Threaten to Set Themselves on Fire to Protect their Brothels', *Associated Press*, 7 June. http://www.nbcnews.com/ id/43650531/ns/world_news-asia_pacific/t/s-korean-sex-workers-threaten-set-themselves-fire-protect-their-brothels/#.UvzW76zlfXQ

Kingdom, E. (1991) *What's Wrong with Rights: Problems for Feminist Politics of Law*, Edinburgh: Edinburgh University Press

Kinnell, H. (2000) *European Network for HIV/STD Prevention in Prostitution: 1998–2000 Final Report (European Commission Programme of Community Action on the prevention of AIDS and certain other communicable diseases)*, London, (SOC.98 20058205F02/98F02PF017)

— (2006) *Murder Made Easy: The Final Solution to Prostitution*, Cullompton: Willan Publishing

— (2008) *Violence and Sex Work in Britain*, Cullompton: Willan Publishing

Kinnell, H. and Griffiths, R.K. (1989) 'Male Clients of Female Prostitutes in Birmingham, England: a Bridge for Transmission of HIV?', 5th International Conference on AIDS, Montreal, June

Kipling, R. (1899) *In Black and White*, New York: R.F. Fenno & Co.

Kloppenburg, J. (1998) *The Virtues of Liberalism*, Oxford: Oxford University Press

Kotiswaran, P. (2011) *Dangerous Sex, Invisible Labor: Sex Work and the Law in India*, Princeton, NJ: Princeton University Press

— (2014a) 'Beyond Sexual Humanitarianism: A Postcolonial Approach to Anti-Trafficking Law', *University of California Irvine Law Review*, 4(1), 353–406

— (2014b) 'Beyond the Allures of Criminalization: Rethinking the Regulation of Sex Work in India', *Criminology and Criminal Justice*, 14(5, November): 565–579

Kulick, D. (1998) *Travesti: Sex, Gender and Culture among Brazilian Transgendered Prostitutes*, Chicago: University of Chicago Press

— (2003) 'Sex in the New Europe: the Criminalisation of Clients and Swedish Fear of Penetration', *Anthropological Theory*, 3: 199–218

— (2005) 'Four Hundred Thousand Swedish Perverts', *GLQ*, 11(2): 205–235

— (2008) 'Good Sex in Sweden', paper presented at "Valg eller Undertrykkelse? Fag eller Forbud?" [Choice or Oppression? Profession or Prohibition?], Conference arranged by the Center for Sexuality Studies at the University of Copenhagen, 1–2 December. http://seksualitetsforskning.soc.ku.dk/pdf/ don_kulick-good_sex_in_sweden.pdf

Kuo, L. (2002) *Prostitution Policy: Revolutionizing Practice through a Gendered Perspective*, New York: New York University Press

Kurbanoglu, E. (2011) 'What Makes Sex Workers Strike: a Comparative Analysis of France (1975) and the UK (1982)', *International Journal of Sociology and Anthropology*, 3(6): 163–179

La Paz (2007) 'Prostitutes Sew Lips Together in Bolivia Protest', *La Paz*, 24 October. http://www.reuters.com/article/2007/10/24/us-bolivia-prostitutes-idUSN2436073120071024

Lacey, N. (1998) *Unspeakable Subjects: Feminist Essays in Legal and Social Theory*, Oxford: Hart Publishing.

Laclau, E. (2004) Ethics, Normativity and the Heteronomy of the Law, in Cheng, S. (ed.) *Law, Justice and Power: Between Reason and Will*, Stanford, CA: Stanford University Press

Laclau, E. and Mouffe, C. (1985) *Hegemony and Socialist Strategy: Towards a Radical Democratic Politics*, London: Verso

Laite, J. (2012) *Common Prostitutes and Ordinary Citizens: Commercial Sex in London, 1885–1960*, Chippenham and Eastbourne: Palgrave Macmillan

Lancet, The (2014), 'HIV and sex workers' (series)

Länsstyrelsen Stockholm (2015) 'Summary: the Extent and Development of Prostitution in Sweden'. http://lansstyrelsen.se/stockholm/ SiteCollectionDocuments/Sv/manniska-och-samhalle/jamstalldhet/ prostitution/SUMMARY-Prostitution-kartlaggning-2014.pdf

Latour, B. and Porter, C. (1993) *We Have Never Been Modern*, Cambridge, MA: Harvard University Press

Laurie, A. (2010) Several Sides to the Story: Feminist Views of Prostitution Reform, in Abel, G. et al. (eds.) *Taking the Crime out of Sex Work: New Zealand Sex Workers' Fight for Decriminalization*, Bristol: Policy Press

Lee, C. (2012) 'Prostitution and Victorian Society Revisited: The Contagious Diseases Acts in Kent', *Women's History Review*, 21(2): 301–316

Lemke, T. (2001) 'The Birth of Bio-politics: Michel Foucault's Lecture at the College de France on Neo-liberalism Governmentality', *Economy and Society*, 30: 190–207

— (2003) 'Comment on Nancy Fraser: Rereading Foucault in the Shadow of Globalization', *Constellations: an International Journal of Critical and Democratic Theory*, 10(2): 172–179

Levinas, E. (1991) *Otherwise than Being, or, Beyond Essence*, ed. Alphonso Lingis, Amsterdam: Kluwer Academic Publishers

Levine, K. and Mellema, V. (2001) 'Strategizing the Street: How Law Matters in the Lives of Women in the Street-level Drug Economy', *Law and Social Inquiry*, 26: 169

Levy, A. (2005) *Female Chauvinist Pigs: Women and the Rise of Raunch Culture*, New York: Free Press

Lewin, B. (ed.) (1998) *Sex i Sverige; Om sexuallivet i Sverige 1996*, Stockholm: Folkhälsoinstitutet

Liberto, H.R. (2009) 'Normalizing Prostitution versus Normalizing the Alienability of Sexual Rights: a response to Scott Anderson', *Ethics*, 120(1): 138–145

Lichtenstein, B. (1999) Reframing 'Eve' in the AIDS Era: the Pursuit of Legitimacy by New Zealand Sex Workers, in Dank, B.M. and Refinetti, R. (eds.) *Sex and Sex Workers*, New Brunswick, NJ: Transaction Publishers

Lim, L.L. (ed.) (1998) *The Sex Sector: the Economic and Social Bases of Prostitution in Southeast Asia*, Geneva: International Labour Organization

Lis, J. (2012) 'Israel Cabinet Approves Bill that Criminalizes Soliciting Prostitution', *Haaretz*, 13 February

Lister, R. (2003) *Citizenship: Feminist Perspectives*, New York: New York University Press

Livneh, N. (2013) 'Meet the Israeli Prostitutes who are Ready to Pay Income Tax', *Haaretz*, 25 July

Lloyd, M. (2005) *Beyond Identity Politics: Feminism, Power and Politics*, London: Sage

— (2007) 'Women's Human Rights: Paradoxes and Possibilities', *Review of International Studies*, 33: 91–103

Loopmans, M. and Van den Broeck, P. (2011) 'Global Pressures, Local Measures: the Re-Regulation of Sex Work in the Antwerp Schipperskwartier', *Tijdschrift voor economische en sociale geografie*, 102(5): 548–561

Lopes, A. (2001) 'Sex Workers of the World Unite!', *Feminist Review*, 67: 151–153

— (2002) Introduction: Strippers of the World Unite!, in Clifton, L. (ed.) *Baby Oil and Ice: Striptease in East London*, London: Do-Not Press

— (2006) Sex Workers and the Labour Movement in the UK, in Campbell, R. and O'Neill, M. (eds.) *Sex Work Now*, Cullompton: Willan Publishing

Lopes, A. and Webber, J. (2013) 'Organising sex workers in the UK: what's in it for trade unions?' www2.uwe.ac.uk/faculties/BBS/BUS/Research/CESR/July_2013_Lopes

Lopes, A., Ditmore, M. and Overs, C. (2002) *Sex Work: Basic Issues*, London: International HIV/AIDS Alliance

Lowman, J. (1992) 'Street Prostitution Control: Some Canadian Reflections on the Finsbury Park Experience', *British Journal of Criminology*, 32(1): 1–17

Lowman, J. and Atchison, C. (2006) 'Men who Buy Sex: a Survey in the Greater Vancouver Regional District', *Canadian Review of Sociology and Anthropology*, 43: 281–296

Luker, K. (1998) 'Sex, Social Hygiene and the Double-Edged Sword of Social Reform', *Theory and Society*, 27(5): 601–634

McClintock, A. (1992) 'Screwing the System: Sex Work, Race and the Law', *Boundary*, 19: 70–95

— (1993) 'Sex Workers and Sex Work', *Social Text*, 37: 1–10

— (1995) *Imperial Leather: Race, Gender, and Sexuality in the Colonial Contest*, London: Taylor & Francis

McCreery, D. (1986) '"This Life of Misery and Shame": Female Prostitution in Guatemala City', *Journal of Latin American Studies*, 18(2): 333–353

McHugh, P. (1980) *Prostitution and Victorian Social Reform*, London: Croom Helm

McIntosh, M. (1978) Who Needs Prostitutes?: The Ideology of Male Sexual Needs, in Smart, C. and Smart, B. (eds.) *Women, Sexuality and Control*, London: Routledge & Kegan Paul

McKeganey, N.P. and Barnard, M.A. (1996) *Sex Work on the Streets, Prostitutes and their Clients*, Buckingham: Open University Press

MacKinnon, C. (1982) 'Feminism, Marxism, Method and the State', *Signs*, 7(3): 515–544
— (1987) *Feminism Unmodified: Discourses on Life and Law*, Cambridge, MA: Harvard University Press
— (1989) *Towards a Feminist Theory of the State*, Cambridge, MA: Harvard University Press
— (1993a) 'Prostitution and Civil Rights', *Michigan Journal of Gender and Law*, 1: 13–31
— (1993b) *Only Words*, Cambridge, MA: Harvard University Press
McLeod, E. (1982) *Women Working: Prostitution Now*, London: Croom Helm
MacLeod, J., Farley, M., Anderson, L. and Golding, J. (2008) 'Challenging Men's Demand for Prostitution in Scotland: a Research Report Based on Interviews with 110 Men who Bought Women in Prostitution', London: Women's Support Project
McNay, L. (1992) *Foucault and Feminism: Power, Gender and the Self*, Oxford: Polity Press
Maginn, P.J. (2011) '(De)Sexing the Suburbs: The Politics and Planning Regulation of Brothels in Perth/WA', paper presented at the State of Australian Cities Conference, Melbourne, 29 November–2 December. http://soac.fbe.unsw.edu.au/2011/papers/SOAC2011_0104_final%281% 29.pdf
Mahood, L. (1990) *The Magdalenes: Prostitution in the Nineteenth Century*, London: Taylor & Francis
Mai, N. (2007) Errance, Migration and Male Sex Work: On the Socio-cultural Sustainability of a Third Space, in Ossman, S. (ed.) *Places We Share: Migration, Subjectivity, and Global Mobility*, Lanham, MD: Lexington Books
Månsson, S.A. (2001) Men's Practices in Prostitution: the Case of Sweden, in Pease, B. and Pringle, K. (eds.) *A Man's World? – Changing Men's Practices in a Globalized World*, London: Zed Books
— (2005a) 'Men's Practices in Prostitution and Their Implications for Social Work'. http://prostitution.procon.org/sourcefiles/mens-practices-in-prostitution-and-their-implications-for-social-work.pdf
— (2005b) Den Köpta Sexualiteten, in Lewin, B. (ed.) *Sex i Sverige: Om Sexuallivet i Sverige*, Stockholm: Folkhälsoinstitutet
— (2006) 'Men's Demand for Prostitutes', *Sexologies*, 15: 87–92
Månsson, S.A. and Backman, M. (1992) *Bordell Europa: Nej Till EGs Skriftserie 3*, Göteborg: Nej Till EG
Månsson, S.A. and Hedin, U.C. (1999) 'Breaking the Matthew Effect: On Women Leaving Prostitution', *International Journal of Social Welfare*, 8: 67–77
Månsson, S.A. and Linders, A. (1984) *Sexualitet Utan Ansikte: Könsköparna*, Stockholm: Carlssons
Marks, S. (2011) 'Human Rights and Root Causes', *Modern Law Review*, 74(1): 57–78
Marshall, J. (2006) 'Feminist Jurisprudence: Keeping the Subject Alive', *Feminist Legal Studies*, 14: 27–51
Marx, K. (1964) *The Economic and Philosophic Manuscripts of 1844*, ed. D.J. Struik, trans. M. Milligan, New York: International Publishers
Mathieu, L. (2001) 'An Unlikely Mobilization: the Occupation of Saint-Nizier Church by the Prostitutes of Lyon', *Revue française de sociologie*, 42 (Supplement: An Annual English Selection): 107–131
— (2003) 'The Emergence and Uncertain Outcomes of Prostitutes' Social Movements', *European Journal of Women's Studies*, 10(1): 29–50
Matthews, R. (1986) Beyond Wolfenden? Prostitution, Politics and the Law, in Matthews, R. and Young, J. (eds.) *Confronting Crime*, London: Sage

— (2005) 'Policing prostitution: Ten Years On', *British Journal of Criminology*, 45(6): 877–895

May, T., Edmunds, M. and Hough, M. (1999) *The Link Between Sex and Drug Markets*, London: Home Office

May, T. and Hunter, G. (2006) Sex Work and Problem Drug Use in the UK: the Links, Problems and Possible Solutions, in Campbell, R. and O'Neill, M. (eds.) *Sex Work Now*, Cullompton: Willan Publishing

Mead, G.H. (1934) *Mind, Self, and Society*, ed. Charles W. Morris, Chicago: University of Chicago Press

Melrose, M. (2007) 'Trying to Make a Silk Purse from a Sow's Ear? A Comment on the Government's Prostitution Strategy', *Community Safety Journal*, 5(2): 4–13

Merlingen, M. (2006) 'Foucault and World Politics: Promises and Challenges of Extending Governmentality Theory to the European and Beyond Millennium', *Journal of International Studies*, 35: 181–196

Merry, S. (2006) *Human Rights and Gender Violence: Translating International Law into Local Justice*, Chicago: University of Chicago Press

Millet, K. (1975) *The Prostitution Papers*, St Albans: Paladin

Milner, N. (1989) 'The Denigration of Rights and the Persistence of Rights Talk: a Cultural Portrait', *Law & Social Inquiry*, 14(4): 631–675

Minow, M.L. (1988) 'Speaking of Silence, Review of Kristen Bumiller, *The Civil Rights Society*', *Miami Law Review*, 43: 493–496

— (1989) 'Introduction: Finding our Paradoxes, Affirming our Beyond', *Harvard Civil Rights & Civil Liberties Law Review*, 24: 1

— (1993) 'Surviving Victim Talk', *University of California Los Angeles Law Review*, 40: 1411–1445

— (1995) Paradoxes of Rights, in Sarat, A. and Kearns, T.R. (eds.) *Identities, Politics, and Rights*, Ann Arbor, MI: University of Michigan Press

— (2002) Instituting Universal Human Rights Law: The Invention of Tradition in the Twentieth Century, in Sarat, A., Bryant, G. and Kagan, R.A. (eds.) *Looking Back at Law's Century*, New York: Cornell University Press

Molyneux, M. and Razavi, S. (eds.) (2002) *Gender Justice, Development and Rights*, Oxford: Oxford University Press

Monto, M.A. (2000) Why Men Seek Out Prostitutes, in Weitzer, R. (ed.) *Sex for Sale: Prostitution, Pornography and the Sex Industry*, New York: Routledge

— (2001) 'Rape Myth Acceptance among the Male Clients of Female Street Prostitutes', *Violence Against Women*, 7(3): 275–293

Morgan, P. (1981) 'From Battered Wife to Program Client: the State's Shaping of Social Problems', *Kapitalistate*, 9: 17–39

Morrison, T. (1987) *Beloved*, Reading: Vintage (reprinted 1997)

Mort, F. (1987) *Dangerous Sexualities: Medico-Moral Politics in England since 1830*, London: Routledge

Mouffe, C. (1992) Feminism, Citizenship and Radical Democratic Politics, in Butler, J. and Scott, J. (eds.) *Feminists Theorise the Political*, London: Routledge

Mullally, S. (2006) *Gender, Culture and Human Rights: Reclaiming Universalism*, Oxford: Hart Publishing

Munro, V.E. (2001) 'Legal Feminism and Foucault – a Critique of the Expulsion of Law', *Journal of Law and Society*, 29: 546–567

— (2007) *Law and Politics at the Perimeter: Re-Evaluating Key Debates in Feminist Theory*, London: Hart Publishing

Munro, V.E. and Della Giusta, M. (eds.) (2008) *Demanding Sex: Critical Reflections on the Regulation of Prostitution*, London: Ashgate

Nagel, J. (1997) *Whores and Other Feminists*, London: Routledge

Neave, M. (1985) *Inquiry into Prostitution: Final Report*, Melbourne: Victorian Government

Nelken, D. (2010) *Comparative Criminal Justice: Making Sense of Difference*, London: Sage

Nestle, J. (1987) Lesbians and Prostitutes: a Historical Sisterhood, in Bell, L. (ed.) *Good Girls/ Bad Girls: Sex Trade Workers and Feminists Face to Face*, Seattle: Seal Press

New South Wales Health Department (2000) *The Health and Welfare Needs of Female and Transgender Street-Based Sex Workers in New South Wales*, Sydney: NSW Government Health Department

Nguyen, L. (2010) 'Prostitution Ruling Stayed in Ontario', *National Post*, 3 December

Nord, A. and Rosenberg, T. (2001) *Rapport: Lag (1998: 408) om Förbudmot Köp av Sexuella Tjänster. Metodutveckling Avseende Åtgärder mot Prostitution*, Malmö: Polismyndigheten i Skåneb

Nozick, R. (1974) *Anarchy, State, and Utopia*, New York: Basic Books

Nussbaum, M. (1998) '"Whether from Reason or Prejudice": Taking Money for Bodily Services', *Journal of Legal Studies*, 27(S2): 693–723

— (1999) *Sex and Social Justice*, New York: Oxford University Press

O'Connell Davidson, J. (1998) *Prostitution, Power and Freedom*, Cambridge: Polity Press

— (2002) 'The Rights and Wrongs of Prostitution', *Hypatia*, 17(2): 84–98

— (2006) 'Will the Real Sex Slave Please Stand up?', *Feminist Review*, 83: 4–22

— (2007) 'Sex Slaves and the Reality of Prostitution', *The Guardian*, 28 December

— (2013) 'Troubling Freedom: Migration, Debt, and Modern Slavery', *Migration Studies*, 1(2): 176–195

— (2014) 'Let's Go Outside: Bodies, Prostitutes, Slaves and Worker Citizens, *Citizenship Studies*, 18(5): 516–532

O'Donovan, K. (1997) With Sense, Consent, or Just a Con? Legal Subjects in the Discourses of Autonomy, in Naffine, N. and Owens, R. (eds.) *Sexing the Subject of Law*, London: Sweet & Maxwell

O'Malley, P. and Valverde, M. (2014) Foucault, Criminal Law and Governmentalization of the State, in Dubber, M.D. (ed.) *Foundational Texts in Modern Criminal Law*, Oxford: Oxford University Press

O'Neill, M. (2001) *Prostitution and Feminism: Towards a Politics of Feeling*, Cambridge: Polity Press

Oakley, A. (ed.) (2007) *Working Sex: Sex Workers Write About a Changing Industry*, Seattle: Seal Press

Oldenburg, V.T. (1990) 'Lifestyle as Resistance', *Feminist Studies*, 16(2): 259–287

Olsen, F. (1983) 'The Family and the Market: a Study of Ideology and Legal Reform', *Harvard Law Review*, 96: 1497–1578

Oppenheim, M. (2014) 'MEPs Vote to Criminalise Buying Sex', *The Guardian*, 26 February

Osbourne, H. (2014) 'Nordic Model of Prostitution Approved by European Parliament', *International Business Times*, 26 February

Östergren, P. (2003) *Synden Ideologiserad: Modern Svensk Prostitutionspolicy som Identitets- och Trygghetsskapare*, unpublished masters thesis, Department of Social Anthropology, Stockholm University. www.petraostergren.com

— (2007) 'Sex Workers Critique of Swedish Prostitution Policy'. http://www.petraostergren.com/pages.aspx?r_id=40716

Otis, L.L. (1985) *Prostitution in Medieval Society: The History of an Urban Institution in Languedoc*, Chicago: University of Chicago Press

Outshoorn, J. (2004a) 'Pragmatism in the Polder: Changing Prostitution Policy in the Netherlands', *Journal of Contemporary European Studies*, 12: 165–176
— (2004b) *The Politics of Prostitution*, Cambridge: Cambridge University Press
— (2012) 'Policy Change in Prostitution in the Netherlands: From Legalization to Strict Control', *Sexuality Research and Social Policy*, 9(3): 233–243
Overall, C. (1992) 'What's Wrong with Prostitution? Evaluating Sex Work', *Signs*, 17(4): 705–724
Overs, P. (1994) 'Prostitution', *New Internationalist*, 252: 114–121
Pakulski, J. (1997) 'Cultural Citizenship', *Citizenship Studies*, 1: 73–86
Palmer, T. (2001) 'No Son of Mine!', Barnados Reporty, London: Barnados
Parent-Duchâtelet, A.J.B. (1836) *De la Prostitution Dans la Ville de Paris*, Paris: J.B. Baillière et fils
Pateman, C. (1983) 'Defending Prostitution: Charges against Ericsson', *Ethics*, 93: 561–565
— (1988) *The Sexual Contract*, Palo Alto, CA: Stanford University Press
Pates, R. (2012) 'Liberal Laws Juxtaposed with Rigid Control: an Analysis of the Logics of Governing Sex Work in Germany', *Sexuality Research and Social Policy*, 9(3): 212–222
Perkins, R. (1991) *Working Girls: Prostitutes, Their Life and Social Control*, Canberra: Australian Institute of Criminology
— (1999) '"How Much are You Love?" The Customer in the Australian Sex Industry', *Social Alternatives*, 18: 38–47
Perkins, R. and Lovejoy, F. (2007) *Call Girls: Private Sex Workers in Australia*, Crawley, WA: University of Western Australia Press
Perkins, R., Prestage, G., Sharp, R. and Lovejoy, F. (1994) *Sex Work and Sex Workers in Australia*, Sydney: University of New South Wales Press
Pheterson, G. (1989) *A Vindication of the Rights of Whores*, Seattle: Seal Press
— (1996) *The Prostitution Prism*, Amsterdam: Amsterdam University Press
Phoenix, J. (1999) *Making Sense of Prostitution*, London: Palgrave Macmillan
— (2002a) 'In the Name of Protection: Youth Prostitution Policy Reforms in England and Wales', *Critical Social Policy*, 22(2): 353–375
— (2002b) Youth Prostitution Policy Reform: New Discourses, Same Old Story, in Carlin, P. (ed.) *Women and Punishment: A Struggle for Justice*, Cullompton: Willan Publishing
— (2007) 'Regulating Prostitution: Different Problems, Different Solutions, Same Old Story', *Safer Communities*, 6: 7–10
— (ed.) (2009) *Regulating Sex for Sale: Prostitution Policy Reform in the UK*, Bristol: Policy Press
Phoenix, J. and Oerton, S. (2005) *Illicit and Illegal: Sex, Regulation and Social Control*, Cullompton: Willan Publishing
Poovey, M. (1995) *Making a Social Body: British Cultural Formation, 1830–1864*, Chicago: University of Chicago Press
Pratt, G. (2005) 'Abandoned Women and Spaces of the Exception', *Antipode*, 37(5): 1052–1078
Pratt, J.D. (2008) 'Scandinavian Exceptionalism in an Era of Penal Excess. Part 1: the Nature and Roots of Scandinavian Exceptionalism', *British Journal of Criminology*, 48(2): 119–137
Prior, J. (2008) 'Planning for Sex in the City: Urban Governance, Planning and the Placement of Sex Industry Premises in Inner Sydney', *Australian Geographer*, 39(3): 339–352

Prior, J. and Crofts, P. (2012) 'Effects of Sex Premises on Neighbourhoods: Residents, Local Planning and the Geographies of a Controversial Land Use', *New Zealand Geographer*, 68(2): 130–140

Prostitution Licensing Authority (PLA) (2004) *Selling Sex in Queensland 2003*, Milton, QLD: PLA

Quan, T. (1990) 'Books about our Business', *Pony X-Press*, 1(1)

Queen, C. (1997) *Real Live Nude Girl: Chronicles of Sex-Positive Culture*, Berkeley, CA: Cleis Press

Rabinow, P. and Rose, N. (2003) *The Essential Foucault*, New York: The New Press

Radin, M.J. (1996) *Contested Commodities: the Trouble with Trade in Sex, Children, Body Parts and Other Things*, Cambridge, MA: Harvard University Press

Randall, V. (1987) *Women and Politics: an International Perspective* (2nd edn.), Chicago: University of Chicago Press

Raymond, J. (1995) *Report to the United Nations Special Rapporteur on Violence against Women: Prostitution and Trafficking*, New York: Coalition against Trafficking in Women International

— (2003) *Ten Reasons for not Legalizing Prostitution*, New York: Coalition against Trafficking in Women International

— (2004) 'Prostitution on Demand: Legalizing the Buyers as Sexual Consumers', *Violence against Women*, 10: 1156–1186

Raymond, J.G., Hughes, D.M. and Gomez, C.J. (2001) *Sex Trafficking of Women in the United States: Links between International and Domestic Sex Industries*, New York: Coalition against Trafficking in Women International

Reynolds, E. (1998) *Before the Bobbies: The Night Watch and Police Reform in Metropolitan London, 1720–1830*, Stanford, Calif: Stanford University Press.

Ridgway, S. (1997) *Sexuality and Modernity*. http://www.isis.aust.com/stephan/ writings/ sexuality/index.htm

Ringdal, N.J. and Daly, R. (2005) *Love for Sale: A World History of Prostitution*, London: Grove Press

Roberts, N. (1992) *Whores in History: Prostitution in Western Society*, London: HarperCollins

Rorty, R. (1989) *Contingency, Irony and Solidarity*, Cambridge: Cambridge University Press

Rose, N. (1985) *The Psychological Complex*, London: Routledge

— (1993) 'Government, Authority and Expertise in Advanced Liberalism', *Economy and Society*, 22(3): 283–299

— (1996) Identity, Genealogy, History, in Hall, S. and du Gay, P. (eds.) *Questions of Cultural Identity*, London: Sage

— (1999) *Powers of Freedom*, Cambridge: Cambridge University Press

Rose, N., O'Malley, P. and Valverde, M. (2006) 'Governmentality', *Annual Review of Law and Social Science*, 2: 83–104

Rose, N. and Valverde, M. (1998) 'Governed by Law?', *Social and Legal Studies*, 7: 541–553

Rosen, E. and Venkatesh, S.A. (2008) 'A "Perversion" of Choice: Sex Work Offers Just Enough in Chicago's Urban Ghetto', *Journal of Contemporary Ethnography*, 37(4): 417–441

Rossiaud, J. (1988) *Medieval Prostitution*, trans. Lydia G. Cochrane, Oxford: Blackwell

Rubin, G.S. (1984) Thinking Sex: Notes for a Radical Theory of the Politics of Sexuality, in Vance, C.S. (ed.) *Pleasure and Danger: Exploring Female Sexuality*, Boston, MA: Routledge & Kegan Paul

Runcis, M. (1998) *Steriliseringar i Folkhemmet* [Sterilization in the Swedish Welfare State], Stockholm: Ordfront

Sanchez Taylor, J. (2001) 'Dollars are a Girl's Best Friend? Female Tourists' Sexual Behaviour in the Caribbean', *Sociology*, 35(3): 749–764

— (2006) 'Female Sex Tourism: a Contradiction in Terms?', *Feminist Review*, 83(1): 42–59

Sandell, G., Pettersson, E., Larsson, J. and Kuosmanen, J. (1996) *Könsköparna: Varför Går Män Egentligen till Prostituerade?*, Stockholm: Natur och Kultur

Sanders, T. (2002) 'The Condom as Psychological Barrier: Female Sex Workers and Emotional Management', *Feminism and Psychology*, 12(4): 561–566

— (2004) 'The Risks of Street Prostitution: Punters, Police and Protestors', *Urban Studies*, 41(8): 1703–1717

— (2005) *Sex Work: a Risky Business*, Cullompton: Willan Publishing

— (2007) 'Becoming an Ex-sex Worker: Making Transitions out of a Deviant Career', *Feminist Criminology*, 2(1): 1–22

— (2008) *Paying for Pleasure: Men Who Buy Sex*, Cullompton: Willan Publishing

— (2009) 'Kerbcrawler Rehabilitation Programmes: Curing the "Deviant" Male and Reinforcing the "Respectable" Moral Order', *Critical Social Policy*, 29(1): 77–99

Sanders, T. and Campbell, R. (2007) 'Designing out Vulnerability, Building in Respect: Violence, Safety and Sex Work Policy', *The British Journal of Sociology*, 58(1): 1–19

— (2008) 'Why Hate Men who Pay for Sex? Exploring the Shift to 'Tackling Demand' in the UK', in Munro, V. and Della Giusta, M. (eds) *Demanding Sex: Critical Reflections of the Regulation of Prostitution*, Aldershot: Ashgate, pp. 163–179

Sanders, T. and Hubbard, P. (2003) 'Making Space for Sex Work: Female Street Prostitution and the Production of Urban Space', *International Journal of Urban and Regional Research*, 27(1): 73–87

Sanders, T., O'Neill, M. and Pitcher, J. (2009) *Prostitution: Sex Work, Policy and Politics*, London: Sage

Sandland, R. (1995) 'Between Truth and Difference: Poststructuralism, Law and the Power of Feminism', *Feminist Legal Studies*, 3: 3–47

Sangera, J. (1997) *In the Belly of the Beast: Sex Trade, Prostitution and Globalization*, unpublished discussion paper for the South Asia Regional Consultation on Prostitution

Santos, B.S. (2002) *Towards a New Legal Common Sense: Law, Globalization and Emancipation*, Cambridge: Cambridge University Press

Sarat, A. and Kearns, T.R. (eds.) (1995) *Law in Everyday Life*, Ann Arbor: University of Michigan Press

— (eds.) (1997) *Identities, Politics, and Rights*, Ann Arbor: University of Michigan Press

— (eds.) (2002) *Human Rights: Concepts, Contests, Contingencies*, Ann Arbor: University of Michigan Press

Satz, D. (1995) 'Markets in Women's Sexual Labour', *Ethics*, 106(1): 63–85

Scibelli, P. (1987) 'Empowering Prostitutes: a Proposal for International Reform', *Harvard Women's Law Journal*, 10: 117–157

Scott Fitzgerald, F. (1936) 'Handle with Care', *Esquire Magazine*, March

Scott, J.G. (2003) 'Prostitution and public health in New South Wales', *Culture, Health & Sexuality*, 5(3): 277–293

— (2005) *How Modern Governments Made Prostitution a Social Problem: Creating a Responsible Prostitute Population*, New York: Edwin Mellen Press

— (2011) 'Governing Prostitution: Differentiating the Bad from the Bad', *Current Issues in Criminal Justice*, 23(1), 53–72

Scott, J., Minichiello, V., Marino, R., Harvey, G.P., Jamieson, M. and Browne, J. (2005) 'Understanding the New Context of the Male Sex Work Industry', *Journal of Interpersonal Violence*, 20(3): 320–342

Scottish Coalition Against Sexual Exploitation (2010) 'Written Submission on the Criminal Justice and Licensing (Scotland) Bill – Stage 2', 16 March. http://archive.scottish.parliament.uk/s3/committees/justice/inquiries/criminaljusticeandlicensing/CJL.S2.44%20Scottish%20Coalition%20Against%20Sexual%20Exploitation.pdf

Scoular, J. (1996) Feminist Jurisprudence, in Jackson, S. and Jones, J. (eds.) *Contemporary Feminist Theories*, Edinburgh: Edinburgh University Press

— (2004a) 'Criminalising "Punters": Evaluating the Swedish Position on Prostitution', *Journal of Social Welfare and Family Law*, 26: 195–210

— (2004b) 'The Subject of Prostitution', *Feminist Theory*, 5(3): 343–355

— (2010) 'What's Law Got to Do with it? How and Why Law Matters in the Regulation of Sex Work', *Journal of Law and Society*, 37(1): 12–39

Scoular, J. and Carline, A. (2014) 'A Critical Account of a "Creeping Neo-abolitionism": Regulating Prostitution in England and Wales', *Criminology and Criminal Justice*, 14(5): 608–626

— (2015) 'Saving fallen women now? Critical perspectives on engagement and support orders and their policy of forced welfarism', *Social Policy and Society*, 14(1): 103–112

Scoular, J. and O'Neill, M. (2007) 'Regulating Prostitution: Social Inclusion, Responsibilisation and the Politics of Prostitution Reform', *British Journal of Criminology*, 47(5): 764–778

— (2008) Legal Incursion into Supply/Demand: Criminalising and Responsibilising the Buyers and Sellers of Sex in the UK, in Munro, V. and Della Giusta, M. (eds.) (2008) *Demanding Sex: Critical Reflections on the Regulation of Prostitution*, London: Ashgate

Scoular, J., Pitcher, J., Campbell, R., Hubbard, P. and O'Neill, M. (2007) 'What's Anti-social about Sex Work? The Changing Representation of Prostitution's Incivility', *Safer Communities*, 6(1): 11–17

Scrambler, G. and Scrambler, A. (eds.) (1997) *Rethinking Prostitution: Purchasing Sex in the 1990s*, London: Routledge

Segal, L. (1994) *Straight Sex*, London: Virago

— (2006) 'A misguided manifesto', *The Guardian*, 28 June 2006. http://www.guardian.co.uk/commentisfree/2006/jun/28/anewsexualmanifestonothan

Self, H. (1999) 'Fair game', *Police Review*, 21 May, 26–7

Self, H.J. (2003) *Prostitution, Women and the Misuse of Law: The Fallen Daughters of Eve*, London: Psychology Press

Sexual Service Providers Advocacy Network (SSPAN) (2006) Response to the Queensland Crime and Misconduct Commission Interim Paper, 31 January. http://www.scarletalliance.org.au/library/sspan06/

Sheldrick, G. (2014) 'Swoop on Roma Brothels as Vice Girls Flood in', *Daily Express*, 18 January

Shrage, L. (1994) *Moral Dilemmas of Feminism: Prostitution, Adultery and Abortion*, London: Taylor & Francis

Silbaugh, K. (1997) 'Commodification and Women's Household Labor', *Yale Journal of Law and Feminism*, 9: 81

Silbey, S. (2005) 'After Legal Consciousness', *Annual Review of Law and Social Science*, 1: 323–368

Simons, J. (1995) *Foucault & the Political*, London: Routledge

Skilbrei, M.L. and Holmström, C. (2011) Is there a Nordic Prostitution Regime?', in Tonry, M. and Lappi-Seppälä, T. (eds.) 'Crime and Justice in Scandinavia', *Crime and Justice*, 40(1): 479–517

— (2013) *Prostitution Policy in the Nordic Region: Ambiguous Sympathies*, London: Ashgate

Smart, C. (1989) *Feminism and the Power of Law*, London: Routledge

— (1995) *Law, Crime and Sexuality*, London: Sage

Smart, C. and Smart, B. (1978) *Women, Sexuality and Social Control*, London: Routledge

Smith, A.M. (1998) *Laclau and Mouffe, The Radical Democratic Imaginary*, London: Routledge

Smith, D. (1990) *The Conceptual Practices of Power: A Feminist Sociology of Knowledge*, Toronto: University of Toronto Press

Smith, F.B. (1971) 'Ethics and Diseases in the Later Nineteenth Century', *Historical Studies*, 15: 118–135

Smith, J. (1989) *Misogynies*, London: Faber

Smith, J. and Honeyball, M. (2014) 'Can the European Parliament Call a Halt to Prostitution as we Know it?', *The Telegraph*, 23 January

Soothill, K.L. and Sanders, T. (2005) 'The Geographical Mobility, Preferences and Pleasures of Prolific Punters: a Demonstration Study of the Activities of Prostitutes' Clients', *Sociological Research Online*, 10(1)

Spelman, E. (1990) *Inessential Woman*, London: Beacon Press

Spivak, G. (1992) French Feminism Revisited: Ethics and Politics, in Butler, J. and Scott, J. (eds.) *Feminists Theorise the Political*, London: Routledge

Spongberg, M. (1997) *Feminising Venereal Disease: The Body of the Prostitute in Nineteenth Century Medical Discourse*, Basingstoke: Macmillan

Sprinkle, A. (1991) *Post-Porn Modernist*, Amsterdam: Art Unlimited

Standing, G. (2011) *The Precariat: The New Dangerous Class*, London: Bloomsbury Academic

Stark, C. and Whisnant, R. (2004) *Not For Sale: Feminists Resisting Prostitution and Pornography*, North Melbourne: Spinifex Press

Stead, W.T. (1885) 'The Maiden Tribute of Modern Babylon', *Pall Mall Gazette*

Steans, J. (2007) 'Debating women's human rights as a universal feminist project: defending women's human rights as a political tool', *Review of International Studies* 33(1): 11–27

Stychin, C. (1997) 'Review of Austin Sarat and Thomas R. Kearns (eds.) *Identities, Politics, and Rights*, University of Michigan Press, 1996', *Social & Legal Studies*, 6: 315–316

Stychin, C. and Herman, D. (eds.) (2000) *Sexuality in the Legal Arena*, London: Athlone Press

Sullivan, B. (1997) *The Politics of Sex: Prostitution and Pornography in Australia since 1945*, Cambridge: Cambridge University Press

— (1999) 'Prostitution Law Reform in Australia: a Preliminary Evaluation', *Social Alternatives*, 18: 9–14

— (2000) Rethinking Prostitution and 'Consent', in Castles, F. and Uhr, J. (eds.) *Proceedings of the 2000 Conference of the Australasian Political Studies*, Canberra: Australian National University

— (2004) Prostitution and Consent: Beyond the Liberal Dichotomy of 'Free or Forced', in Cowling, M. and Reynolds, P. (eds.) *Making Sense of Sexual Consent*, London: Ashgate

— (2007) 'Rape, Prostitution and Consent: the Australian and New Zealand Situations', *Journal of Criminology*, 40(2): 127–142

— (2010) 'When (Some) Prostitution is Legal: the Impact of Law Reform on Sex Work in Australia', *Journal of Law and Society*, 37: 85–104

Sullivan, E. and Simon, W. (1998) The Client: a Social, Psychological, and Behavioural Look at the Unseen Patron of Prostitution, in Elias, J.E. and Brewer, G. (eds.) *Prostitution*, New York: Prometheus Books

Sullivan, M. (2005) 'What Happens When Prostitution Becomes Work? An Update on Legalisation of Prostitution in Australia', New York: Coalition Against Trafficking in Women

— (2007) *Making Sex Work: A Failed Experiment with Legalised Prostitution*, North Melbourne: Spinifex Press

Sullivan, M.L. and Jeffreys, S (2001) 'Legalizing Prostitution is not the Answer: the Example of Victoria, Australia', New York: Coalition against Trafficking in Women International

— (2002) 'Legalization: the Australian Experience', *Violence against Women*, 8: 1140–1148

Sullivan, R. (2001) The Schizophrenic State: Neo-liberal Criminal Justice, in Stenson, K. and Sullivan, R. (eds.) *Crime, Risk and Justice: The Politics of Crime Control in Liberal Democracies*, Cullompton: Willan Publishing

Surratt, H.L., Inciardi, J.A., Kurtz, S.P. and Kiley, M.C. (2004) 'Sex Work and Drug Use in a Subculture of Violence', *Crime & Delinquency*, 50(1): 43–59

Svanström, Y. (2004) En Självklar Efterfrågan? Om Torskar och Sexköpare Under Hundra År, in Svanström, Y. and Östberg, K. (eds.) *Än Män Då? Kön och Feminism i Sverige under 150 År*, Stockholm: Atlas

Svensson, G. (2003) 'Att Köpa Sex Kan Vara Rop på Hjälp', *Dagens Nyheter*, 28 October

Swedish Government, Ministry of Industry, Employment and Communications (2003), *Prostitution and Trafficking in Women Fact Sheet*, 2 April

Swedish National Police (2013) 'Supervision Report 2013: 7: The Inspection of Police Forces' Ability to Investigate Cases of Trafficking for Sexual Purposes and the Purchase of Sexual Services' [Inspektion av polismyndigheternas förmåga att utreda ärenden om människohandel för sexuella ändamål och köp av sexuell tjänst]. http://polisen.se/Global/www%20och%20Intrapolis/Rapporter-utredningar/01%20Polisen%20nationellt/Ovriga%20rapporter-utredningar/Inspektioner-tillsyns% 20rapporter/2013/Tillsynsrapp_7_Manniskohandel_13.pdf

Szymanski, A.-M. (2000) 'Book Review of *Diseases of the Will: Alcohol and the Dilemmas of Freedom*, by Mariana Valverde', *The Law and Politics Book Review*, 10(10): 558–561

Tadros, V. (1998) 'Between Governance and Discipline: the Law and Michel Foucault', *Oxford Journal of Legal Studies*, 18: 75–103

Tierney, T. (2006) 'Suicidal Thoughts: Hobbes, Foucault, and the Right to Die', *Philosophy and Social Criticism*, 32: 601–638

Truong, T.D. (1990) *Sex, Money, and Morality: Prostitution and Tourism in South-East Asia*, London: Zed Books

Twining, W. (2000) *Globalization and Legal Theory*, Cambridge: Cambridge University Press

UK Home Office (2000) 'Setting the Boundaries: Reforming the Law on Sexual Offences', London: HMSO

— (2003) 'Vital to Help Victims of Prostitution Break out of the Violent Circle of Abuse – David Blunkett', Press Release, 27 June. http://www.cjp.org.uk/ news/archive/vital-to-help-victims-of-prostitution-break-out-of-the-violent-circle-of-abuse-david-blunkett-27-06-2003/

— (2004) 'Paying the Price: A Consultation Paper on Prostitution', London: HMSO

— (2006) 'A Coordinated Prostitution Strategy', London: HMSO

— (2007a) *Crime Reduction Briefing, Prostitution*, London: Home Office

— (2007b) *Campaign to Deter Kerb-Crawling*, London: Home Office

— (2008) 'Tackling the Demand for Prostitution Review', London: HMSO
Ulrich, B. (1992) *Risk Society: Towards a New Modernity*, London: Sage
US State Department (2005) *Trafficking in Persons Report: June 2005.* http://www.state.gov/documents/organization/47255.pdf
Valverde, M. (1987) Too Much Heat, Not Enough Light, in Bell, L. (ed.) *Good Girls/Bad Girls: Sex Trade Workers and Feminists Face to Face*, Seattle: Seal Press
— (1989a) 'Beyond Gender Dangers and Private Pleasures: Theory and Ethics in the Sex Debates', *Feminist Studies*, 15(2): 237–254
— (1989b) 'The Love of Finery: Fashion and the Fallen Woman in Nineteenth Century Social Discourse', *Victorian Studies*, 32(2): 167–188
— (1991) *The Age of Light, Soap and Water: Moral Reform in English Canada, 1885–1925*, Toronto: Toronto University Press
— (1998) *Diseases of the Will: Alcohol and the Dilemmas of Freedom*, Cambridge: Cambridge University Press
Valverde, M. (1999a) 'The Harms of Sex and the Risks of Breasts: Obscenity and Indecency in Canadian Law', *Social & Legal Studies*, 8: 181–197
— (1999b) 'Derrida's Justice, Foucault's Freedom: Ethics, History, and Social Movements', *Law and Social Inquiry*, 24(3): 655–676
— (2003) *Law's Dream of Common Knowledge*, Princeton, NJ: Princeton University Press
— (2007) 'Genealogies of European States: Foucauldian Reflections', *Economy & Society*, 36(1): 159–178
— (2010) 'Spectres of Foucault in Law and Society Scholarship', *Annual Review of Law and Social Science*, 6: 45–59
Van der Meulen, E., Durisin, E.M. and Love, V. (2013) *Selling Sex: Experience, Advocacy, and Research on Sex Work in Canada*, Vancouver: UBC Press
Van der Poel, S. (1995) 'Solidarity as Boomerang: the Fiasco of the Prostitutes' Rights Movement in the Netherlands', *Crime Law Change*, 23(1): 41–65
Van der Veen, M.K. (2002) *Rethinking Prostitution: Analyzing an Informal Sector Industry*, PhD thesis, Amherst: University of Massachusetts
Vance, C.S. (1993) (ed.) *Pleasure and Danger: Exploring Female Sexuality*, Boston, MA: Routledge & Kegan Paul
— (1993) 'More Danger, More Pleasure: A Decade after the Barnard Sexuality Conference', in Carole S. Vance (ed.) *Pleasure and Danger*, Pandora Press
Vanwesenbeeck, I., (1994) *Prostitutes' Well-being and Risk*, Amsterdam: VU University Press
Vanwesenbeeck, I., Honing, P. and Vennix, P. (2002) *The Social Position of Prostitutes in the Regulated Circuit a Year after the Change*, Utrecht/Den Haag: Rutgers Nisso Groep/WODC, Ministerie van Justitie
Veitch, S. (1997) 'Law and "Other" Problems', *Law and Critique*, 8(1): 97–109
Veitch, S., Christodoulidis, E. and Farmer, L. (2007) *Jurisprudence: Themes and Concepts*, New York: Routledge-Cavendish
Vogel, S. (2002) 'Fifth Annual Sex Workers' Art Show (Review)', *Theatre Journal*, 54(3): 496–498
Walby, K. (2007) 'Contributions to a Post-sovereigntist Understanding of Law: M. Foucault, Law as Governance and Legal Pluralism', *Social and Legal Studies*, 16: 551–571
Walker, G. (1990) *Family Violence and the Women's Movement: the Conceptual Politics of Struggle*, Toronto: University of Toronto Press
Walkowitz, J. (1980) *Prostitution and Victorian Society: Women, Class, and the State*, Cambridge: Cambridge University Press

— (1982) 'Male Vice and Feminist Virtue: Feminism and the Politics of Prostitution in Nineteenth-century Britain', *History Workshop Journal*, 13(1): 79–93

Wall, I. (2011) *Human Rights and Constituent Power: Without Model or Warranty*, London: Routledge

Waltman, M. (2011) 'Sweden's Prohibition on the Purchase of Sex: the Law's Reasons, Impact and Potential', *Women's Studies International Forum*, 34: 449–474

Ward, H., Day, S., Green, A., Cooper, K. and Weber, J. (2004) 'Declining Prevalence of STI in the London Sex Industry, 1985 to 2002', *Sexually Transmitted Infections*, 80(5): 374–376

Warner, M. (2000) *The Trouble with Normal: Sex, Politics, and the Ethics of Queer Life*, Cambridge, MA: Harvard University Press

Weatherall, A. and Priestley, A. (2001) 'A Feminist Discourse Analysis of Sex "Work"', *Feminism and Psychology*, 11(3): 323–340

Weber, M. (1949) Objectivity in Social Science and Social Policy, in Shils, E. and Finch, H. (eds.) *The Methodology of Social Science*, Wilmington, IL: Free Press

Weeks, J. (2012) *Sex, Politics and Society: The Regulation of Sexuality Since 1800* (3rd edn.), Harlow: Pearson Education Ltd

Weeks, K. (2011) *The Problem with Work: Feminism, Marxism, Antiwork Politics, and Postwork Imaginaries*. Durham, NC: Duke University Press

Weitzer, R. (1991) 'Prostitutes' Rights in US: the Failure of a Movement', *Sociological Quarterly*, 32: 23–41

— (ed.) (2000) *Sex for Sale: Prostitution, Pornography and the Sex Industry*, New York: Routledge

— (2007) 'The Social Construction of Sex Trafficking: Ideology and Institutionalization of a Moral Crusade', *Politics & Society*, 35(3): 447–475

— (2012) *Legalizing Prostitution: From Illicit Vice to Lawful Business*, New York: New York University Press

West, D.J. and de Villiers, B. (1992) *Male Prostitution*, London: Taylor & Francis

West, J. (2000) 'Prostitution: Collectives and the Politics of Regulation', *Gender, Work and Organization*, 7: 106–118

White, L. (1990) *The Comforts of Home: Prostitution in Colonial Nairobi*, Chicago: University of Chicago Press

Whowell, M. (2010) 'Male Sex Work: Exploring Regulation in England and Wales', *Journal of Law and Society*, 37(1): 125–144

Whowell, M. and Gaffney, J. (2009) Male Sex Work in the UK: Forms, Practices and Policy Implications, in Phoenix, J. and Pearce, J. (eds.) *Regulating Sex for Sale: Prostitution Policy Reform in the UK*, Cambridge: Polity Press

Williams, J.C. (1991) 'Domesticity as the Danger Supplement of Liberalism', *Journal of Women's History*, 2: 69–76

— (2000) Rorty, Radicalism, Romanticism: The Politics of the Gaze, in Pettegrew, J. (ed.) *A Pragmatist's Progress? Richard Rorty and American Intellectual History*, Lanham, MD: Rowman & Littlefield

Williams, J.C. and Zelizer, V.A. (2005) To Commodify or Not to Commodify: That is *Not* the Question, in Erman, M. and Williams, J.C. (eds.) *Rethinking Commodification: Cases and Readings in Law and Culture*, New York: New York University Press

Wittgenstein, L. (1970) *Philosophical Investigations*, trans. G.E.M., Oxford: Blackwell

Wolstenholme Elmy, E. (1897) in *Shafts*, March: 87

Woodward, C., Fischer, J., Najman, J.M. and Dunne, M. (2004) *Selling Sex in Queensland 2003: A Study of Prostitution in Queensland*, Research Study published by the Prostitution Licensing Authority

Woodward, W. (2007) 'Harman Calls for Prostitution Ban to Tackle Trafficking', *The Guardian*, 21 December

World Health Organization (2013), *Implementing comprehensive HIV/STI programmes with sex workers: practical approaches from collaborative interventions*, WHO. http://apps.who.int/iris/bitstream/10665/90000/1/9789241506182_eng.pdf

Wotton, R. (2005) 'The Relationship between Street-based Sex Workers and the Police in the Effectiveness of HIV Prevention Strategies', *Research for Sex Work*, 8: 11–13

Yngvesson, B. (1988) 'Making Law at the Doorway: The Clerk, the Court, and the Construction of Community in a New England Town', *Law and Society Review*, 22(3): 409–448

Zatz, N. (1997) 'Sex Work/Sex Act: Law, Labor and Desire in Constructions of Prostitution', *Signs*, 22: 277–308

Zelizer, V.A. (2005) *The Purchase of Intimacy*, Princeton, NJ: Princeton University Press

Legal materials

Acts etc.

Adulteration of Food and Drink Act 1860, c. 84

Contagious Diseases Act 1866, c. 35

Contagious Diseases Act 1869, c. 96

Contagious Diseases Prevention Act 1864, c. 85

Criminal Code of Canada, RSC 1985, c. C-46

Criminal Justice and Police Act 2001, c. 16

Criminal Law Amendment Act 1885, c.69

Hansard, HC Public Bill Committee, 9th Sitting, col. 318 (10 February 2009)

Nuisances Removal Act for England (Amendment) Act 1863, c. 117 (often referred to as the Diseased Meats Act 1863)

Policing and Crime Act 2009, c. 26

Prohibition of the Purchase of Sexual Services Act 1998 (Sweden)

Prostitution (Public Places) (Scotland) Act 2007, asp 11

Prostitution Reform Act 2003 (New Zealand)

Public Health Act 1875, c. 55

Reference re ss. 193 & 195.1(1)(c) of Criminal Code (Canada), (the Prostitution Reference), [1990] 1 SCR 1123, Supreme Court of Canada

Sanitary Act 1866, c. 90

Sections 2 and 7 of the Canadian Charter of Rights and Freedoms, Part 1 of the Constitution Act, 1982

Street Offences Act 1959, c. 57

Vaccination Acts Amendment Act 1861, c. 59

Cases

Bedford vs. *Canada* (2010) ONSC 4264

Canada (Attorney General) vs. *Bedford* (2012) ONCA 186

Canada (Attorney General) vs. *Downtown Eastside Sex Workers United Against Violence in Society* [2012] 2 SCR 524

Canada (Attorney General) vs. *Bedford* 2013 SCC 72
DPP vs. *Bull* [1994] 4 All E.R. 411
DML vs. *Montgomery and MT Enterprises Ltd* [2014] NZHRRT 6
R vs. *Arjumand Hussein* [1996] EWCA 606
R vs. *Barker* (1829) 172 ER 558
R vs. *Charles Grenville Shaw* [1997] EWCA 165
R vs. *Clark* [1987] 1 NZLR 380
R vs. *Harris* 1981 (unreported), Victorian Supreme Court, Court of Criminal Appeal
R vs. *Heros Hakopian* BC9100584 Supreme Court of Victoria Court of Criminal Appeal 168 & 871 of 1991
R vs. *Kevin Davis* [1997] EWCA 3655
R vs. *Krausz* (1973) 57 Cr App R 466
R vs. *Leary* BC 9302383 Supreme Court of NSW Court of Criminal Appeal CCA 060254 of 1992
R vs. *Myers and Ward* BC 9300725 Supreme Court of Victoria Court of Criminal Appeal 40 & 83 of 1993
R vs. *R* [1991] UKHL 12
Stallard vs. *HM Advocate* 1989 SCCR 248
TR vs. *Bashir* [1969] 1 WLR 1303

Index

For Product Safety Concerns and Information please contact our EU representative GPSR@taylorandfrancis.com Taylor & Francis Verlag GmbH, Kaufingerstraße 24, 80331 München, Germany